DR. MASQUELIER's MARK ON HEALTH

Dr. Jack Masquelier

DR. MASQUELIER's MARK ON HEALTH

**How & Why
MASQUELIER's Original OPCs
Work in**

Macular Degeneration
Diabetes
Skin Care
Inflammations
Allergies
Premenstrual Syndrome
Hemorrhoids
Cardiovascular Health
Sports Injuries
Stroke
Varicose Veins
Eyesight
Retinopathy
Premature Aging
Edema
Cerebrovascular Health
TIA, Transient ischemic attack
Impaired Vision
Impaired Circulation

By Bert Schwitters

Table of Contents:

1. MASQUELIER AND THE UNIVERSAL OPCs	7
2. MASQUELIER's CHILDHOOD AND YOUTH	17
3. THE DISCOVERY OF OPCs	22
4. THE FIRST VASCULAR PRODUCT	35
5. JACK AND JACQUES	44
6. VITAMINS C AND P	49
7. DEFINITION OF A VITAMIN	52
8. COLORLESS ISN'T YELLOW OR RED	56
9. OPCs FROM THE BARK OF THE MARITIME PINE	64
10. TEACHER AND STUDENT AND A NEW PINE BARK PRODUCT	69
11. AMAZING EFFECTS OF FLAVAN	76
Case Study 1	78
Case Study 2	78
Case Study 3	79
Case Study 4	79
12. THE OLIGOMERIC PROANTHOCYANIDINS	84
13. WHERE ARE OPCs IN NATURE?	95
14. ANTHOGENOL	98
15. VASCULAR PROTECTION	104
16. OPCs' PLACE IN NUTRITION	115
17. ARE OPCs VITAMINS?	124
18. OPCs AND BIOFLAVONOIDS: THE ESSENTIAL DIFFERENCES	131
19. NEW CLINICAL HIGHLIGHTS	140
Recommended Daily Dosage	140
Capillary Resistance	141
Cirrhosis of the Liver	143
Venous Problems in the Legs/Varicose Veins	143
Decreasing Vision	146
Retinopathy	147

Retinopathy and Diabetes	148
Age-Related Macular Degeneration	150
Premenstrual Syndrome	153
Sports Injuries	154
Edema After Facelift	155
Lymphedema After Removal of Breast Tissue	156
20. STROKE, TRANSIENT ISCHEMIC ATTACK, AND ALZHEIMER's	158
21. BEAUTY AND THE SIGNS OF AGING	163
22. COLLAGEN	172
23. THE NO. 1 KILLER, OPCs, AND CHOLESTEROL	183
24. ARTERIOSCLEROSIS AND INFARCTIONS	203
25. REGULATING INFLAMMATORY AFFAIRS	208
26. HISTAMINE, STOMACH ULCERS, AND ALLERGIES	218
27. RHEUMATOID ARTHRITIS	221
28. OPCs, THE MIGHTIEST SCAVENGERS OF FREE RADICALS	227
29. SURVIVING THE RADICAL COMBAT ZONE	238
30. TUMOR PREVENTION AND CANCER	248
31. RED WINE DRINKERS LIVE HAPPIER AND LONGER	256
32. OPCs AND THE REBOUND EFFECT	268
33. ALCOHOL, WHAT ELSE TO SAY?	279
34. WHY THE JAPANESE OUTLIVE THE FRENCH	283
35. TANNINS, TOO BIG TO HANDLE	290
36. GRAPE SEED EXTRACT, THE DREADED SCENARIO	296
37. THE U.S. PATENT REVISITED	306
38. CELEBRATE YOUR OWN 120TH BIRTHDAY	312
39. OPCs, VITAMIN C, AND THE FACTS OF *e*-LIFE	319
40. APPLICATION, DOSAGE, AND SAFETY	333
41. LITERATURE	343
42. PUBLICATIONS AND PATENTS OF DR. JACK MASQUELIER	357

1 MASQUELIER AND THE UNIVERSAL OPCs

The scope of Dr. Jack Masquelier's inventions and discoveries is infinitely wide in that they occurred in the European aftermath of World War II, amid poverty, famine, and complete lack of scientific equipment. At that time, all people wanted was food. During the decades of increasing wealth and abundance that followed, Masquelier's research came to fruition. Awareness of the relation between nutrition and health was growing.

It is paradoxical that the discovery of one of the best-performing micronutrients took place when food was lacking and that the relevance of this discovery is coming to be fully appreciated when supermarkets are filled to the brim with a quantity of food products the world has never before seen under one roof. Yet, many of today's industrially processed food products are considered as lacking quality and as unhealthy. Modern ways of large-scale agriculture produce tasteless fruits and vegetables that many consider "empty" when it comes to essential nutrients. The microwave oven and easy-to-prepare or instant meals and food products allow us to spend less time in the kitchen. Knowledge of the origins of our food is completely lost to younger generations. Our dietary habits have been dramatically altered. In reaction, many consumers have begun to develop a preference for the organically grown traditional whole foods, and they supplement their diet with pure-form vitamins, minerals, and other essential nutrients such as oligomeric procyanidins (OPCs).

The food industry follows the new needs by fortifying empty products with ingredients one normally finds in whole foods. Marketeers and scientists invent terms such as "customized nutrition" to individualize dietary recommendations and consumption of specific foods to match an individual's health needs. All this is very interesting and well meant, but an NBC News survey conducted during August 2002 gave a revealing answer. When people were asked, "Would you be prepared to restrict your calorie intake by one-third in order to live longer?" 73 percent of the respondents said no. When questioned, 65 percent of the respondents said that they were not interested in living to extreme old age, even if it were possible.

When Masquelier took his first pharmacy classes at Bordeaux University, pharmacy was not yet an industry. Then, individual pharmacists, almost exclusively, indulged in the art of preparing and dispensing practically all medicines. Pharmacists shared their skills and knowledge, but they did not share a vested interest. Since those days, the world of medicines has drastically changed. Magistrally prepared medicines have been replaced by drugs that are manufactured by a multibillion-dollar industrial conglomerate that strictly obeys the terms set by investors and shareholders. In a very literal sense, for the financial masters of the pharmaceutical cartel, a healthy person is of no interest because they earn their living by selling drugs. Many of those drugs would become redundant if people took dietary supplements and improved their eating habits. The free sale of vitamins, minerals, and other nutrients such as OPCs through channels not monopolized by the pharmaceutical industry significantly disturbs that industry's profits and profit potential. In an attempt to master the situation, the pharmaceutical industry forcefully imposes itself on scientists, doctors, media, politicians, and authorities to obtain drug status for nutrients. If nutrients were under the industry's control as drugs, pharmaceutical executives would no longer fear nutrients as the loose cannons that could negatively affect their personal bonuses, their companies' profits, and their shareholders' dividends. As long as the pharmaceutical industry fails to get nutrients redefined as drugs, it will continue to inform consumers that high dosages of vitamins are worthless or dangerous.

Although proud of his work, Masquelier never sought to place his discoveries and inventions in a scope broader than the framework of his own day-to-day "magistral" work at the university. He never tried to lift himself to Nobel Prize heights by stressing his research's implications for millions of people. Yet, the implications of his work are so profound that one cannot simply sum up the many varied health aspects of the products he developed just to serve the reader who is looking for a miracle cure.

In this age of quick answers to brief questions, reading *Dr. MASQUELIER's Mark on Health* involves more than having our health-related questions answered in some one-liners that promote more than they explain. In his work, Masquelier challenges with wits. Rather than bluntly promoting his OPCs, he simply explains how and why they work. He is always a gentleman scientist, never a salesman. His explanations take unexpected turns, leading the student or interviewer from botany to biochemistry, from medicine to cosmetics, and always to a better understanding of OPCs. That's why a book that renders tribute to this eminent scientist and to his inventions must challenge the wits and attention of the reader. To narrow the focus of this book to the problems of aging or to the treatment of varicose veins would be an insult to Masquelier, especially because no other scientist in his field understands the art of simplicity. Therefore, a book about OPCs must also describe the personality of their discoverer.

When Masquelier looks back on his life, more than 81 years after he was born, it appears to him as straightforward and consistent. For Jack, his discoveries always were the logical consequence of his research. In his day-to-day work at the University of Bordeaux, he dealt with vegetal ingredients and, in an evenly intensive manner, also with wine. Part of the enjoyment of drinking a glass of wine with Masquelier is the wisdom he shares without teaching. Primarily, though, what made the results of his work so consistent was his determination to devote all his professional efforts to a colorless, "invisible" vegetal nutrient that fascinated him practically every day of his entire life: oligomeric procyanidins (OPCs).

Though colorless, OPCs have colored the lives of millions of people as well as practically all aspects of Professor Masquelier's life. And OPCs impart much color when it comes to what they can achieve in the human body. In terms of human health, OPCs are truly a color in that they are particles of gold, hidden in the whirl of the enormous variety of micronutrients and phytonutrients until Masquelier discovered them in 1947. Isolated, defined, tried, and tested, OPCs turned out to be the most colorful phytonutrient on today's nutritional palette.

OPCs' discovery and extraction were dramatic enough, but the exploration of their applications in human health was a series of "to be continued" episodes because the effects of OPCs influenced so many seemingly unrelated conditions. At first, right after their discovery, it became obvious that OPCs were a high-performing vasoprotective nutrient that provided relief in practically all vascular disorders and diseases. ("Vaso-" means vascular, or relating to a blood vessel.) In France, Dr. Masquelier's discovery of OPCs gave rise to three medicinal products that have been successfully used against vascular disorders for many decades.

The finding that OPCs provide protection to collagen and contribute to the making of it explained why OPCs exert a positive influence on all structures in the body where collagen plays a supportive role. This brings into perspective not only the vascular wall but also bones, muscles, tendons, connective tissue, joints, skin, and mucous membranes. In fact, it brings into perspective every tissue of the body because collagen acts as a "ground substance" in all tissues.

Even more options in the application of OPCs in the human body became apparent as research continued. Masquelier was better able to explain the broad and intense effect that OPCs have on the body when he discovered that OPCs neutralize the common cause of many seemingly unrelated conditions: free radicals. OPCs are tremendously strong antioxidants. This discovery is extremely significant in a time when an increase in life expectancy is accompanied by a dramatic increase in cardiovascular and other degenerative diseases. Those in western and westernized societies live much longer now than any preceding generations lived, yet this longevity makes it imperative that people spend their lives in good health. And this is precisely where OPCs come into play — they provide a means to live not only longer but also better so that we may fulfill our lives without being crippled by traditional ravages of old age.

The anti-aging battle is ferociously fought by many and eventually lost by all. Everyone knows that aging is inevitable, so it makes sense to abandon the frantic pursuit of eternal youth and instead age gracefully and harmoniously by staying physically and mentally fit. Yves Montand, one of France's most famous singers of Masquelier's generation, sang in one of his songs: "Il faut boire jusqu'à l'ivresse ... sa jeunesse!" In English, it means, "One must drink one's youth until exhilaration." There is more to anti-aging than taking antioxidants. Unless one drinks one's youth until exhilaration, all the health gained in later life will be lost. In the spirit of Montand's immortal song, Masquelier's work is brought to full bloom only when people let the results of his scientific endeavors inspire them to drink their youth until exhilaration.

I vividly remember some conversations with Masquelier regarding the enormous importance of his products in today's time frame. I reiterated that half a century after his discovery of OPCs, his work has a crucial effect on the lives of many people, that it improves their well-being, spares them diseases, and provides relief for or cures the most varied illnesses. I insisted that he be proud of and content with the results of his scientific research. In typical Masquelier style, he said, "No, not really! Contentment is not something that is part of my character. All my life I have done my work, engaged in research, kept searching, erred, abandoned wrong tracks, looked for new ones, had my doubts ... In the course of my life, results presented themselves that were the logical consequence of my work. Every work bears fruit. I dedicated myself to research because I was curious, because it was my profession. I did my job, conscientiously, also with passion, but not necessarily with the abstract objective in mind 'to save mankind' or for any other similarly noble goal."

Masquelier has always been a scientist who looked for truth and facts. A scientist in the real meaning of the word, he made his contribution to society without the express motive and intention to make such a contribution. He didn't discover and invent so that he could "do good." Masquelier had no political, financial or social agenda. He is a scientist "pur sang." It was thus that he encountered his moments of drama and intensity, moments when he had to face people who did not rise the way his students did when he entered the lecturing halls of universities. He did not escape the reality that life is a series of highs, turning points, and lows, of situations that do not always respond to the laws of nature that he applied in his research in his laboratory.

It was precisely in the straightforwardness of his scientific work that Masquelier recognizes the scientific drama. Everybody who is preoccupied with the history of science and its discoveries will be familiar with this professional suspense. In the case of Masquelier, this suspense was produced by the simplicity with which he always approached complex and difficult matters. Instead of indulging in formulating obscure and incomprehensible theories, Masquelier was satisfied only when simplicity produced results.

When Masquelier started his research right after World War II in 1945, there existed practically nothing that he needed and wanted for his scientific laboratory work. Sometimes he even had to blow his own beakers. This forced simplicity, however, had one advantage. Those miserable working conditions were conducive to the creative mind. They made him into an exceptionally imaginative and practical scientist. Simplicity thus became the "leitmotiv" of his life. Despite their far-reaching consequences for humanity, his discoveries have always been simple to explain and simple to understand. Yet, it is only in retrospect that one recognizes the simplicity and wonders, "Why didn't someone think of that earlier?"

Dr. Jack Masquelier in his laboratory (1950)

In today's world, science has become a marketing tool. Science and scientists are used to sell products. The sales and marketing divisions of the big companies that now govern the health food industry always need "something new": new formulas, new ingredients, new research ... If it isn't new, it won't sell. In the minds of those who are preoccupied with sales, research that is older than a year is being regarded as stale and unfit for use in promotional campaigns and unfit for sending out a press release.

This book is different. I take you on the journey I made after I came to know the work and person of Professor Jack Arthur Masquelier. We track his many discoveries and inventions, starting at the very origins of his research. Masquelier discovered OPCs when the oldest of today's baby boomers were babies. OPCs were born in the same spirit of freedom, love, adventure, and happiness that laid the foundation for most of that generation. In the truest sense, OPCs are also baby boomers and have grown, not only in age, but also in potential and relevance. Every time a new health topic hit the front pages over the past 55 years, OPCs were found to be of unique relevance.

OPCs have grown in relevance in a world that has fundamentally changed since their discovery. There are no more unknown continents. There are no undiscovered desert islands. There is no square yard that cannot be spotted by some satellite. We know where the poor people are who starve for no good reason. We know where the rich people are who die of cancer. Some people worry about what they will eat tomorrow. Others worry about *whether* they will eat tomorrow.

The one thing that all people have in common, though, is their will to survive. For some this means waiting in a desert for a meager cup of foreign aid food. For others it means waiting in a hospital corridor to learn the date of a bypass operation. Some of us fight every day for a cup of soup. Others fight McDonald's for its failure to stop them from overeating. Others fight cigarette companies for having enjoyed too many of their addictive products. The millions who struggle for no more than a piece of bread are not on the time sheets of the attorneys who go where the money is.

Sixty-one percent of all Americans are overweight, and the health costs to treat obese American children have risen to $100 billion. In Germany, every third child under age 12 and every fifth teenager is overweight. In Greece, more than 70 percent of adult men and women are above their ideal weight. Around the world,

300 million adults and 35 million children are overweight. Poverty doesn't mean lean. High-calorie junk food is cheap and tempting, even for those who live on a couple of dollars per day. In all its empty cheapness, junk food symbolizes Western wealth to the deprived. When the party is over, reality hits with cardiovascular diseases, obesity, diabetes, premature signs of aging, and the rest of the welfare problems the "Cola" societies are coping with. It makes OPCs the lynchpin of health in many different cultures. When Masquelier isolated the first OPCs in his bare and ill-equipped university lab, he could not have foreseen that 55 years later, his "high-performance phytonutrient" would be just as relevant for an American Boomer as for a child growing up in China.

2 MASQUELIER's CHILDHOOD AND YOUTH

In 1922, Jack Arthur Masquelier was born the son of simple people in Paris. His mother was a worker from Paris and his father a bricklayer from Lille, a town in the North of France, close to the Belgian border. Although very French, his parents preferred the English name Jack to the French Jacques.

Jack remained an only child, which certainly molded his life-long solitary working manner. Even today, he is still convinced that teamwork — currently so favored and praised — is nonsense, an illusion. According to Masquelier, the group always consists of individuals with varied skills. Its progress is inhibited by the weakest member. In science, there is no such thing as a result produced by a team of researchers. The decisive idea is invariably the product of one single mind, not of the entire group. Masquelier realizes that this opinion may not enjoy great popularity in today's world, but from his earliest childhood, he was forced to resort to his own abilities, to learn to work alone and to rely on himself. This tendency was promoted by the numerous moves made by the Masquelier family during Jack's childhood.

Jack's father built houses as accommodations for miners in the north of France. The region around Lille, Roubaix, Tourcoing, and Lens up to the Pas-de-Calais, that is Dunkerque on the coast, held huge coal deposits. Once the mining settlement of a town was completed, the family moved to the next town. In Lens, there was a long Masquelier Street named after Jack's father, a very active, industrious man who could build an entire house with his own hands. The Masquelier family always lived in homes that Jack's father had personally constructed.

As a self-reliant only child, Jack was accustomed to occupying himself alone. Literature, the vast realm of imagination, interested him as much as everything he could touch, move, and change. During his school days, he became increasingly engrossed in the natural sciences, in physics, and primarily in chemistry. He experienced combining the material aspects of life with the world of the mind, his mind. In the small laboratory that he had created at home, he performed tests that resulted in occasional explosions startling his parents, especially his mother. But his interest was not limited to achieving amusing effects. He wanted to understand causes and relationships. He bought books to learn what exactly happens when two substances react, generating a third one.

His father suggested that Jack study pharmacology. In those days, a pharmacist was someone who, after five years of study, was permitted to sell medicines prepared in the pharmacist's own laboratory. At that time, a pharmacist still worked with generic substances, preparing and mixing them in the manner the physician had prescribed rather than dispensing the packaged industry-made medicines we know today. People often visited their pharmacist before seeing a physician.

Jack liked the idea of studying pharmacology. He had just finished his A-level (high school) exam in Dunkerque and was free to study wherever and whatever he wanted. Then something happened that severely restricted his options. The Germans invaded the north of France; for Jack Masquelier the Second World War had begun. Jack's parents, who had experienced the First World War, knew that in the event of war, the north of France would be in extreme danger. They decided to move as far away from the Germans as possible, gave up their residence in

Dunkerque, and in 1939, settled in Arcachon, on the South Atlantic coast near Bordeaux. Their decision was certainly right since vast regions of the north were destroyed, and then practically all of France was occupied by the Germans. This move, nevertheless, had tragic consequences. As soon as Jack's father left his beloved homeland, he fell ill and died that same year. From then on, Jack and his mother were on their own.

In order to be able to begin his pharmacology studies, Jack had to do a one-year internship in a pharmacy. Unfortunately, he was not the only one to have fled to the southwest of France. Many northern French people, especially Parisians, resided there too. As a result, all trainee positions in the pharmacies of Arcachon, Bordeaux, and that area were taken. Jack did not want to waste his time waiting for a position and therefore began his medical studies.

In those days, the first year of medical studies consisted of training in natural sciences, ending with an examination in physics, chemistry, and biology. Thus he avoided losing precious time. Moreover, he was a tremendous step ahead when he finally took up his pharmacology studies after his first year of practical training. The initial phase of pharmacology studies provided training in the very subjects with which he was already familiar. He completed the first year with outstanding grades and was considered top of the class during the further course of his studies. He had become enthralled with both fields and wanted to become both physician and pharmacist.

He found his studies increasingly fascinating, especially because he was aware that he was being trained in a profession that he perceived less as work and more as vocation and joy. He did what he enjoyed doing and realized that this is the secret of happiness: to be able to do as an adult what you did in your childhood games. But then again, life did not proceed as smoothly as Jack had hoped it would. His plans and his studies were thwarted by the fact that he belonged to the age group that was recruited in 1943 for deportation to work in Germany. After four years of war, Germany had a shortage of medically trained staff, and everybody who had followed medical, pharmaceutical, or surgical training in the occupied territories was conscripted to work in Adolf Hitler's "motherland." Refusing or running away was not a solution because pressure would then be exerted on one's family. If Jack had not gone to Germany, his mother might have been arrested. Thus he ended up in Erfurt in Thuringia, where he assisted in a pharmacy for more than one year.

In contrast to original promises, the Germans did not let Masquelier and those who shared his fate return to France. Since they had taken his papers, he was trapped. Yet, shortly before the end of the war, he fled Germany without documents, without money, and without a chance to earn any food. Hunger, which by then haunted all of Europe, was a horrid experience he shared with millions. Only after the liberation of Bordeaux in 1944 was Masquelier able to resurface from the underground and resume his studies. However, he now had to give up medicine. Medical studies take six to seven years. He had completed only two years and simply lacked the time to study both pharmacology and medicine. He had to make money to survive and so completed his pharmacology studies by learning the material of two years of study in only one year. He passed his examination in 1945.

After 1945, he remained enrolled at the university to prepare for his Ph.D. He earned a living by filling in as a pharmacist. Since he had passed several examinations in natural sciences, including chemistry, biochemistry, and physics, he was also able to make some money by performing analyses for hospital laboratories. Owing to his versatility, he could choose between a Ph.D. in pharmacology and a Ph.D. in natural sciences. In those days, natural sciences comprised the fields of physics, chemistry, biochemistry, biology, and botany. The degree in natural sciences no longer exists because it is regarded as excessively comprehensive and challenging.

With his pharmaceutical examination done and certificates in several of the natural sciences in his pocket, he had applied for a Ph.D. at the pharmaceutical and medical faculty, which at that time was one and the same. The faculty suggested a thesis in natural sciences. Masquelier's doctoral advisor, Professor Francis Tayeau, who soon became the faculty's dean, gave him three topics from which to choose. Masquelier selected a study about the pigments in the skin of the peanut. Unimportant and trivial as the peanut skin may seem, by making it the object of his doctorate studies, Masquelier planted the seeds for an impressive career at the Biological and Medical Research Faculty of Bordeaux University, a part of the French National Center for Scientific Research (CNRS). The publication of his doctorate thesis on July 12, 1948, also marked the birth of the nutrient we have come to know as OPCs.

3
THE DISCOVERY OF OPCs

Jack Masquelier's doctoral studies on the pigments of the peanut skin had a very practical social relevance. After World War II, Europe was in ashes. All countries, including France, were bled out. Many millions suffered from hunger, poor nutrition, and the emotional shock created by the loss of family and friends. An entire continent was to emerge from a state of destruction and severe depression. Uncountable numbers of people who had been displaced by events were trying to get back home, crossing Europe without regular means of transportation. The distribution of food was limited and rationed until several years after 1945. Scientific research was almost impossible for the lack of equipment and utensils.

Devastated, France had lost the agricultural potential for which it had been envied by the rest of Europe just a few years earlier. The French even had to look for sources of food not normally grown in their country. In 1940, foreseeing what seemed to be inescapable, the French government had commissioned the laboratory where Masquelier came to work five years later to determine the nutritional value of peanut residue. This residue is the mass that remains after the pressing of the peanut oil and was traditionally used as an ingredient for fodder for livestock. Under the war and post-war circumstances, the idea had arisen to use the compact residue as food for humans because it was a rich source of protein. First, though, two questions had to be answered.

Some farmers had found that their cattle refused to eat the de-oiled peanut food. Maybe it was because these residues had a fairly high content of the red skin that surrounds the nut. No one knew for sure. People had eaten peanuts for ages, but if the peanut residue were to serve as human food, it was necessary to make sure that the skins were not potentially toxic or otherwise dangerous. Also, the University team needed to establish whether the proteins of the peanut residue contained a sufficient number of amino acids essential for humans. Amino acids make up proteins, and the peanut residue consisted mostly of proteins. If the peanut residue was to serve as food for humans, it seemed logical to determine which amino acids could be found in the residue.

The protein part of these investigations was performed by Masquelier's doctoral advisor, Professor Tayeau, who was an expert in the chemistry of proteins and intensively preoccupied with peanuts as a source of proteins for humans and animals. Masquelier vividly remembers how Tayeau never ceased to feed his students all kinds of peanut butters. Their taste left a lot to be desired, but they certainly reduced the latent feeling of hunger. Apart from having to taste his tutor's peanut butters, Masquelier was given the task to investigate the peanut skins, especially to find out whether the coloring agents of the thin peanut skin might be potentially toxic.

When Masquelier joined the laboratory for biological and medical chemistry in October 1945, he had no idea that more than half a century later he would still have his attention focused on the subject of his first research project and that the phytonutrient he managed to isolate would provide relief to millions of people. The Arachis hypogaea, the peanut plant, and more especially its nuts, were not unknown to him. From his school days in the harbor town of Dunkerque, he still had fond memories of long walks that invariably took him and his friends to the harbor on free days. When they felt hungry, they headed for the pier where freight ships from Africa were moored and whose holds where filled with peanuts. They had to only bend down and pick up the peanuts that had dropped to the ground during unloading.

Years later, destiny caused him to live in Bordeaux in a house on the bank of the Garonne River not far from the spot where overseas trade had been resumed after the end of the war. Again, deliveries of peanuts from Senegal, earmarked for the major oil presses of the town, presented a familiar element. Therefore, it does not come as a surprise that when offered three research subjects by his doctoral tutor, he decided in favor of the peanut. The student Masquelier was also fascinated by the many different aspects of a study that involved complicated analytical techniques, botany, plant-chemistry, toxicology, and nutrition as well as the testing of biological effects of the substances he was to isolate from the peanut skins. Most of all, he loved this kind of research because he could practice artisanship.

Strangely and unexpectedly, Masquelier's work tied in with the research that was done by Tayeau on the nut's proteins. To separate and isolate the amino acids of a protein, one must split the protein by way of a chemical process called hydrolysis, which is just splitting something in water. The proteins are heated in acid water, which is an aqueous (watery) mixture of the very strong acid hydrogen-chloride, or hydrochloric acid. Hydrochloric acid is also a normal constituent of the gastric juice. At body temperature, hydrolysis of proteins naturally happens in our stomachs, where hydrochloric acid aids in dissolving the proteins before they are split by the enzymes (pepsins) of the gastric juice. Under laboratory conditions, heat replaces the function of the pepsins. When Tayeau's team performed the hydrolysis by heating the proteins of the peanuts with hydrochloric acid, they were quite surprised when with the various colorless amino acids a bright red coloration appeared.

At first, they could only explain the reddening by simply assuming that a coloring agent attaches itself to the proteins while the peanut grows and that this pigment then detaches itself when the proteins are being split. The appearance of a red substance gave rise to the idea that something similar might be present in the red-brown peanut skin. Because they still had to determine whether the red-brown skin contained something toxic, they had become equally cautious with regard to the contents of the nut, especially now that all of a sudden something red appeared. Could the something red that showed up while they were breaking the proteins down into amino acids also be present in the skin? And if so, was it toxic? Tayeau wanted to obtain a clear picture of the identity of the pigments in the skin and of those that seemed to be invisibly present in the proteins. He assigned the research of these pigments to Masquelier and requested that his student find a quick and simple way to solve these "colorful" issues.

In those days, it was well known in the botanical sciences that in plants a red, pink, violet, or blue coloration generally hints at the presence of a pigment named anthocyanin. It had also been found that the color of the anthocyanin pigment can vary with the degree of acidity or alkalinity in the plant. Acidity and alkalinity are expressed by the symbol pH on a scale where a pH of 7 marks the neutral point. In an acid environment, the pH is lower than 7 and the anthocyanins are red. In an alkaline environment, the pH is higher than 7 and the anthocyanins are blue. In old Greek, "anthos" means flower and "kuanos" or "cyano" means blue. From alkaline blue to violet, the "cyano" colors in flowers derive the name of anthocyanin ("flower-blue"). In his doctorate thesis, Masquelier describes how botanists managed to turn red geranium flowers blue by bringing them in contact with an alkaline substance and how, in reverse, the violet's flowers could be switched to red when brought in contact with an acid substance. These colorful matters were known beyond botanical circles. Cabbage comes in many colors, ranging from blue to red, and when a blue cabbage is cooked with a touch of vinegar, it turns red in the magical transformation of anthocyanins.

The bright red substance that appeared following the hydrolysis of the peanut's proteins behaved in a strikingly identical manner. It changed from red to blue in accordance with the changes in pH Masquelier produced. This was anthocyanin. But where did the anthocyanin come from? Nobody knew the exact composition and structure of anthocyanin. Although the biochemical identity of the precursor that gives rise to anthocyanin was still unknown, scientists had called this phantom substance "chromogen," not so much on the basis of what it is but more on the basis of what it does. "Chromo" means "color" and "gen" comes from generating. Chromogens generate colors.

Chromogens were known in the botanical sciences. Those who studied plants attributed the reddening of the leaves in autumn to these yet unidentified substances. As early as 1908, the botanist J. Laborde had proposed the idea that autumn puts enzymes into action that make the chromogens produce their color in vivo — that is, in the living organism — while the activation of such chromogens in the laboratory (ex vivo) requires heat and acid hydrolysis. In 1920, Otto Rosenheim had coined the term "leucoanthocyanin" for chromogen. By using the term "leuco," which means white or colorless, Rosenheim tried to suggest that there existed some colorless pigment, a white form of anthocyanin, that manifests itself under the influence of an acid and simultaneous heating.

In the 1930s, the famous couple of biochemists, Lord and Lady Robinson, took up Rosenheim's studies. Their interest was primarily in botanical aspects. They determined and classified plants by means of chemical analysis of certain plant constituents. Of special and obvious importance were plant pigments and their precursors as a means to classify by color. The Robinsons, however, concentrated on describing and classifying the substances. They were not interested in their extraction or application. In 1933, Lord Robinson suggested a theoretical chemical structure for chromogen (leucoanthocyanin), but he never came up with any proof.

When Masquelier began his research project, nobody had yet extracted anthocyanin's chromogen in its pure state and nobody had proposed a realistic clue for its chemical structure, for its biological properties, and for the way it could transform itself into anthocyanin. Knowing he was onto something, Masquelier made it his primary goal to close the gaps in all these theories, opinions, and suggestions. Equipped only with the most elementary tools, Masquelier had to confront these complex chemical issues while at the same time overcoming various difficult analytical and technical problems. First of all, he had to somehow remove the oil from the peanut skins because the oil would complicate and obstruct all further steps. Another cautionary measure turned out to be equally important. During the removal of the oil from the skins as well as during all the steps that followed, Masquelier had to avoid heating the material in the presence of an acid because doing so would have transformed the chromogen into anthocyanin. Thus, the chromogen would have gone up in color.

After much study and preliminary work, Masquelier managed to obtain a de-oiled fraction of the skin. Because he had used ether to remove the oil, he also managed to get rid of impurities that are soluble in ether. What remained was the insoluble de-oiled fraction, which he called fraction insoluble, or F.I. The red-brown F.I. material had a strong astringent taste, which reminded Masquelier of the extract made from the ratanhia. Ratanhia is a South American medicinal plant used because it is rich in tannins. Masquelier figured that the de-oiled extract from the peanut skin probably contained tannins because the taste was strikingly tannic. As with the chromogen, tannins were known by what they did, rather than by what they were in terms of their chemical structure. Scientists detect and identify tannins by simply tasting them or by making them insoluble by bringing them into contact with gelatin or other proteins such as casein. In contact with proteins, tannins become insoluble by irreversibly binding to the proteins. "Their ability to combine with proteins is the basis of the process known as vegetable tannage, by which animal fibre is converted into leather," is how the scientist M. Nierenstein had described tannins already in 1934. The more astringent the tannin, the better and quicker it transforms skin into leather. Years before Masquelier went to work, the leather industry already knew standardized methods for determining the strength and purity of tannic materials by making them insoluble with gelatin, casein, or hide powder.

But first, Masquelier had to further fraction his raw F.I. peanut material to determine its components. Chromatograpy is the common name for various laboratory methods used to separate complex mixtures into individual fractions and components. In 1947 and 1948, chromatography was still in its infancy. But the crude method that did exist enabled Masquelier to discover that when percolated through an aluminum chromatography column, the de-oiled peanut skin material, the fraction insoluble, clearly split into two fractions: a pale yellow fraction, which he named f1, and a red-brown fraction, which he named f2. f1 responded instantly when it was heated in a mildly acid solution, leading to the conclusion that f1 was the pure chromogen that generates anthocyanin. f2 turned out to be tannins because Masquelier was able to render f2 completely insoluble by putting it in contact with gelatin.

It was still too early to cry victory. Being a practical man, Masquelier wanted to figure out how he could obtain considerable quantities of the pale fraction without the intervention of the time-consuming and complex chromatography, which permitted the isolation of only infinitely small quantities. During the many months he worked on this project, Masquelier had been struck by the idea that it might be possible to isolate larger quantities of the pure pale chromogen (f1) by mixing the raw de-oiled peanut skin material (F.I.) with water that had been saturated with table salt.

And indeed, this "salting" resulted directly in the precipitation of a fraction that turned out to be identical to the tannic f2 fraction he had produced by way of chromatography. Thus, he could "salt out" the tannins by making them insoluble and filtering them out of the crude raw material. What remained in the solution was the pale yellow fraction that showed all the chromogenic qualities of the corresponding yellowish solution (f1) he had separated in the chromatography column. Heating of the f1 fraction in hydrochloric acid immediately caused the formation of anthocyanin.

Now having sufficient and reproducible amounts of chromogen at his fingertips, Masquelier sent some samples to the Laboratory for Organic Microanalysis and to the Collège de France to find out how much carbon, hydrogen, oxygen, and combinations of these three atoms could be counted. Combining the results he got back with the results of a number of other tests and with the theoretical work done by the Robinsons, Masquelier then succeeded in formulating the chemical structure of chromogen as well as the chemical reaction through which the colorless chromogen turns into the red anthocyanin.

Apart from formulating chromogen's chemical structure, Masquelier demonstrated that chromogen exists in its pure form in that it is not bound to a sugar. Part of the tannins, anthocyanins, and similar compounds are found in plants in the form of complexes with sugars. The properties of these so-called heterosides can differ very much from the properties of the pure substances. Therefore, Masquelier had to see whether chromogen also exists in the form of a chromogen-sugar complex. He found that there is no heteroside of chromogen and that it exists only in pure form. In addition, he showed that chromogen dissolved in water and then left in open contact with air gradually forms an insoluble reddish deposit. When analyzed, this deposit turned out to be tannins. The oxidation of chromogen transforms it into tannins. In other words, tannins are made out of chromogen by way of oxidation.

Were these then the only constituents of the peanut skin? No. During his many tests, Masquelier was able to find small traces of other substances, such as flavonon and phlobaphen. Flavonon is a colorless bioflavonoid that turns yellow. The yellow flavonoids were not unknown, but their chemistry and biological activity were still largely unexplained. Phlobaphen is an intensely red insoluble substance found in the brownish tannic fraction. Masquelier's method of isolating the chromogen eliminates these pigments as well as the tannins. Remarkably, Masquelier did not find any anthocyanin in the peanut. All the reds and browns in the peanut skin are tannins and a little bit of phlobaphen. The chromogen is colorless and thus "invisible."

As Masquelier told me many times, when he succeeded in these operations for the first time, he sensed tremendous joy and excitement. And every time he explained to his students the procedures he had followed to obtain the chromogen, he relived the emotions and sensations the discovery of chromogen (now OPCs) had stirred up in his soul. Numerous researchers before him had dedicated themselves to studying leucoanthocyanins, but as botanists, they were concerned only with achieving results that were of interest to those who studied plants. They did not think of chromogen as a phytonutrient. Masquelier, on the other hand, had made the choice to work at a medical faculty where he could immediately apply his research in the field of nutrition and

31

human health. The moment he knew he could standardly reproduce pure chromogen, he became convinced that this nutrient, now known as OPCs, had the potential of becoming the subject of numerous examinations about what it could accomplish in the human body.

All this was fundamental nutritional research in its infancy — born out of famine, the quest for better understanding the nature of the individual components that make up our food, and also pure professional curiosity. It was the very beginning of a development that has brought us "nutraceuticals," vitamin-enriched foods, and shelves filled with hundreds of dietary supplements that contain a multitude of natural, fermented, and synthetically produced micronutrients. This was an unimaginable world for the young Masquelier and is still an unimaginable world for the millions for whom hunger has remained or has become a reality. It was also an unimaginable world for the pioneers who had put forward the notion of "vitamins" not long before Masquelier isolated chromogen. It was in this emerging field of health and nutrition that Masquelier concluded that his discoveries fell within the framework of a vitamin that had become known under the letter P.

In 1828, the French scientist M. Lebreton published in the *Journal of Pharmacy and Chemistry* an article about "the crystalline material in oranges and yet undeveloped analyses of this fruit." Lebreton had isolated a complex of hesperidin and sugar (a hesperidoside) from the peels of oranges, but at the time, he had no idea of the nutritional relevance of his discovery. Hesperidin is a bioflavonoid similar to the flavonon of which Masquelier had found traces in the peanut skins. In 1936, these bioflavonoids had been brought to the attention of the world in the form of a product named citrin. Citrin was the result of the scientific work of the great Hungarian scientist Albert Szent-Györgyi into the nature and effects of the vitamins C and P.

Albert Szent-Györgyi

Citrin was an extract made from citrus fruits. It had been developed by Szent-Györgyi, who thought that his citrin contained or actually was a vitamin he had named P after the protective effect that the citrin product sometimes had on the permeability of capillaries. The compound had received a name for what it did and not for what it was because Szent-Györgyi had not been able to isolate and chemically define Vitamin P. He had also failed to reach consistent results with it, mainly because the name vitamin P described more a biological effect than that it defined a specific substance. This is why Masquelier and others sometimes referred to the vitamins P. Szent-Györgyi and his team never resolved the many uncertainties surrounding vitamins P, and the notion that there was a vitamin called P was gradually abandoned. What remained was the vitamin P effect. The vitamin that did survive was vitamin C, especially because a few years after Szent-Györgyi had isolated and defined vitamin C, American scientists discovered an industrial way to produce it.

The essential merit of Masquelier's early research lay and still lies in his finding that chromogen (now OPCs) has an intense

33

capacity to protect the blood vessels. In fact, one could say that by discovering OPCs, Masquelier discovered the real vitamin P because he isolated it, chemically identified it, showed that it is safe, and proved that it *consistently* has an intense vitamin P effect.

4 THE FIRST VASCULAR PRODUCT

Apart from testing OPCs for possible toxicity, Masquelier performed a whole series of other tests to see what biological effects f1 produced in guinea pigs. Because vitamins P were still on many a scientist's agenda, Masquelier got the idea to see if he could observe a shortening of the bleeding time in the test animals. In the simple test he chose for this purpose, one briefly pricks the animal's ear in a process comparable to an inoculation and catches the emerging blood every 15 seconds on a strip of paper until the bleeding has stopped by itself and no blood is left to stain the paper. The number of spots x 15 seconds represents the total duration of the bleeding (hemorrhage). By way of injection, Masquelier gave one group of the animals 1 mg of OPCs daily over five consecutive days. Before the test, the average bleeding time of all animals was 108 seconds. Twenty-four hours after the last dosage, he found that in the group of untreated animals, the bleeding time remained unchanged; the guinea pigs that had received the OPCs stopped bleeding after only 55 seconds. Fifteen days later, the treated animals' bleeding time was at an average of 62.5 seconds. One month after the administration of 1 mg OPCs per day, the bleeding time of the treated animals was still under 100 seconds. The bleeding time of the untreated animals did not significantly change as shown on the next page.

From these preliminary experiments, Masquelier ascertained that OPCs were innocuous and they shortened the bleeding time by half. Although not yet knowing the precise mechanism that so significantly reduced the duration of the hemorrhage, Masquelier arrived at the conclusion that the vascular

N[b]	Weight (g.)	Sex	Initial bleeding time (seconds)	After 24 hours	After 15 days	After 30 days
1	640	M	120	60	60	90
2	570	M	120	45	60	90
3	540	M	105	60	60	105
4	737	F	90	45	75	90
5	628	F	105	60	60	90
6	580	F	105	60	60	120
7	718	M. Reference	120	120	120	105
8	655	F. Reference	105	105	120	105
average			108	55	62.5	97.5

system would present a perfect field for further experimentation if one intended to determine the physiological properties of OPCs. However, the easily measurable shortening of the duration of bleeding he induced by pricking an animal's ear presented him with more problems than he was able to solve right away. Did OPCs influence the permeability of the blood vessel? In other words, did OPCs really have a vitamin P effect? Making a wound affects the blood's vessel as well as its content, the blood itself. Two mechanisms come into play: the strength of the damaged vessel as well as its ability to seal a leak and the coagulation of the blood itself, or its ability to stop the bleeding process. Which was the decisive mechanism?

In 1936, when Szent-Györgyi presented the concept of vitamin P, he left no doubt as to what it was that this vitamin did. By definition, the vascular permeability vitamins influence the permeability of the capillary. In a way, the use of the word permeability is not 100 percent correct because it does not take into account the fluidity of the blood. Assuming that the fluidity of the blood is constant, the capillary becomes the decisive permeability factor. In that sense, Szent-Györgyi was correct in labeling vitamin P. Taking into account that the blood's fluidity may vary, it would have been more correct to name the new vitamin with the letter F, for *fragility*. In any case, Szent-Györgyi proposed that the vascular wall was not sufficiently strong to prevent the blood's fluid from seeping through. His staff and whole legions of scientists dedicated themselves to researching the new vitamin(s) and especially to measuring its (their) effect on what is called vascular resistance. In light of this, and to understand better what happened during the simple bleeding time test, Masquelier then decided in favor of another technique that gave more precise results than could be obtained by pricking an animal's ear.

The problem was that no reliable measuring tool existed to do what Masquelier had in mind. So, he constructed the tool himself. In his doctoral thesis, we find a drawing of this measuring device. Simple though efficient, it shows the unsophisticated ways in which Masquelier had to perform his research. His device enabled him to put a small suction hood on the shaven skin of a guinea pig. Then a pressure lower than that of the surrounding atmosphere is generated in the hood and measured by a manometer. The lowered pressure in the hood results in the formation of mini-leaks (micro-hemorrhages) in the capillaries. The leaks manifest themselves as tiny red spots under the skin and confirm that the minute blood vessels, the capillaries, have been ruptured by the decompression of the surrounding tissue. At the exact moment of the appearance of the red spot, the pressure in the hood is measured in centimeters of mercury and noted. The term "capillary resistance" thus refers to the point at which the capillary loses its resistance and can no longer contain the blood. In guinea pigs as well as in humans, the lowest point of intact capillary resistance rests at about 25 cm of mercury.

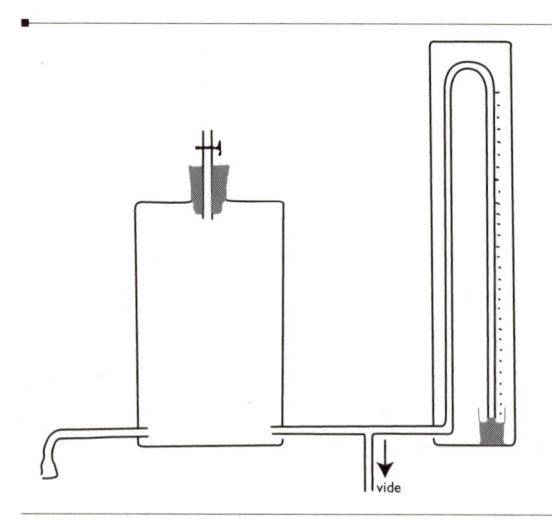

In his doctoral thesis, Masquelier printed this sketch of the device he built to perform his first tests on capillary fragility.

From a group of approximately 100 animals Masquelier selected those with low capillary resistance (between 10 and 14 cm). After he injected varying dosages of OPCs (between 0.10 and 4 mg), the resistance of the blood vessels (capillaries) doubled, making the capillaries twice as strong. It was now clear that OPCs have an excellent and consistent vitamin P effect; in fact, it was proven that OPCs are *the* vitamin P. These results, which he published in his doctoral thesis in 1948 (see the table on the next page), formed the basis of all his subsequent research and of the first human applications of OPCs. Having finished his thesis, the newly inaugurated Dr. Masquelier knew that he faced the immense task of combining these insights into a comprehensive theory and illustrating the far-reaching effect of OPCs on our health.

N[b]	Injected amount (mg.)	Initial Capillary Resistance (cm. of Hg)	Capillary Resistance after:						
			2 h.	6 h.	24 h.	36 h.	48 h.	96 h.	120 h.
1	4 >	10	14	15	19	24	18	12	12
2	2 >	11	13	15	16	18	20	14	14
3	2 >	10	12	12,5	15	17	21	17	13
4	2 >	13	15	16	18	27	29	18	16
5	1 >	13	14	15	21	30	28	20	17
6	1 >	11	14,5	16	20	30	25	25	25
7	1 >	13	14	15	18	30	24	23	20
8	0,50	12	13	13,5	15	17	24	24	23
9	0,50	10	13,5	15	18	23	24	30	24
10	0,25	14	14,5	15	17	30	30	24	20
11	0,25	11	11	13	15	21	25	20	14
12	0,10	12	12	12,5	14	15	17	16	14
13	reference	11	10	13	11	11	12	13	12
14	reference	13	14	10	11	13	10	13	12

Masquelier had administered to guinea pigs the OPCs he could now produce and reproduce from the peanut skins in quantities sufficient to be tested in animals and to be used in humans. Because Masquelier was able to simultaneously prove that OPCs are absolutely safe and highly effective, Professor Tayeau encouraged him to prepare sufficient quantities of it to help Tayeau's wife. She was pregnant and suffered from edema in the legs (from a swelling produced by serous fluid), a not-uncommon condition in pregnant women. She often felt tired, and her swollen legs caused her difficulties in walking. Forty-eight hours after Madame Tayeau took Masquelier's OPCs, she was relieved from these symptoms. The amazing vascular effects of the extract, which would be refined, identified, tested, and perfected during the many decades that followed, incited Masquelier to continue his research and development. This is how, in 1950, he developed Resivit, the first vasoprotective medicine based on OPCs.

In 1950, the field of nutrition and medicine was not yet ready to acknowledge such insights. The relationship between nutrition and health was nowhere near as advanced as it is today. Food was food and medicines were medicines. If one was ill, one took a pill. What medical doctors and pharmacists did not condone was referred to as folk medicine. Food preparation was left to the women, who then still spent many hours of each day in the kitchen. Processed food, instant food, snacks, microwaves, and all the other "blessings" that were unleashed during subsequent decades were unknown. And whatever the "folks" and the housewives believed was of no relevance to science. The precise relationships between food and health were still largely unmapped. Even the discoverer of vitamin C, Szent-Györgyi, had no idea when he made his first discoveries in the years before the Second World War that scurvy and infarction are rooted in a deficiency of the same vitamin. It was not until later in the second half of the 20th century that scientists around the world finally began to accept the notion that nutrition and health are integrally related fields and that certain nutrients have a profound effect on many conditions.

This is how, in the days of young Masquelier, his experiments that showed that OPCs produced improved lowered capillary resistance in guinea pigs could only lead to the conclusion that his research was relevant for the medical field. This is how, although discovered as a phytonutrient in peanuts, OPCs found their first use in the form of a medicine. Masquelier's doctoral advisor, Professor Tayeau, was a medical man. Excited by the improvement in his wife's condition, he was the first to come up with the idea of systematically trying OPCs on human subjects. The experiments were performed at the Saint-André

Hospital in Bordeaux. Several women, among them Madame Tayeau, were injected with the substance dissolved in liquid. The effects on the state of their vascular system were overwhelming. Madame Tayeau's edema disappeared after 48 hours, and remarkably positive changes were also recorded in the other women.

In 1948, Jack Masquelier registered the French patent for the process of producing leucoanthocyanin (now OPCs) from the peanut skin (French patent no. 968.589). Clinical tests were performed to check the effect of the patented product on various disorders due to capillary weakness: hemorrhage, increased tendency to bleeding, bleeding gums, and other vein-related disorders including varicose veins, heavy legs, and edema. After the positive effect of OPCs on weakened blood vessels had been

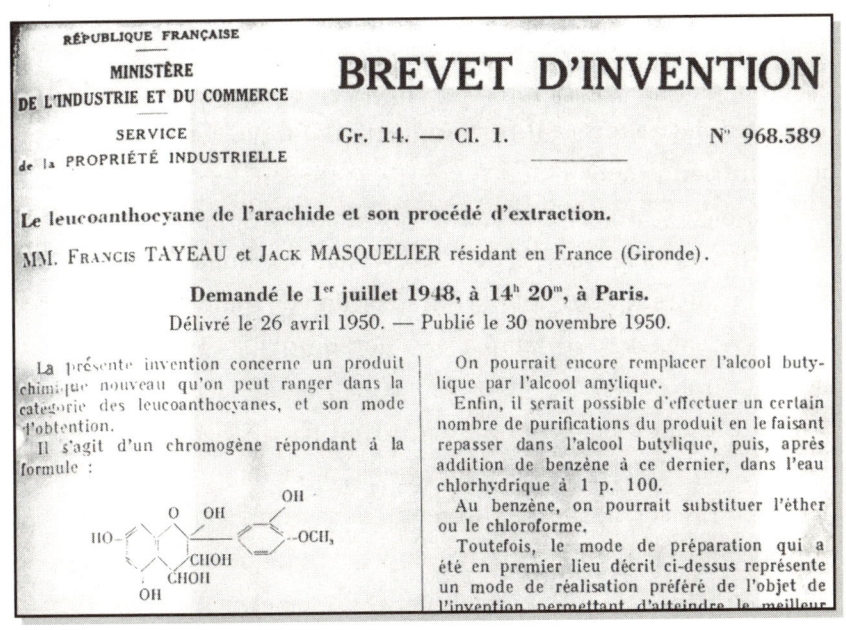

French patent no. 968.589

confirmed and the required series of tests had been concluded, Masquelier assigned the Oberlin Laboratory in Paris to develop an appropriate medicine. The first OPCs product was called Resivit (vitamine de résistance, or resistance vitamin). It was presented in liquid form and was put in ampoules. To extend its shelf life and to prevent the OPCs from forming tannins through oxidation, Masquelier suggested adding a small quantity of sodium sulfite acid. Thus the Resivit medicine was given a slight antioxidant "twist." Up to the present day, Masquelier has kept some of the ampoules from that time. Their content has not changed color and there are no sediments.

Resivit entered the market in 1950 and was used primarily by women who worked in jobs that required them to stand or walk for long periods, including factory workers, waitresses, and sales clerks. At the time, many doctors prescribed this medicine for such indications. Dentists used it before extracting teeth, injecting the medicine into the appropriate spot in the gums to prevent excessive bleeding. Although its active principle was a phytonutrient, Resivit was given the status of a medicine. It had been subjected to all analytical, physiological, and clinical tests required for admission. A few years ago, Resivit was discontinued, but in the 1997 edition of the *VIDAL*, the official French reference book for medicines, we still find the following indications for Resivit:

- Symptoms related to venolymphatic weakness
- Functional problems: heavy legs
- Paraeshtesia (burning, pricking, itching, or tingling)
- Cramps
- Pain and primodecubitis (restlessness)
- Edema (swelling)

- Cutaneous capillary fragility
- Ecchymosis (blue spots)
- Petechia (small pinpoint hemorrhages)
- Functional signs related to hemorrhoid attacks

On July 12, 1948, when Masquelier was promoted to Dr. Masquelier on the basis of the doctoral thesis in which he described his discovery of chromogen and their amazingly strong vasoprotective effect, he could not have foreseen that he had laid the groundwork for the development of several of these medicinal products. What had begun as an investigation of the nutritional aspects of the pigments in the peanut skin had unexpectedly taken on much greater dimensions, showing enormous promises.

5 JACK AND JACQUES

The profound historic and nutritional significance of Jack Masquelier's discovery of OPCs can best be illustrated against the background of the horrible experiences of seafarers of earlier centuries who were away on long voyages. Several weeks after going out to sea, sailors invariably began to suffer from the first symptoms of a condition that would eventually and inescapably turn into the often-fatal disease we know as scurvy. Today, we know that scurvy is caused by a serious deficiency in vitamin C. In earlier times nobody knew what caused scurvy, so the disease was considered to be a curse against which there was no cure or defense.

All those who were at sea for more than two months without consuming any fresh fruit or vegetables were at risk. Hemorrhages, sore joints, bleeding gums and loss of teeth, bone deformation, tissue degeneration, and in severe forms, death from weakness were inevitable. Many historical examples confirm the devastating consequences for sailors who were struck by the curse. When sailing around the Cape of Good Hope in 1498, Vasco da Gama lost almost two-thirds of his crew to this dreaded disease, which at the time was also called "the gruesome one," "the big one," or simply "fatality."

Even though the English, Portuguese, Dutch, and Spanish played prominently in discovering foreign continents, the French played their role in conquering the world. France's major success in this respect was the discovery of the western shores of Canada. It was there, in the beginning of the 16th century, that the French explorer Jacques Cartier had an enlightening experience. Among other regions, he explored the territory of Quebec, where he searched out the St. Lawrence Bay and sailed up the St. Lawrence River. During Cartier's second voyage in the winter of 1534-1535, he was caught by a sudden cold spell. The river froze over, trapping Cartier and his crew of over 100 men in the ice where they had to spend the entire winter. Cartier's logbook makes for fascinating reading. We learn about the horrid details of his men's slow decay, their increasing weakness and the horrible death of an increasing number of the group. In his helplessness the captain allowed one of the dead bodies to be dissected. They found a white, decomposed heart surrounded by reddish fluid.

But fortunately, not all members of the ship's crew ended their lives in this manner. When 25 of the 110 sailors had already died, 50 were in a critical condition. Only three sailors seemed to be spared from the disease. The surviving crew members were so weak that they could not even bury their dead companions but only covered them with snow. In this bleak situation, during his excursions, Cartier met an Indian. He had had regular encounters with the man because he had engaged in trading with the natives. This Indian had drawn Cartier's attention because he had shown symptoms of scurvy, but after a while the symptoms had disappeared and the man looked completely healthy. Cartier questioned him and found out that the Indians knew a tree called Anneda, which provided help.

The Indian directed Cartier to the tree and explained how he could concoct a drink from its bark and needles. The solid leftovers of bark and needles had to be put on the afflicted body parts as a poultice. Cartier followed the Indian's instructions and ordered his people to drink the "pine tea." Although they were skeptical, they obeyed their captain. And those who drank the tea miraculously recovered within a few days. Open wounds and edema were treated with the poultice and healed wonderfully. Within 48 hours after this application of the tea residue, the scurvy symptoms had considerably subsided. In his biography, Cartier comments that only God's intervention could have caused this concoction to cure the dreaded disease. God may have intervened to let Cartier meet the Indian, but as explained 400 years after the event by Masquelier, Cartier's men were actually saved by the OPCs from the bark in combination with the vitamin C from the needles.

Cartier had assumed that his people were infected by Indians who had displayed similar symptoms. The fact that scurvy wasn't an infectious disease but a vitamin deficiency was discovered only much later. Even though Cartier reported in detail how the remainder of his crew survived, his experience did not lead to the eradication of scurvy. It took another 200 years before a British Navy doctor by the name of James Lind found that sailors could avoid the dreaded disease by consuming citrus fruits. For this reason lemon juice has been regularly administered to British seafarers from the 19th century onward. Their healthy habit gave them the nickname "limeys." The habit survived the test of time in that a slice of lime still crowns many drinks.

Crusaders, seafarers, explorers, soldiers, prisoners, whole populations in times of famine — everybody knew the ravages caused by scurvy, if not by personal experience, then most certainly through the tales of others. Scurvy was never far from people's doorstep. Canadian Indians brewed tea from pine bark. The British Navy squeezed limes. Sauerkraut seemed to do some good. Red wine was drunk not only for pleasure; it was known also for its medicinal effects. But it wasn't until the 1920s that the Hungarian scientist Albert Szent-Györgyi succeeded in isolating from lemon juice the substance that became known as the nutrient that cures and prevents scurvy: ascorbic acid.

There is a widely spread fantasy that Masquelier became interested in OPCs after having read the works of Cartier, even though the French explorer never made any mention of peanut skins. This fantasy was created by a misinterpretation of historic events and even a reversion of cause and effect. Some tried to give a twisted explanation of the fact that a few years after having isolated OPCs from peanut skins, Masquelier discovered that OPCs could also be isolated from the bark of the Maritime Pine, which abundantly grows in the Les Landes area southwest of Bordeaux, also known as Gascony. No matter how interesting Cartier's diary may be, it certainly isn't a guide to the Les Landes forest and a description of how to isolate OPCs from pine bark. Masquelier had discovered OPCs years before he discovered that OPCs could also be isolated from pine bark. The Cartier diary had absolutely nothing to do with the work that took place at Bordeaux University. It played no role whatsoever in Masquelier's discoveries.

What is the real relationship between the works of Jack and Jacques? What really happened is that Jack Masquelier put the French explorer's reports in the perspective of his OPCs research. It was Masquelier who explained the events that occurred on the shores of Canada's St. Lawrence Bay and described how Cartier's men were cured of scurvy. This explanation took place many years after Masquelier had found out how he could isolate OPCs from the bark of the Les Landes pine tree. From 1963 to 1974, more than 15 years after his discovery of OPCs, Dr. Masquelier had lecturing assignments about phytochemistry in Quebec, the very place where the Cartier drama took place many centuries before.

During his frequent stays in Quebec, this story came to Masquelier's mind. Teaching Canadian students about his own experiences with the Les Landes pine tree, he began to wonder from what tree the Indians and Cartier could have made their concoction. Was it a pine tree? If so, what was its botanical name? Masquelier became preoccupied with these questions and began some detective work. The Indian had shown the tree to Cartier in winter. The men had used not only the bark, but also the green parts to prepare a tea and poultice. Therefore, it must have been a conifer. It was not difficult for Masquelier to analyze the content of polyphenols in various conifers native to the Quebec region. Only the tree that the people of Quebec call pruche with the botanical name Tsuga canadensis presented a high content of the active ingredients. The vitamin C contained in the needles and the OPCs contained in the bark of the Tsuga canadensis formed a strong indication that Cartier's crew was healed by this tree. There was no doubt in Masquelier's mind that Tsuga canadensis was the tree he was looking for. As professor at the Pharmaceutical Faculty in Quebec, he then initiated a doctoral thesis. In this paper, Masquelier's student Pierre Claveau, who eventually obtained his doctor's degree in Bordeaux, presents all details of the research performed on this subject.

VITAMINS C AND P

A truly milestone scientific event in the quest for understanding the relationship between nutrition and health took place in 1928, when Szent-Györgyi isolated the first ascorbic acid. Initially, Szent-Györgyi focused his studies on paprika, which turned out to be rich in vitamin C and were grown in his homeland, Hungary, in large quantities. Szent-Györgyi's major accomplishment was that he isolated ascorbic acid from the vegetable, preserved it in its pure form, crystallized it, and defined its molecular structure. In 1932, the American researchers W.A. Waugh and C.G. King named this substance, which they had also isolated from lemon juice, vitamin C. It did not take other scientists long to synthetically produce vitamin C because its structure is fairly simple. In 1933, the Englishman H.C. Haworth and the Swiss T. Reichstein produced the first synthetic version. Even though his work on Vitamin C made Szent-Györgyi a Nobel Prize winner, he was never completely satisfied with the discovery. This feeling stemmed from the fact that he knew that vitamin C could not be the sole cause for curing scurvy. There was a phantom cofactor.

In animal tests, Szent-Györgyi had discovered that pure ascorbic acid was less effective in fighting scurvy symptoms than was vitamin C in its natural context. One of the main symptoms of this deficiency disease is the collapse of the vascular wall. Ascorbic acid was less effective alone in preventing this collapse than in combination with the extract Szent-Györgyi had prepared from lemon peel and called Citrin. Citrin (first mentioned in *chapter 3: The Discovery of OPCs*) consisted of a mixture of various substances, mostly of the so-called bioflavonoids.

Sometimes Citrin was able to enforce Vitamin C's anti-scurvy effect on the vascular wall. But the results obtained with Citrin were very inconsistent, and Citrin alone did not invariably cure scurvy.

Szent-Györgyi failed to identify the citrin mixture in its entirety, but he realized that one or more of citrin's components had to be the co-factor(s) of vitamin C. Since the combination of vitamin C and citrin was more suitable than pure ascorbic acid to prevent the collapse of the vascular wall, he believed that in addition to vitamin C, he had discovered: vitamin P. P is the first letter of permeability, by which was meant the permeability of the wall of the hair vessel or capillary. Szent-Györgyi never managed to prove the existence of such a vitamin P, which was, to a certain extent, a personal tragedy for him. He was highly regarded as the discoverer of vitamin C, although he considered vitamin C only a nutritional element. On the other hand, he was convinced that he had discovered vitamin P, but his failure to systematically produce a vitamin P deficiency carried this vitamin to an early grave.

Masquelier encountered the very fascinating Szent-Györgyi a couple of times and had the opportunity to discuss his work with him. In 1947, Masquelier met Szent-Györgyi in Oxford at the first International Physiology Congress that took place after World War II. On April 12, 1961, the two also saw each other in Bordeaux, where Szent-Györgyi was awarded an honorary degree. Masquelier's Hungarian colleague showed great interest in his work because OPCs always did what Citrin did only from time to time: increase capillary resistance and regulate capillary permeability. Fourteen years after the discovery of OPCs, while meeting with Masquelier in his Bordeaux laboratory, Szent-Györgyi said to him, "But Mr. Masquelier, are you still interested in this issue? Don't you know that in the United States no one believes in the effects of bioflavonoids (citrin) anymore?" Obviously, even the man who had coined the notion of vitamin P had abandoned his track. The unresolved mystery of this vitamin had left Szent-Györgyi with a feeling of regret. Joking about his discoveries, he said, "It is unbelievable. They have made me the father of vitamin C, although I wasn't, and they refused to make me the father of vitamin P, which I was."

With all due respect to the great Szent-Györgyi, it cannot be denied that the research that was performed as a result of Szent-Györgyi's coining of bioflavonoids as vitamin P kept producing conflicting and unclear results. In 1950, the International Vitamin Committee finally decided to completely abandon the term vitamin P. Yet, Szent-Györgyi never accepted this decision. He knew that people could best prevent and overcome the deficiency disease called scurvy by taking a combination of the vitamins C and P. Szent-Györgyi deeply regretted that he had never been able to lay his finger on the actual vitamin P. Had he looked outside the realm of the yellow bioflavonoids, he might have found what Masquelier found: OPCs. Unfortunately for the progress of nutritional science, vitamin P was equated with the yellow bioflavonoids, and this is how the scientific relevance was lost. Until this very day, the wrinkles created by the demise of vitamin P blur the work of those who try to identify the real vitamin P. The pursuit kept Masquelier busy all his life. It has kept me busy since I met Masquelier.

7 DEFINITION OF A VITAMIN

Why was Citrin not recognized as a vasoprotective vitamin? How did vitamin P end up in an early grave? Vitamins are organic compounds called micronutrients. The human organism cannot produce vitamins itself, yet vitamins are essential for maintaining vital functions. We consume them in small quantities during food ingestion. Vitamins differ from the macronutrients fats, proteins, and carbohydrates in that we need them in only relatively small "micro" quantities, expressed in micrograms and milligrams. An imbalanced or improper diet may result in a vitamin deficiency as may an increased need. Vitamins are stored in the body for different periods of time. Vitamin A is stored for up to two years, whereas our vitamin C deposit needs to be replenished every two to six weeks. If a vitamin is being withheld from the body for an extended period of time, the body responds to the lack of that essential nutrient by displaying a specific set of deficiency symptoms. A lack of vitamin D, for instance, causes rickets in children and osteoporosis in adults. A thiamin (vitamin B1) deficiency produces loss of appetite and, in the worst cases, beriberi. A lack of vitamin C results in lessened concentration, impaired immune defense, digestion problems, cardiovascular and cholesterol problems, and in extreme cases, scurvy.

To demonstrate that a micronutrient merits the status of vitamin, one must be able to produce a condition that can be directly related to withholding that specific nutrient from the body. Although increased capillary permeability most certainly is a symptom of a food-related condition, scientists could not produce capillary fragility by depriving test animals of the yellow bioflavonoid components to which Szent-Györgyi and his colleagues had given the name vitamin P. In animals, they tried to produce a vitamin P deficiency, a so-called avitaminosis, but they did not obtain consistent results.

The animals were administered a Citrin-free diet, but during many tests, nothing happened. No change in the permeability of the capillaries was observed. In other tests, however, a weakening of the capillaries was observed. It became clear that something influenced the results of the tests — something that was present at some times and absent at other times. Having their focus completely on bioflavonoids, the researchers stepped on their own tails. Being convinced that bioflavonoids were the cause of the P effect, they had given them the status of vitamin, excluding the possibility that perhaps other substances deserved vitamin P status. It was thus that, not being familiar with the Bordeaux OPCs research, the bioflavonoid people completely overlooked the real vitamin P (= OPCs) and mistakenly concluded that vitamin P did not exist.

This series of mishaps illustrates the confusion that has haunted the field of bioflavonoids ever since. In addition, because researchers attributed a vitamin effect to the wrong substance and then declared that that substance *is* the vitamin, all research done with that wrongly labeled substance ended up in a dead-end street. The bioflavonoid researchers were tricked by the absence or presence of something of which they were completely unaware. In other words, during the deficiency tests, they failed to remove the real vitamin P factor from the diet because they were pushing the "delete bioflavonoids" button. They should have pushed the "delete OPCs" button, but that button was not yet on their keyboards.

As the result of Masquelier's scientific work, we now know that the vitamin P researchers did not take into account the presence or absence of OPCs in their search for the co-factor of vitamin C. When coincidentally present in the flavonoid-free diet, the unaccounted OPCs prevented the creation of the deficiency condition, which is the decreased permeability of the capillaries. When OPCs were coincidentally absent, a condition of scurvy produced itself. Overlooking OPCs as the co-factor of vitamin C, Szent-Györgyi and others failed to figure out why the Citrin-free diet did not standardly produce a decreased capillary permeability. Their failure to create a vitamin P not only discredited the bioflavonoids but had as another dramatic consequence the implicit abandoning of the idea that a weakened vascular system is related to a nutritional deficiency. Thus, everything that did improve capillary permeability was automatically classified as a medicine, even though that medicine is a phytonutrient.

Another reason it is difficult to generate the scurvy deficiency in animals is that, apart from a few exceptions, animals are able to produce vitamin C. Mice, rats, and rabbits are unsuitable for such experiments because they synthesize ascorbic acid themselves, which means that vitamin C is not a micronutrient for them. They don't depend on food for the intake of this vitamin. For most animals, vitamin C is not a vitamin! Other than humans, only a few creatures require food as a source of vitamin C. These include guinea pigs, bats, a Madagascan bird species, gorillas, chimpanzees, and orangutans. During the 1930s, the synthetically produced vitamin C had not been launched as a vitamin. Initially, vitamin C was used mostly as a preservative in many foods and drinks and not so much as an individual vitamin supplement. This is the reason Szent-Györgyi's idea that vitamin

C worked better as a vitamin in the presence of a co-factor named vitamin P never received much attention in scientific and industrial circles. With the rise of vitamin supplements, Szent-Györgyi's vitamin research encountered a rebirth in the form of combined vitamin C and bioflavonoids tablets, promoted, sold, and taken with the idea that bioflavonoids are vitamin C's co-factor.

8 COLORLESS ISN'T YELLOW OR RED

Why did OPCs escape the eye of even great scientists like Szent-Györgyi? First, in unscientific terms, many researchers made a mess that could be cleaned up only by someone who put things where they belong. In most households, that someone is a parent whose children's rooms are a mess. But in a developing field of science, many scientists have different scientific and personal opinions as to where things must be put and what these things actually are and are not. The most crucial contribution that Masquelier has made in putting things where they belong was his discovery that OPCs *essentially* differ from citrin-bioflavonoids, making them two distinctly different categories of plant compounds. The term flavonoid is derived from the Latin word flavus, which means yellow. Every substance that was or formed yellow was a "yellow-oid." Originally, the term flavonoid denoted only the yellow and yellow-forming plant pigments. These pigments were found to have in common a core chemical "backbone" structure that thus received the name flavan nucleus. Everything that had this flavan core was thus ranked a flavonoid. These pigments are abundantly found in citrus fruits, which is why they are also referred to as *citro*flavonoids. Citroflavonoids are found in all citrus fruits, such as oranges, lemons, and grapefruit.

It is quite evident that while working on the peanut project, Masquelier found himself in the arena of the red pigments. Anthocyanin led Masquelier to the colorless substance then defined as chromogen or leucocyanidin. Thus, he was led to the isolation and characterization of the colorless substance that turns into the red. Later, the German scientists Freudenberg and

Weinges proposed to give leucocyanidin a name that somewhat better reflects its chemical behavior: proanthocyanidins, or the precursor of anthocyanin. Sometimes the term anthocyanoside is used for anthocyanin to indicate that anthocyanin contains a sugar part. The sugarless anthocyanin is called anthocyanidin. In comparison, it was found by Masquelier that there are no sugar-containing proanthocyanosides or proanthocyanins. There are only sugarless proanthocyanidins.

From only their core chemical *structure*, proanthocyanidins can be classified as bioflavonoids because they contain the flavan core. Even though proanthocyanidins are colorless and cannot generate a yellow pigment, biochemists never adjusted the classification. They never replaced the term bioflavonoids, which had become a blunt misnomer when non-yellow substances were found to have the flavonoids' chemical backbone. Unhindered by what their eyes could see, most researchers blindly kept classifying non-yellow compounds as "yellow-oids." Replacing the "flav-" prefix with what it means in current language — yellow! — makes the mistake glaringly obvious. However, those who didn't want to change their textbooks and scientific publications were not as concerned.

This is how proanthocyanidins were classified as flavanols and flavanols were classified in the group of flavonoids. After this U-turn was taken, the proanthocyanidins, mislabeled as yellow-oids, erroneously ended up as bioflavonoids. OPCs ended up as identical to citrin. Ever since, Masquelier has fought against this madness, first because proanthocyanidins aren't yellow and do not generate yellow; they distinctly turn red. More important to him, though, are the essential *biological* differences between bioflavonoids and proanthocyanidins, differences that are occluded when one incorrectly classifies proanthocyanidins as bioflavonoids. From the perspective of nutrition and health, these differences are vital.

Although the biochemist who has specialized in bioflavonoids is well aware of the essential differences in chemical behavior between flavonoids (yellow-oids) and flavanols (non-yellow-oids), the two terms are too close for comfort. Even for use among the specialists, the terms are too similar to avoid confusion. Many well-respected authors still use the *o* where the *a* is the correct letter. And even when the terms are correctly applied, the difference between the letters makes almost meaningless and trivial the crucial difference on which rests the enormous importance of all of Masquelier's flavanols research: establishing the differences and the similarities between flavanols and other flavonoids. He found that there are more differences than similarities.

Contrary to Masquelier, Szent-Györgyi dealt exclusively with the yellow pigments, the bioflavonoids, to which he erroneously attributed the results he haphazardly achieved when he tested citrin as a vasoprotective factor. He did not know that in reality, his results must have been influenced by the colorless proanthocyanidins. Because they are colorless, they escaped attention in the way they had escaped attention for endless millennia as the origin of one of the most impressive natural phenomena.

In France and in many other regions with a moderate climate, an amazing and beautiful phenomenon happens before our very eyes every fall, or autumn: The trees turn color. Of particular splendor is this spectacle of nature in the magnificent forests of North America. The "Indian Summer," when the green ocean of trees is suddenly ablaze, attracts visitors from all over the world. The green leaves that owe their color to their high chlorophyll content suddenly turn red. In some cases this amazing change takes place overnight. The cause of this phenomenon puzzled scientists for a long time because the red coloration occurs only in leaves that are on the verge of dying. They are therefore unable to initiate from their own waning power a biochemical process of such magnitude.

The simplest, although unfortunately incorrect, explanation assumed that the chlorophyll is hiding an already existing red pigment. Then, when the leaf begins to die, the red supposedly emerges when the green color vanishes. The error is simply demonstrated. If the chlorophyll of the leaves that are still green in early autumn is dissolved in benzol, there is no remaining red coloration whatsoever. In reality, the leaves contain proanthocyanidins, the chromogen or colorless precursor, which turns red on the moment of the leaves' death. This event finds its cause in a biological, enzymatic transformation. The proanthocyanidins in the leaves are suddenly altered by enzymes that become active on the dying of the cells in the leaves. They transform proanthocyanidins into anthocyanins.

Antho is the ancient Greek word for flower. Cyanin (not to be confused with the toxic cyanide) is a blue coloring agent or pigment. Anthocyanin denotes the class of pigments ranging from red to blue found in flowers and other plant parts. It is also the pigment found in red wine. In the Anglo-Saxon languages, the

59

precursor to anthocyanin is *pro*anthocyanidin. In other languages, such as French and German, the "antho" part is not used, which results in the term "procyanidin." The autumnal coloration in nature is not a synthesis but a programmed transformation that requires only minimal energy because enzymes are involved. Naturally, this phenomenon does not affect all plants but only those that contain proanthocyanidins. The colorless proanthocyanidins *always* turn red, never yellow. They invariably become red, both in the chemical process conducted in the laboratory and during the spontaneous enzymatic red coloration of leaves in fall.

The reddening of proanthocyanidins in the laboratory is referred to as the Bate-Smith reaction. E.C. Bate-Smith's name was given to this reaction not because he invented it, but because he used the reaction to botanically classify plants that provoke the reaction. To determine whether a plant contains proanthocyanidins, all you have to do is to expose it to acid and heat. If it turns red, the presence of proanthocyanidins is confirmed. This experiment is so inexpensive and simple that an amateur chemist can easily perform it. You cut, for example, grape or maple leaves into small pieces, put these into an Erlenmeyer beaker, add a diluted mineral acid (a 10 percent solution of hydrochloric acid), and heat the mixture. While it is being heated, a red coloration will appear. Following filtration, you can recover this color in a solution. When isoamyl alcohol is added and the solution is shaken, all of the red coloring will float to the top. This is how proanthocyanidins behave in the laboratory. Whenever they are subjected to a Bate-Smith test, they transform into anthocyanins, into red pigments.

One doesn't need more than this simple set of laboratory equipment to perform the Bate-Smith reaction. Please note that the Bate-Smith reaction is not OPCs specific, but it will indiscriminately reveal the presence of all procyanidins, oligomers, and polymers (tannins).

The red coloration of leaves in fall, however, is caused by a natural enzymatic process. If we do not want to use the Bate-Smith test to determine whether plants contain proanthocyanidins, we have to wait until fall and observe which plant leaves turn red. The problem with this natural way of determining whether plants contains proanthocyanidins is that it is a rather time-consuming process, and in many areas of the world, there is no fall season that witnesses the changing colors of the leaves. Do tropical plants contain any proanthocyanidins, even when they do not change colors? They do. The coconut tree is filled with proanthocyanidins. But since the tropical climate is not subject to major seasonal changes, there exist no Nordic autumnal conditions that cause the leaf to die. Thus the enzymes required for the coloring do not emerge, and a Bate-Smith test is required to confirm the presence of proanthocyanidins in tropical plants.

There is another aspect that needs to be explained in this chapter, even though the details appear later in this book. Not all proanthocyanidins sit and wait in the leaves and other parts of plants to turn red during autumn. Remember how, during his earlier research, Masquelier separated the pale yellow fraction (f1) from a dark red-brown fraction (f2) by precipitating the brown impurities with the use of salt? These brown impurities are tannins. The pale fraction is OPCs. During the latter part of his doctorate research, Masquelier observed that OPCs gradually form tannins when they are being oxidized. OPCs and tannins belong to the same family in that they are both proanthocyanins. But tannins have no biological value. Yet tannins are procyanidins just like OPCs. In other words, OPCs are proanthocyanidins but not all proanthocyanidins are OPCs! The normal fate of OPCs in the plant is that they self-condense into ever-thicker clusters called tannins.

Confusion between tannins and OPCs can easily arise when the Bate-Smith reaction is used as a way to determine the presence of OPCs. Like OPCs, tannins respond well to the Bate-Smith reaction by turning red. So one doesn't have to be a biochemist to understand that because the Bate-Smith reaction reveals the presence of all proanthocyanidins, it is not a method to distinguish OPCs from tannins. To the unsuspecting reader, this may seem a highly academic and boring issue. Yet, when buying a product that states on the label that it contains procyanidins, you may be looking at worthless tannins instead of valuable OPCs. Don't think that it doesn't happen. Certain manufacturers happily inflate their extracts by leaving in what Masquelier took out: tannins. And what's even worse, they invoke the Bate-Smith reaction as proof of OPCs content. The truth is that the Bate-Smith reaction cannot tell an OPC from a tannin.

Because both substances are proanthocyanidins, OPCs are always found together with tannins in plants. Unless OPCs are first separated from tannins by the Masquelier method, determining the presence of OPCs by way of simple analytical methods such as the Bate-Smith reaction is a meritless effort. This is quite critical because OPCs are phytonutrients and tannins are not. And within the context of this chapter, it is another reason OPCs have remained hidden for so long.

9 OPCs FROM THE BARK OF THE MARITIME PINE

During the early days, and according to the first Masquelier patent and initial research, the manufacturer of Resivit used peanut skins to isolate the product's OPCs. The unshelled peanuts were delivered from Senegal to the oil mills in Bordeaux where they were laboriously shelled and skinned. This practice began to change shortly before 1950 when Senegal no longer exported to France the whole peanuts but only shelled and skinned ones. Therefore, another vegetal source for producing leucocyanidin had to be found. Masquelier managed to find an alternative rather quickly through a mixture of work, intuition, and good luck.

One day he happened to pick up a piece of bark from the Maritime Pine and he was struck by the fact that it was dark brown-red on the outside but light brown-yellow on the inside. The Maritime Pine is found all around Bordeaux, especially southwest of the city in the vast Landes region. It is a tree with a long straight stem and branches only in the upper part. The vast Maritime Pine forests in Les Landes were planted some 200 years ago and they came to serve as a source of lumber and of all kinds of terpenes and resins. If Masquelier had lived elsewhere, he might have never picked up the answer to his problem. The pine bark reminded him of the peanut skin. It, too, is red on the outside and light yellow on the inside. In the peanut, the bioactive part containing the OPCs is located in the inner lining of the "wrapping," where the skin is in contact with the nut.

Masquelier's line of reasoning was as follows. In the peanut, OPCs are located in the inner part of the skin, probably because this is the best place for the OPCs to protect the oils in the nut against turning rancid under the influence of oxygen. OPCs form an antioxidative sheath. In the pine tree, it seemed to Masquelier that a similar bioactive part with OPCs might be located in the inner lining of the bark, protecting the stem and especially the fluids that flow through it. Comparing the composition of the pine and the peanut, Masquelier concluded that the resin in the pine was also an easily oxidizable substance that was protected by a similarly placed sheath: the bark. When the resin becomes oxidized, it turns hard and sticky and it is no longer of any use for the tree. So the resin must be protected against oxidation. The assumption that OPCs provided this antioxidative protection logically presented itself, and Masquelier and his colleagues came to regard the pine bark as a huge peanut skin. As a source of leucocyanidin, pine bark presented an essential advantage. It did not contain any oils, so the step to remove oily parts could be eliminated from the production process. In laboratory tests, the bark of the Maritime Pine turned out to be a viable source of leucocyanidin.

This is how the manufacturer of Resivit began to use the bark of the Pinus Maritima as the raw material for the production of OPCs. Until this very day, OPCs are being made from pine bark. However, the production method was successively improved by Masquelier and his colleagues since they filed the first French Patent (No. 968.589) describing the production of OPCs from peanuts. During those earliest "peanut days" of Resivit, the production method consisted of a multitude of steps. On May 9, 1951, one year after French Patent 968.589 was granted, a second patent was filed by Masquelier, describing an equally complicated method to produce OPCs from the bark of the French Maritime Pine. French Patent 1.036.922, which was granted on April 29, 1953, still shows the complex nature of the extraction process. During the 1960s, Masquelier found that the process of producing a product from pine bark, which was sufficiently rich in OPCs, could be reduced to some essential steps.

Extracting OPCs from the bark of the French Maritime Pine tree instead of from peanut skins had the great advantage that, at least until recently, this plant material was abundantly available in Les Landes southwest of Bordeaux. There, the Maritime Pine forests extend over an area of 2.5 million acres. During December 2000, those Landes acres were heavily struck by gales that brought down an enormous number of trees, leaving fewer trees from which to collect the bark. The bark from a fallen tree is worthless within a few weeks. In addition, the demand for raw pine bark had steeply increased because it has become a popular ingredient in many gardens, where it covers the soil to keep down weeds. All in all, there is less mature and thick bark today than there was when it was first used as a source of leucocyanidin.

For every production process that aims at the isolation of one or more ingredients from vegetal material such as pine bark, the rules of economy dictate that the relationship between raw material and the eventual isolated ingredient should be as favorable as possible. Because the yield of OPCs production from Maritime Pine bark is 0.3 to 0.5 percent, one needs an enormous amount of bark, preferably not far from the factory. Still, with all the economic factors considered, pine bark is a raw material that yields reasonably acceptable quantities of the phytonutrient OPCs. This is how the Oberlin Laboratories in Paris managed to continue sales of Resivit when the supply of peanut skins ran dry. Resivit was sold until just a few years ago, a rare accomplishment in the pharmaceutical market, which is subject to constant change. This is also how the "antique" term leucocyanidin survived during almost half a century as the generic name of Resivit's active ingredient, also called "vitamin P factor" in Masquelier's 1953 French Patent. Although the name leucocyanidin remained in use, it was not until newer analytical methods became available that Masquelier and his coworkers were able to show that leucocyanidin was a complex of phytonutrients rather than one single compound.

In the western world, few people consider bark a component of our food. Yet, as Cartier found during his involuntary stay in Quebec, the bark of trees served and still serves as an ingredient for wholesome teas in traditional and in modern societies. In times of hunger, bark even serves as food. In the part of India known as Rajasthan, more specifically in the Thar Desert, the Khejri tree is considered the Tree of Life because it survives in conditions of extreme drought. The tree is the source of firewood, fodder, and traditional medicines. During the

Rajputana famine that struck India during 1868-1869 the bark of the Khejri tree was ground to flour that kept many from starvation. In traditional cultures, food still includes components that western culture has discarded or eliminated. This process of eliminating has brought us the empty food that may seem nutritious and tasteful but lacks many of the essential nutrients required for optimum health. Lacking industrial ways of first emptying and then enriching foods, traditional cultures are still "blessed" with foods that we no longer find on our civilized tables.

10 TEACHER AND STUDENT AND A NEW PINE BARK PRODUCT

Soon it became clear that Jack Masquelier was not only a proficient scientist but also an equally proficient teacher. After completing his doctoral thesis, he was appointed "chef de travaux" in 1948. From then on, he was responsible for the practical training of physicians and pharmacists. One year later, he won the Concours National, a national scientific competition that had been initiated in May 1949, and subsequently, he became "maître de conférence agrégé." Masquelier was the youngest person to be appointed university instructor in France. Parallel to his work at the university, he gave lectures at the Oenological Institute in Bordeaux on the subject of wine and nutrition. In 1956, he was appointed professor and awarded a chair in the field of Matière Médicale. The following year, Professor Masquelier became vice-dean of the medical and pharmaceutical faculty. In 1970, he was appointed dean of the pharmaceutical faculty at Bordeaux University where he stayed, except for his research assignments in Canada, until his retirement from the academic chair in 1984.

Teaching has always been of major importance for Masquelier. He feels that one cannot share if one doesn't have anything to give and that one who gives is surrounded by happy people. He loved to spend his time with the young students whether they were studying in his classes or working on research projects. This constant contact with young people has always kept him young and active. As the new generations absorbed his knowledge, he received important stimulation in return. In Masquelier's teaching days, there was a great mutual respect between the teachers and the students. In those days, when a professor entered the lecture hall, the students stood up!

Masquelier lecturing at the University of Dakar, Senegal 1980

When one experiences the excellent speeches and lectures of Masquelier, one wonders why he thinks of himself as an introvert who found it difficult to speak in front of a large audience. "Actually," says Masquelier, "I am a rather shy man, and in the beginning, teaching presented quite a challenge for me. But I discovered a possibility to deal with this situation by deciding to never base my lectures on memory aids, cribs, or even detailed papers. This required fastidious preparation of every single seminar. But in the long term, this method proved effective. On the one hand, it gave me the required security, and on the other hand, I quickly earned my students' respect since they invariably experienced a lecturer who had done his homework with perfection and was never rummaging through papers for having lost direction."

Although he placed high demands on his students and was regarded as strict, Professor Masquelier always was a popular teacher. This popularity can be attributed to his competence and his simplicity as well as his efforts at description. He always tried to present even the most complex and dry subjects in a vivid manner. Thus his courses were always well attended, and many of his students stayed in touch with him for a long time. Among them was also the one who, after he had completed his studies, undertook the development and marketing of a new herbal medicine based on the OPCs discovered by his professor.

Compared with today's recommended daily dosages, Resivit offered the relatively low dosage of 2.5 mg per 1 ml; that is, 5 mg of pine bark leucocyanidin per 1 vial. Despite this low dosage, Resivit proved to be an effective product against capillary fragility. But some indications, such as hemorrhoid prolapse, require a much higher dosage. Therefore, Masquelier and his team felt the need to improve the efficacy of OPCs products by increasing their dosage. Other than the dosage problem, the vial is a rather expensive and troublesome way of presenting and taking OPCs. Even though it allows injecting OPCs, which works well in a hospital or dentist's office, simpler product forms, such as the tablet, were the obvious way to go. To make this step to a new product, from vial to tablet and from low to higher dosage, Masquelier needed more OPCs than could be made with the first methods.

As a result of the need for changes, Masquelier filed another French Patent for an improved production method on December 14, 1964, describing the making of OPCs from the bark of the Maritime Pine. In French Patent 1.427.100, which was granted on December 27, 1965, Masquelier had reduced the extraction method to some essential steps. These most important steps were employing a sodium chloride (salt) solution to separate the large molecules (the tannins) from the OPCs and then "picking" the OPCs from the solution by means of a harmless organic solvent called ethyl acetate. In the same patent, Masquelier shared with the world some new insights on the complex nature of leucocyanidin.

French patent 1.427.100

In the 17 years that separated the first from the third French Patent, Masquelier and his colleagues had delved deeper into the nature of leucocyanidin. They had found that leucocyanidin was not one single substance but that there existed a series of consecutive complex forms of leucocyanidins in degrees of condensation ranging from two units to 10 or more. Not yet knowing the precise details and mechanisms of this condensation, Masquelier had hinted at the complex nature of leucocyanidin when, in his doctorate work, he had observed how leucocyanidin turned into tannins under the influence of oxidation. In fact, this condensation process is the natural life cycle of the leucocyanidins. Gradually, taking on one new unit at the time, they neatly condense into thicker and thicker tannins and eventually phlobaphens. In 1948, Masquelier had described how this bonding or polymerization takes place. Masquelier's 1965 patent explains how the improved production method could separate the slightly condensed leucocyanidins from the thicker tannins. In that patent, Masquelier defines for the first time the *biologically active* leucocyanidins as clusters of two to five units.

On March 12, 1965, Masquelier also patented the many vasoprotective effects of the product he defined as follows: "a new bioflavonoid or vitamin P factor containing essentially as its active ingredient tetrahydroxy 5, 7, 3', 4' flavan 3,4 diol." His use of the word bioflavonoids and of flavan 3,4 diol demonstrates that during the 1960s, Masquelier could not escape the use of the existing incorrect scientific terminology, even in his own writings. The flavonoid "canon" inescapably prescribed the words to be used between scientists. Unable to solve the dilemma, Masquelier nevertheless abbreviated tetrahydroxy 5, 7, 3', 4' flavan 3,4 diol to Flavan in the 1965 French Patent. Flavan was also the name chosen for the product that would be introduced in France in 1968 in the form of tablets each containing 20 mg of leucocyanidin.

In the 1965 patent, Masquelier lists an impressive range of vascular conditions that respond well to Flavan:
- Capillary fragility
    - Tendency to ecchymosis (hematoma or "blue spots" occurring spontaneously or after bruising or sports injuries)
    - Vascular problems in those with high blood pressure
    - Diabetic retinopathy (eyesight problems due to impaired circulation of the retina in diabetics)
    - Capillary fragility caused by renal insufficiency, hepatic insufficiency, or infectious diseases
- Abnormally high capillary permeability
    - Swollen legs, "heavy legs"
    - Varicose conditions, varicose ulcers
    - Sequels of phlebitis (vein inflammation)
    - Edema in premature infants
    - Edema caused by hepatic insufficiency
    - Pleural cardiac effusion
    - Pleurisy
    - Periarthritis
    - Allergic reactions (urticaria, eczema, Quincke's edema, dishidrosis)
    - Dermatoses (pemphigus – "water blisters," psoriasis)
    - Cellulitis

All these indications claimed for Flavan fall well within the scope of the vitamin P effect. Although the claims were the result of some 15 years of research and experience, they needed to be confirmed by observations in a clinical setting. The responsibility for obtaining such clinical confirmation was taken by Gueyne Laboratories. Gueyne undertook the mission of placing Flavan on the French market, in which it succeeded in 1968. The clinical tests, which prior to the admission of Flavan as medicine had to be performed for an extended period of time, comprised most of the vascular applications claimed in the French Flavan patents.

11 AMAZING EFFECTS OF FLAVAN

All the basic scientific tests required for the admission of pharmaceutical substances with respect to toxicity, long-term effects, and so on were performed for Flavan. And so it happened that in the 1960s, the clinical evaluations and results became available, confirming and acknowledging the efficacy of OPCs that had been observed ever since its discovery. According to its official product description, Flavan is made from the bark of the Pinus Maritima, and it displays vasoprotective properties by increasing the resistance of the blood vessels and balancing their permeability. The following table shows the significant improvement in just a few of the cases of patients who underwent testing of their capillary resistance.

Patient	Age, in years	Initial Capillary Resistance, in cm per Hg	Posology	Capillary Resistance After 24 Hours, in cm per Hg	Improvement
Miss J.T.	30	30	2 tablets x 20 mg	36	20%
Mrs. N.D.	40	30	1 tablet x 20 mg	37	23%
Mrs. L.B.	56	20	2 tablets x 20 mg	30	50%
Mrs. L.D.	39	20	1 tablet x 20 mg	30	50%
Mrs. J.M.	42	25	2 tablets x 20 mg	40	60%
Mrs. M.L.P.	41	19	2 tablets x 20 mg	26	36%
Mrs. P.F.	34	25	1 tablet x 20 mg	35	40%

The Effects of Flavan on Capillary Resistance

The improvement of capillary resistance expresses itself in all kinds of conditions caused by venolymphatic weakness, such as heavy legs, cramps, pain, tingling and numbness of extremities (paresthesia), edema, capillary fragility of the skin (including bruises and teleangiectatic rosacea/"spider veins"), hematoma (ecchymosis), eye troubles, circulatory disorder of the retina and choroid (see *chapter 19: New Clinical Highlights*), and hemorrhoid prolapse. All these conditions are considered indications for use of Flavan in dosages that range as shown in the following table.

Symptom	Number of 20 mg Tablets Daily	Number of Days	Recommended Daily Maintenance Dosage	Subsequent Dosage in mg
Eye disorders	8	20	4 tablets daily	160 - 80
General application	6	6	3 tablets daily for 20 days	120 - 60
Acute hemorrhoid prolapse	10 - 12	1	-	200 - 240

Conditions Responding Well on Flavan

The following sections detail the results of some case studies from the clinical report issued by Professor Jacques Leng-Levy, Dr. Edouard Bessiere, and Professor Pierre Sourreil. They performed tests from 1963 to 1965 as part of an effort to learn about Flavan's status as an herbal medicine.

Clinical report issued by Professor Jaques Leng-Levy, Dr. Edouard Bessiere, and Professor Pierre Sourreil.

Case Study 1

A 76-year-old patient suffered from a macular lesion and inflammation of the choroid and iris in the right eye. Her condition was atheromatous, which means her blood vessels showed plaque deposits. She suffered from high blood pressure (220/120) and had frequent headaches in the morning. In her right eye, she had small black spots in her field of vision. These constant floaters result from the deposit of cholesterol crystals in the vitreous body of the eye.

- *Treatment:*
  Two Flavan tablets (20 mg) prior to each of the two main meals over a period of three months.
- *Clinical course:*
  Her vision improved and her morning headaches disappeared.
- *Result:*
  Satisfactory.

Case Study 2

Subsequent to previous venous inflammation, a 54-year-old patient had a history of suffering from major disorders of venous post-phlebitic circulation in the lower left limb, with wine-colored cyanic pigmentation. Marked starburst varices were visible, and she endured pain when she stood upright for prolonged periods. Previous treatment with different medication was without any appreciable result.

- *Treatment:*
  Two Flavan tablets (20 mg) prior to each of the two main meals over a period of four months.
- *Clinical course:*

She saw manifest regression in the starburst varices, and the pain she had suffered when standing upright disappeared.
- Result:
Excellent.

Case Study 3

A 42-year-old patient had suffered from vascular disorders in the legs since puberty. She had persistent reddening of the ankles, which turned into chilblains during the winter. She also suffered from subcutaneous hematomas ("blue spots"), which appeared either spontaneously or as a result of minor injury in the thighs and the legs.
- *Treatment:*
  Two Flavan tablets (20 mg) prior to each of the two main meals over a period of three months.
- *Clinical course:*
  There was no change in the morphology of the legs; the spontaneous or induced hematomas were eliminated.
- *Result:*
  Excellent.

Case Study 4

A 44-year-old patient was suffering from varicose ulcers surrounded by widened capillaries and severe itchy skin eruptions (eczematoid dermatitis).
- *Treatment:*
  Two Flavan tablets (20 mg) prior to each of the two main meals over a period of two months.

- *Clinical course:*
  The varicose ulcer has improved. The itchy skin (pruritus) has disappeared, and the capillarosis (inflamed capillaries) is less marked.
- *Result:*
  Satisfactory.

In the course of this study conducted by Professor Leng-Levy, many additional cases were treated with Flavan. Treated disorders included capillary fragility; venous-related ailments such as varicose legs, phlebitis (venous inflammation), and their consequential disorders; hemorrhoid prolapses; hemorrhage in connection with sclerosis of the liver; skin diseases such as urticaria (itching red patches), angiospasm (contraction of the walls of a blood vessel under the skin), and Quincke's edema (small swellings on the skin as from an insect bite); retinitis (retinal inflammation); and others. With one exception, patients' conditions significantly improved subsequent to the taking of Flavan. The product was tolerated extremely well, and patients were free from any toxic or other side effects. The only unexpected and unpredicted side effect the researchers mentioned was the reduction and shortening of strong menstrual bleeding!

All required toxicity tests were performed on different types of animals. No incompatibilities with respect to digestion, liver, kidneys, blood, or skin manifested themselves. Therefore, the study conducted by Professor Leng-Levy concludes with his explicit recommendations: "We must point out the persistency with which patients requested to be supplied with this drug. In the opinion of some, this would be regarded as a highly relative criterion. Lengthy experience with clinical drug trials allows us to declare peremptorily that this criterion is valid. If patients do not see convincing results from a drug, they will readily abandon it. This has not been the case with Flavan. In response to precise indications, this new vitamin P factor, perfectly developed in chemical terms by Masquelier after lengthy studies, in collaboration with Tayeau, is worthy of being introduced into clinical therapy. In our opinion, of all vitamin P factors available, this preparation has produced the most satisfactory results."

After concluding his series of clinical tests Professor Pierre Sourreil, who had been recommending Flavan to patients of his dermatology and phlebology practice, arrived at the following conclusion:

"No intolerance was recorded, irrespective of the treatment period. We are pleased to note:
- o The rapid disappearance of painful symptoms
- o The regression or arrest in the development of lesions

When Flavan was used in association with other therapies in patients presenting essential varices ...., and in post-phlebitic disease, the drug performed a valuable adjuvant (helpful) function in:
- o Painful phenomena
- o The resorption of edema and inflammatory phenomena
- o Improvements in the quality of sclerosis (hardening caused by inflammation)

In our opinion, Flavan is a vitamin P active product of particular benefit and efficacy for disorders of capillary resistance and permeability."

A Flavan study conducted by ophthalmologists with patients suffering from conjunctivitis, macular degeneration, retinopathy, and lesions ends with a recommendation by Bessiere: "The medication appears especially effective when the lesion is moderate and if prolonged treatment can be prescribed. We must stress the favorable effect of Flavan in conditions of doubtful prognosis in spite of conventional therapy. In particular, the comparison with other vitamin P factors hitherto used is very much in the product's favor."

"In addition to certain beneficial physiological properties currently under study (modification of electrogenesis and visual acuity curve in low luminosity), we consider Flavan, of all the vitamin factors currently available, to have the most intense and reliable action on disorders affecting capillary resistance and permeability."

PATENT SPECIFICATION
NO DRAWINGS

1,092,269

Date of Application and filing Complete Specification: Dec. 3, 1965.
No. 51398/65.
Application made in France (No. 998508) on Dec. 14, 1964.
Application made in France (No. 9054) on March 12, 1965.
Complete Specification Published: Nov. 22, 1967.
© Crown Copyright 1967.

Index at acceptance: —C2 C3A13D; A5 B(2S, 12B)
Int. Cl.: —C 07 d 7/18

COMPLETE SPECIFICATION

Hydroxyflavan 3,4-Diols and Medicaments based thereon

We, SOCIETE CIVILE DE RECHERCHE PHARMACEUTIQUE ET THERAPEUTIQUE, a body corporate organised under the laws of France, of 33, Rue de Turenne, Bordeaux, Gironde, France, do hereby declare the invention for which we pray that a patent may be granted to us, and the method by which it is to be performed, to be particularly described in and by the following statement:

van 3,4 - diols from groundnuts and pine bark have already been described, particularly in French patent Specifications Nos. 968,589 and 1,036,922. In these known processes use is first made of an organic solvent which dissolves all the polyphenols of the drug. Undesirable substances are then eliminated either by selective solvation or by adsorption followed by elution. Finally, the product is puri-

British patent no. 1,092,269

> **United States Patent Office**
>
> 3,436,407
> Patented Apr. 1, 1969
>
> 3,436,407
> **HYDROXYFLAVIN 3,4-DIOLS, A METHOD OF PRODUCING THEM AND MEDICAMENT BASED THEREON**
> Jacques Masquelier, Bordeaux, France, assignor to Societe Civile de Recherche Pharmaceutique et Therapeutique, Bordeaux Gironde, France, a corporation of France
> No Drawing. Filed Dec. 10, 1965, Ser. No. 513,118
> Claims priority, application France, Dec. 14, 1964, 998,508
> Int. Cl. C07d 7/24; A61k 27/00
> U.S. Cl. 260—345.2   12 Claims
>
> **ABSTRACT OF THE DISCLOSURE**
>
> Hydroxyflavan 3,4-diols or leucoanthocyans are extracted in isolated but undergraded condition comprising the less polymerized forms of the hydroxyflavan 3,4-diols comprising, in particular, the monomer, the dimers, trimers, tetramers, and pentamers, while eliminating the more condensed forms ranging from tannin to phlobaphene, by successive stages of elimination of impurities. The compounds are active elements of a bioflavanoid or vitamin P factor, effective in the treatment of venous, vascular, and capillary diseases.
>
> The present invention relates to hydroxyflavan 3,4-diols, a method of producing them, and to medicaments
>
> phene type, and the process according to the invention has the advantage of isolating the less polymerised forms of the hydroxyflavan 3,4-diols, comprising in particular the monomer, the dimers, trimers, tetramers, and pentamers. Moreover, the process according to the invention eliminates the more condensed forms, ranging from tannin to phlobaphene.
>
> The process according to the invention comprises the steps of: treating vegetable material such as groundnuts or pine bark with an aqueous solution of sodium chloride; separating the resulting aqueous solution from the solid impurities; extracting said aqueous solution with ethyl acetate to obtain a solution of hydroxyflavan 3,4-diols in ethyl acetate; treating said solution with an excess of chloroform; separating the precipitated hydroxyflavan 3,4-diols; purifying said hydroxyflavan 3,4-diols by a plurality of stages each consisting of solution in ethyl acetate followed by precipitation from solution by addition of chloroform.
>
> The hydroxy flavan 3,4-diols have the following general formula:

U.S. patent no. 3,436,407

Following all these impressive results, Masquelier obtained patents for the Flavan product in Great Britain in 1967 (Patent No. 1,092,269) and in the United States in 1969 (Patent No. 3,436,407). These patents, which were based on the original French Flavan patents, were expanded to include a number of the case studies mentioned above. By 1970, the vascular properties of OPCs, then still referred to as leucocyanidin, had become well established.

12. THE OLIGOMERIC PROANTHOCYANIDINS

By the time Flavan had hit the French market during 1968 and 1969, the term leucocyanidin, though still used to describe Flavan's active ingredient, had become obsolete. Science had progressed to a level that finally permitted a much more precise analysis of leucocyanidin. The new findings confirmed that the name leucocyanidin was no longer appropriate because it gave the idea that leucocyanidin was a single substance, which it wasn't. The era of OPCs had arrived. Out of all the complexities, mistakes and errors, OPCs now emerged as the short name for small proanthocyanidins. OPCs could be identified, fingerprinted, defined, and steadily produced in consistent quality because on June 16, 1970, Masquelier had filed another French Patent describing a method to produce OPCs in their finest form.

Expensive research is worthwhile only when the material being used is known and of a constant quality. This is especially so when the material a researcher is using is made from plants. Variations in the raw material must be minimized and the production method must be focussed and rigidly applied in an invariable way. The more knowledge one has regarding the composition of the researched material, the higher the value that may be attributed to the research's results. The enormous advantage of Masquelier's new patent was that the research could now be done with a material that could be better defined than ever before. In the case of OPCs, this is especially relevant because each OPC that forms part of OPCs is a proanthocyanidin, but not every one of these OPCs has the same size. Some OPCs are homogeneous in that they consist of only catechins or epicatechins. Other OPCs are heterogeneous in that they consist of catechins and epicatechins.

The new patent thus opened the way for a new herbal medicine that has as its active ingredient: oligomeric proanthocyanidins. Readers who are interested in learning more about the nature of OPCs should read on. After all, defining OPCs formed an essential part of Masquelier's and his colleague Professor Jean Michaud's work. A book about OPCs should allow readers to also connect with that less accessible aspect of Masquelier's life.

Readers who are more interested in what OPCs do than in their composition may well skip this chapter and go to *chapter 13: Where Are OPCs in Nature?* to pick up the story from there.

To reiterate briefly what was explained in previous chapters, when judged purely from the core of their structure, OPCs are classified as flavonoids. Flavonoids, or bioflavonoids, is the name of a group of plant compounds distinguished by an identical structure in the molecule's center: the flavan nucleus. Flavus means yellow, and the "flav-" term came into use because the early research concerned yellow pigments. Later, many non-yellow substances were found to have a flavan nucleus. Yet the term bioflavonoids remained in use, confusing generations of scientists because the admission of one chemical similarity does not overcome the many essential differences between flavonoids and OPCs. A subclass of the flavonoids is the flavanols. OPCs are in the flavanols subclass.

Not only are many bioflavonoids not yellow, but a classification on the basis of core chemical structure is of no great help in the field of health and nutrition because the range of this group of bioflavonoid plant compounds is extremely broad. From a biological, nutritional, and medicinal viewpoint, the various individual bioflavonoids may present substantially different properties, such as with respect to their absorption and their biological effects. This is why, in the course of his research, Masquelier became increasingly convinced that the flavanols should no longer be regarded as a subcategory of flavonoids but rather as a separate, independent class that is equivalent to flavonoids. This group of flavanol compounds comprises single flavanols as well as clusters of two, three, or more flavanol units. The following sections discuss the kinds of flavanols that exist.

In nature, some flavanol units are destined to remain single. These "bachelor" flavanols are called catechins. Catechins remain single for the duration of their existence. The catechin has a mirror-image flavanol called epicatechin. The difference between them is like the difference between your left hand and your right hand. Both the catechin and epicatechin are single flavanols. Both forms of catechin remain bachelors. How is it then that clusters of two, three, four, or more "bachelors" come into being? To understand, this we must take one step back in the process of the formation of flavanols in plants. Before there is catechin, there is an "almost catechin" called carbocation. On the road from carbocation to catechin, there is a fork with a sign that points in the direction of proanthocyanidins. Once the decision to go left or right has been made, there is no way back. A carbocation that "goes catechin" ends up as irreversibly single. A carbocation that "goes proanthocyanidin" ends up as irreversibly married catechins. There remains an intriguing question. On the way to marriage, is there a single proanthocyanidin? Coupled catechins behave differently from the way they behave as singles. Coupled, they behave as proanthocyanidins. Catechins differ sufficiently from proanthocyanidins to warrant a different name.

Does nature know a single proanthocyanidin? It does, but its existence is somewhat theoretical in that it is hard to isolate a single proanthocyanidin. Theoretically, a single proanthocyanidin is a flavanol, and its structure is similar to but not identical to that of the single flavanols named catechin and epicatechin. As the multiple proanthocyanidins, the singles behave as true proanthocyanidins. The primary and most visible difference is that the proanthocyanidins are unlike the catechins in that a catechin does not produce red anthocyanin under the Bate-Smith reaction, while all the proanthocyanidins do. You can heat catechins in an acid solution for days, and they will not turn red. There has been confusion about this issue up to the present day because the proanthocyanidins so abundantly found in nature are clusters (pairs, triples, quadruples, etc.) of catechins and epicatechins.

Single proanthocyanidins are hardly found in nature because once they exist, they find another single proanthocyanidin to marry. Once married, they find another proanthocyanidin to be married, and so the proanthocyanidins form bigger and bigger proanthocyanidolic clusters. Paradoxically, these clusters consist of catechins, but these catechins don't speak for themselves as individuals. They can express themselves only as proanthocyanidins, in complete bondage, so to speak. The bonding is the process described by Masquelier in 1948 as he observed how chromogen evolved into tannins. Many years later, Masquelier realized that he had been observing the formation of proanthocyanidins.

What process in nature decides whether the carbocation, the precursor that catechins and proanthocyanidins have in

Carbocation

Catechin

Epicatechin

Proanthocyanidins

Single proanthocyanidin
(1 unit)
(Hypothetical monomer)

Dimer (2 units)

Trimer (3 units)

Tetramer (4 units)

Pentamer (5 units)

Tannins (Polymers) (six or more units)

OPCs

Mirror image — Catechin (A)
Mirror image — Epicatechin (B)

Dimers of Proanthocyanidins

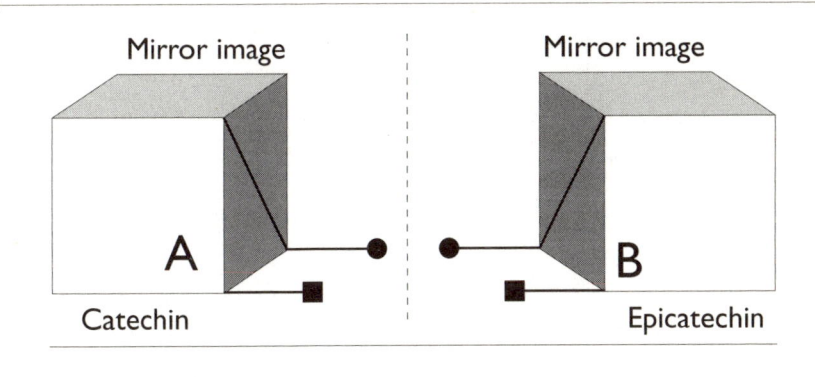

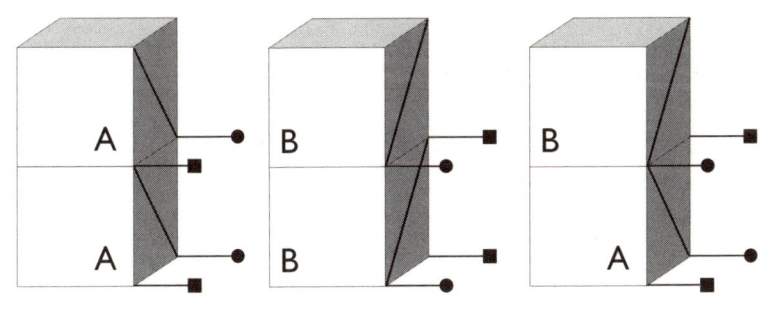

Trimers of Proanthocyanidins

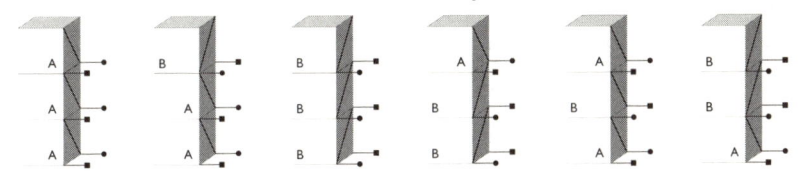

This figure shows how complex OPCs can be, because they can consist of the catechins (A) and epicatechins (B). Catechin and epicatechins are isomers, that is mirror images of each other. Therefor, the combination of the 2 isomers can give rise to 3 different proanthocyanidolic dimers: AA, BB, AB. When it comes to forming combinations of 3 isomers (trimers of proanthocyanidins) the number of combinations increases: AAA, BAA, BBB, ABB, ABA, BBA. In the proanthocyanidins that consist of 4 isomers (the tetramers) the number of possible combinations is much higher. And so it goes on and on with the growing of the numbers of isomers per proanthocyanidin. This is why we now use the plural OPCs instead of the single OPC. Although all OPCs are similar in activity, their make-up can vary in terms of combinations of catechins and epicatechins.

common, "goes single" and becomes a catechin or turns into a single proanthocyanidin to marry another proanthocyanidin to form clusters? Masquelier and his colleagues have tried to unravel this secret because they wanted to see if they could synthesize OPCs in the laboratory. Many attempts were made, but they found that proanthocyanidins cannot be stably produced in the laboratory, which means that OPCs cannot be synthetically produced. OPCs can only be isolated from plant materials. This is an important aspect of OPCs because many of the phyto- and micronutrients present in today's foods and food supplements have been synthetically produced. Practically all commercially available vitamins are synthetic. Even substances such as CoQ10 are not extracted but fermented. In contrast, OPCs are truly phyto because they are always made from plant materials.

Whether a carbocation becomes a single "starter proanthocyanidin" depends on the presence of a certain enzyme. If a plant that contains catechins also contains this enzyme, it presents a marked propensity to condensation of flavanols and produces OPCs and thicker "polymerized" clusters of catechins, the tannins. So far, nature alone has decided on the plant's enzymatic composition. Recent studies indicate that influencing the plant's propensity to form procyanidins by way of "engineering" enzymes into plants that lack OPCs and tannins seems to be a possibility. The reason for this research will probably not be of interest to most readers because it concerns the inhibiting of "pasture bloating" in cattle. According to these genetic engineers, tannins increase the amount of protein that leaves the animal, thus diminishing the bloating caused by proteins. This kind of research touches on another very important distinction we must make: that between OPCs and tannins.

The final step that we must make in distinguishing OPCs is to determine at what point the process of thickening turns the proanthocyanidins from valuable phytonutrients (OPCs) into useless, antinutritional tannins. To make that final distinction, I must take you a few steps further into the process of condensation or polymerization. The Latin word merus or ancient Greek meros means part. When identical parts form pairs, triples, quadruples, major clusters, or even chains, this process is referred to as polymerization, with poly standing for many. Plastics are a common household example of such polymers in that plastics are the result of polymerization. Smaller groups consisting only of several identical parts are called oligomers; in ancient Greek oligo means few. The single part is called a monomer, mono meaning single or one.

We can now distinguish the various proanthocyanidolic compounds by way of the words polymers, oligomers, and monomers. The single proanthocyanidin (the starter unit) is a monomeric proanthocyanidin. Two bonded flavan-3-ol parts constitute a "dimer." Three bonded flavan-3-ol parts are referred to as "trimers," four constitute a "tetramer," and five, a "pentamer." All proanthocyanidins consisting of two, three, four, and five units are the oligomeric proanthocyanidins. To simplify this complicated terminology, Masquelier and his team began referring to the oligomers of proanthocyanidins as OPCs during the 1960s. According to Masquelier, clusters of six and more units belong to the polymers or tannins. One could call them PPCs. As is explained in this book, only the OPCs and the catechins have nutritional value. Only OPCs and catechins are phyto*nutrients*. Compared with catechins, OPCs are by far the superior phytonutrient. PPCs or tannins are considered to be antinutritional because they interfere with the digestion and absorption of proteins.

Researchers have had heated discussions about whether the term oligo really stops at five units or may be conveniently stretched to the level of 10-unit compounds (decamers) to extend the merits of OPCs to worthless products. Because these discussions are often fought on commercial rather than on scientific grounds, *The American Heritage Dictionary of the English Language* is probably the best authority to resolve this discussion. Its Third Edition defines an oligomer as "a polymer that consists of two, three, or four monomers." According to the dictionary, which is even stricter than OPCs' discoverer, the procyanidolic pentamers (five units) and higher polymers are not OPCs but PPCs or tannins.

> **o•lig•o•mer** (ə-lĭg′ə-mər) *n.* A polymer that consists of two, three, or four monomers. —**o•lig′o•mer′ic** (-mĕr′ĭk) *adj.* —**o•lig′o•mer′i•za′tion** *n.*

Masquelier always explains this chemistry by way of a simple comparison representing catechins as the bricks used to build a house. In their catechin state, these bricks remain loose elements, with which one cannot construct a house. The bricklayer needs mortar to bond the bricks. The enzymes that can influence the formation of single starter proanthocyanidins are like the bricklayers who put mortar between the bricks. Once they have created a starter unit, the bricklaying proceeds almost automatically because the units cluster spontaneously. Without the enzymes (bricklayers) we find nothing but catechin-bricks that remain loose elements that cannot be used to build OPCs (the house). In plants that lack these "bricklaying" enzymes, we may find catechins, but we will not find OPCs. In plants that have these enzymes, we find catechins and OPCs. This is why Masquelier's OPCs products always contain a certain amount of the loose catechins (bricks), which naturally "come" with the OPCs during the manufacturing process.

In this procyanidolic context, there exists a widespread, persistent but incorrect use of the term "monomer." By definition, a monomer is a molecule that can combine with other identical molecules to form a polymer. A catechin is not a monomer because a catechin lacks the capacity to combine with other catechins to form oligomers of proanthocyanidins. The true monomer of proanthocyanidins is the single starter proanthocyanidin, which is made from the carbocation under the influence of enzymes. Monomers of proanthocyanidins are so rare that it is safe to say that no product contains them. In the context of products containing proanthocyanidins, it is a mistake to speak of monomers. I know because I have made the mistake myself, thinking that catechins are the monomers of proanthocyanidins. There are catechins and epicatechins. There are oligomeric (OPCs) and polymeric (tannins) proanthocyanidins. The monomers exist in theory only. You won't find them in any commercially available product. Product labels that mention "monomers" are incorrect.

Throughout the many years of Masquelier's research, he and his colleagues developed an ever-clearer understanding of all these substances. Yet the problem remained that the scientific community never fully resolved the confusion caused by the fact that flavanols were wrongly classified in the large family of bioflavonoids, although they definitely deserved to be classified as a separate family because of the wide differences between the two groups. Until this very day, the confusion haunts scientific articles as well as the labels of many herbal medicines and dietary supplements.

13 WHERE ARE OPCs IN NATURE?

In the course of the long years of Masquelier's studies, he discovered that OPCs exist in practically every plant. An examination of 500 different plant species confirmed the broad distribution of OPCs in the vegetal kingdom. Dr. Marie-Claude Dumon, who became one of Masquelier's loyal collaborators after having been his student first, wrote in her 1990 doctoral thesis, "Study of 500 species belonging to 175 different families shows the wide distribution of these substances (OPCs). This analysis confirms that in certain families, there is a particular abundance of species containing catechic tannins, like Anacardiaceae, Caprifoliaceae, Ericaceae, Fagaceae, Saxifrageae, Hamamelidaceae, Lauraceae, Leguminosae, Myrtaceae, Rosaceae, Rubiaceae. ... Together with the oligomers, we find monomeric molecules, which are particularly abundant in the areas of active metabolism."

Dr. Dumon then describes how OPCs "accumulate in the woody parts of the plant. In fact, they are isolated most often from wood and bark (Pinus Pinaster [pine tree], Aesculus hippocastanum [chestnut tree], Cinchona succirubra [cinchona tree], and Viburnum prunifolium). We find them, however, also in the *leaves* (Rubus fructocisus [raspberry], Aesculus hippocastanum [chesnut tree], Vaccinium myrtyllus [blueberry], Quercus robur [oak tree]), the *seeds* (Cola nitida [kola nut], Theobroma cacao [cacao], Persea gratissima [avocado], Vitis vinifera [vine]), the *fruit* (Rubus fructicosus [raspberry], Malus sylvestris [apple], Sorbus aucuparia [rowan tree], Crataegus oxyacantha [hawthorn], Cupressus semper-virens [cypress]), and the *roots* and *rhizomes* (Fragaria vesca [strawberry], Krameria triandra [ratanhia]) as well as in the *stems* and *flowers* (Tilla officinalis [linden tree],

Crataegus oxyacantha [hawthorn])." In brief, OPCs are found in many familiar (remedial) plants, such as linden, hawthorn, chestnut, oak, vine, and pine.

Plants create OPCs in the leaves from which they migrate to those parts of the plant in which they are required for protection against oxidization. By 1970, Masquelier had developed isolation methods that make it possible to obtain OPCs from practically every plant and from every part of plants. In an industrial setting, care must be taken that there is a reasonable relationship between the quantity of raw plant material and the yield of OPCs. Because the finest OPCs cannot be produced in quantities exceeding 0.5 to 1 percent of the crude plant material, that crude material must be abundantly available and its industrial processing must be feasible as well as ecologically meaningful in its exploitation. It would, for example, make no sense to cut entire forests just to obtain the bark. The use of the bark of the Maritime Pine is meaningful only because pines are cut and replanted for wood and paper processing. In that process, the bark is actually wasted or used in gardening. Nevertheless it can be observed that pine trees are chopped down ever earlier in their growth. The bark of younger trees is, of course, not as thick as that of older ones, so younger pine trees yield fewer OPCs.

After having fully explored the manufacturing of OPCs from peanut skins and Maritime Pine bark, Masquelier discovered another even more meaningful source of OPCs: the seeds of the Vitis Vinifera grapes. The seeds that are suitable for OPCs' production process are the seeds that remain after the pressing of the grapes during the production of white wines. This does not necessarily mean that the seeds must be from white grapes. Some white wines are made from red grapes. For Masquelier, living in the Bordeaux region, which is one of the largest wine-growing areas in the world, this crude plant material was abundantly at his fingertips. The seeds that are left in the mash after the grapes are pressed are a mere waste product, although a certain volume of those seeds is being used for pressing oil and for making the "marc" distillate. Although it lacks any trace of OPCs, the "marc de raisin" is an "eau-de-vie," which is quite popular in France for digestive help.

Masquelier's Patent filed in 1970 (French Patent 70.21940) envisioned the isolation of OPCs from all possible plants. From then on, it was possible to obtain high-quality OPCs from various kinds of plant materials without risking any loss in quality. The 1970 patent was the gateway to a third French herbal medicine on the basis of OPCs obtained from Vitis Vinifera seeds. With the finest OPCs now available, Masquelier would conclusively demonstrate the bioavailability of OPCs, in turn setting in motion further exploration of the analysis of this substance and its fingerprinting.

French patent no. 70.21940

14 ANTHOGENOL

The production process that was invented by Jack Masquelier and gives us the product known as MASQUELIER's Original OPCs concentrates on the isolation of that narrow section of the plant's micronutrients, which is characterized by the plant's most active one: the OPCs. In the production of MASQUELIER's Original OPCs, great care is taken that few or no other compounds end up in the product. Aiming at OPCs, isolation begins of course with selecting from the plant the specific part that is rich in it. In this way, we minimize the problem that other known or unknown plant substances would end up in MASQUELIER's Original OPCs, blurring its purity. The bulk of the problem of making OPCs is their separation from the big procyanidolic molecules, the tannins.

The selection of the plant from which the crude parts are used is of great importance because even though Masquelier's production method is "sharp," plant materials such as pine bark contain polyphenols of which small traces come with the OPCs during production. Pine bark contains noticeable amounts of taxifolin and caffeic acid. It is hard to eliminate their presence in Masquelier's Pinus Maritima OPCs. The seeds of Vitis Vinifera grapes, on the other hand, do not contain taxifolin, caffeic acid, or other related polyphenols, so the OPCs isolated from this raw material are of a finer quality. This does not mean that Flavan, which is made from the bark of the Maritime Pine, is of a lesser *biological* quality than MASQUELIER's Original OPCs made from Vitis Vinifera. Flavan's efficacy has been demonstrated beyond a shadow of a doubt, even though in terms of OPCs, the product is not "fine" in the absolute chemical meaning of the word.

In the industry, the term fine means free from impurities. Most certainly, OPCs are the predominant active principle in Flavan, but the product does contain other elements that make it more of a complex of phytonutrients than one fine phytonutrient. In terms of OPCs, yes, taxifolin and caffeic acid are impurities, and as individual substances, they do not interest us. Their presence in traces in Masquelier's Pinus Maritima product is no cause for concern because they have never given rise to any negative effect. International Nutrition Company (INC), the worldwide supplier of Masquelier's Pinus Maritima product, distinguishes Flavan as MASQUELIER's French Pine Bark *Complex*. Because the OPCs material made from Vitis Vinifera seeds is finer, INC refers to this phytonutrient as MASQUELIER's Original OPCs. The latter product is trademarked as ANTHOGENOL®.

Apart from being a proficient scientist and teacher, Masquelier has a knack for coining new scientific terms as well as for coining trademarks and other terms to distinguish his products — not that he always reaps the fruits of his creative skills. Some trademarks fell by the wayside, and others were left unused, mostly because Masquelier has more affinity for the creative process itself than with the struggles that come with using and defending the results of his creativity. Although Masquelier did not coin the ANTHOGENOL trademark, he readily gave it his irrevocable blessings because ANTHOGENOL describes quite precisely the phenomenon that condensed flavan*ol*s will *gen*erate the red pigment *antho*cyanin. Moreover, the Greek word anthos means not only flower but also blossom, young greenery, or the best, strongest, highest of something as best expressed in the French words "fine fleur." Fine fleur stands for pride or flower as in flower of the nation. Surely, OPCs generate youth in the figurative sense of the Greek word anthos. And aren't OPCs the colors, the grains of gold in the field of nutrition and human health? The fact that MASQUELIER's Original OPCs are sold under the ANTHOGENOL trademark combines very well with the fact that these products rank as the fine fleur in the fields of medicine, cosmetics, and dietary products.

INC does not use the word extract to distinguish its MASQUELIER's products because that term is so imprecise that its use to identify and describe products can only give rise to confusion and unfair competition. From one particular plant, one can make many kinds of extracts in many different qualities, ranging from worthless to beneficial. Classifying all these different extracts as extracts is counterproductive in that it gives the false impression that all these extracts are identical. As a consequence of such indiscriminate use of the term extract, the lowest-priced, lowest-quality worthless extract will eventually drive out and destroy the higher-priced, finest-quality efficient extract. Then, the lowest-quality extract will wipe out itself because consumers abandon products that don't give results. In disservice to public health, this is how a large part of the health food industry works. In disservice to itself, this is why the health food industry provokes attacks on itself. This is why the supplier of MASQUELIER's French Pine Bark Complex doesn't use the word extract to describe a product for which the outstanding vasoprotective effects have stood steady since 1968.

The plant parts that are rich in OPCs are always abundantly rich in tannins. Because of their size, tannins are antinutritional and serve no useful purpose other than to stop diarrhea.

They have such biological strength that they would do harm to the body if they passed from the intestines into the bloodstream. When nutrition contains both proteins and tannins, the latter bind with the proteins, making them no longer available to the body. That's why tannins are regarded as antinutritional. Fortunately, Masquelier invented ways to precisely separate tannins from OPCs — for instance, by making tannins insoluble through the addition of large amounts of salt to the solution in which the crude plant material has been dissolved. Following this procedure, the tannins can be filtered out.

In contrast to the tannins, catechins are not eliminated during the production of Masquelier's products. Catechins are left in ANTHOGENOL, because their removal is unnecessary and expensive, and they might even make the OPCs unstable. In ANTHOGENOL, catechins are not only free from undesirable effects, they are even useful. According to Masquelier, catechins (and epicatechins for that matter) contribute to the effectiveness of OPCs. In their pure crystalline state, catechins are not soluble, but in the presence of OPCs, they become soluble and display their beneficial effects without the slightest degree of toxicity. Masquelier is firmly convinced that in coexistence with OPCs, catechins become particularly effective. Obviously, Masquelier's opinion pertains as much to ANTHOGENOL as to MASQUELIER's French Pine Bark Complex.

All scientists who deal with a complex mixture of ingredients are driven by the urge to analyze it, dissect it into its individual components, characterize these components, and eliminate all parts they deem undesirable. In the case of Masquelier's products, the urge to further refine and purify them turned out to be a waste of precious time and energy. Unintentionally, Dr. Michel Bourzeix, a French professorial colleague of Masquelier's, showed that Masquelier's mixtures of catechins and OPCs should not be "disintegrated" further through separation and isolation of their individual components. Bourzeix, who worked at the National Agronomical Research Institute (INRA), had undertaken the painstaking effort to isolate, identify, and correctly "label" OPCs. Once he had obtained a good number of individual OPCs, he withdrew all water from them to try to protect them against oxidation and aging. He intended to analyze their chemical profile and find out how the isolated OPCs behave in living organisms.

It took Bourzeix at least two years to separate a good number of the smaller OPCs. When he then began to examine the OPCs he had first isolated, to see how they had developed, he found they had changed completely. Instead of producing on chromatographic paper one single stain, as any pure substance will do, the OPCs produced two or three stains. They had fallen apart. The whole effort had been a waste of time, except that it showed that by themselves, the individual OPCs are not stable. We must simply respect the plant in that once we have industrially isolated its naturally occurring slice of catechins and OPCs, we should not try to make any further separation of what seems to be a family of happily coexisting flavanols. Separating OPCs into individual ones may be interesting from an analytical viewpoint, but doing so completely disintegrates the quality, stability, and efficacy of ANTHOGENOL.

It is meaningless to further split the product into purer fractions because the section of catechins and OPCs that

Masquelier "cut" seems to form the perfect combination of quality, stability, economy, and efficacy. Nature has obviously intended these molecules, which are all members of the family of flavanols, to be together and to jointly unfold a number of highly important biological activities. Catechins are weaker than OPCs, but there is good reason to let them be together. The various members of this family can be compared to horses that are harnessed to a coach. They may be different breeds, but they all pull the coach in the same direction. No single horse swerves or pulls the other way. These molecules belong together; they protect and support one another, much like trees that keep together in a forest and avoid being uprooted during a thunderstorm.

15 VASCULAR PROTECTION

Pregnant Madame Tayeau, to whom Masquelier had administered his first OPCs at the beginning of his scientific career, felt immediate relief when the edema in her legs receded within 48 hours. During the decades that followed, especially in France, OPCs were primarily dealt with as vasoprotective remedies. Before discussing the third vasoprotective herbal remedy that was developed in France during the 1970s, let's see which disorders and complaints are attributable to vascular problems. How would you know if you were suffering from a vascular problem?

When your gums bleed as you brush your teeth, when brief exposure to a cold draft causes the tiny veinlets in the whites of your eyes to burst and your eyes to redden, when your legs hurt because of varicose veins, when hardly noticeable pressure such as pinching or nipping results in a hematoma (blue spot), when at the end of a long flight your shoes are too tight, when you've been standing all day and your ankles are swollen ... you are facing a vascular problem. You could also have a vascular problem if a weakened blood vessel that is only slightly strained "bursts" and blood plasma (fluid) containing larger solid particles extravasates into the surrounding tissue. In people with weakened vessels, there is a continuous impaired permeability. Uncontrollably, the blood leaks from the vascular system and accumulates in the tissues, resulting in swellings, or edema. Such impaired permeability occurs only in the tiny and very delicate capillaries, where the arterial system containing oxygen-rich blood coming from the lungs and heart turns into the venal system, in which the carbon-dioxide-rich blood flows back to the lungs and heart. At the point of the capillaries, the blood releases oxygen into and picks up carbon dioxide (CO_2) from the tissues. A well functioning vascular system is of ultimate importance to your health.

This circulatory system has the task of channeling blood and lymph through the entire organism, allowing the transportation, delivery, and pick-up of their particles. It is a matter of pumping and keeping everything flowing while controlling volume and allowing particles to leave and enter the system. The arteries and veins, the capillaries and the lymphatic system — the whole circulatory system pervading the tissues at cell level is embedded in the connective tissue, which provides structure, strength, and resilience. The circulatory system does not have disparate or diverging features. The entire structure and all functions of this system are aligned and completely focused on one goal: transportation.

The arteries and their small terminal branches, the arterioles, transport the blood, which is rich in oxygen and free from toxic components, to the cells and provide them with everything they require for life. Owing to their structure, the arteries and the arterioles possess dynamic properties that enable them to regulate blood pressure by absorbing the flow of blood that is pumped into the circulatory system by the heart 70 to 150 times per minute. Sportsmen at peak performance and pilots during take off and landing rate 190 beats per minute. A healthy arterial system flexibly responds to the differences in volume so that blood pressure does not fluctuate too much. To allow this to happen, the structure of the arterial wall consists primarily of muscle cells and connective tissue.

The veins not only permit the backflow of blood to the places of cleansing, such as the liver and the kidneys, they also fulfill the functions of storage and temperature regulation. The venous endothelium (the layer of the vascular wall that forms the interface between the blood and the inner layers of the vascular wall) plays a complex part in the origin of certain processes, especially blood clotting. Owing to their structure, veins are able to perform only a very limited degree of contraction and expansion, but their tone contributes significantly to regulating the mass of blood.

In the tiny capillaries that form the connection between the arterial and the venous system, the exchange between blood and tissues takes place. Oxygen and nutrients pass into the tissues, and CO_2 and waste pass into the blood. Capillaries have an average diameter of 10 microns, which is about the size of a single red blood cell. The red blood cells must make their way through the capillaries in single file. The capillaries consist of a layer of endothelial cells that is glued on a basal membrane. The endothelial cells form the coating of the cavities of the heart and of the blood and lymph vessels. At the point where the arterial and the venal system connect, the vascular wall consists of nothing more than its endothelial coating surrounded by a membrane, forming a fragile permeable network: the capillary or hair vessel. When in good condition, this network precisely controls and checks the passing through of liquid and certain dissolved particles (nutrients, waste materials). The total length of these hair vessels adds up to several miles, providing every single cell in the body with the necessary nutrients.

The hair vessel must be permeable to the precise degree that it will allow the crossing of nutrients and waste materials. But if the hair vessel is too permeable, it will impair the strict separation between the blood and the tissues, which will lead to swelling and pain. The results would be hemorrhage, hematoma, or edema. In severer cases, the leaking may turn into a rupture of the capillary. This accident is called a stroke when it takes place in the brain. A stroke may be the result of not only a burst capillary or artery, but also of a blockage by a blood clot. In the latter case, the stroke is called ischemic. In a vascular incident, the stroke is called hemorrhagic. In any case, the reduction of, or disruption in, blood flow in the brain for even a short period of time can be disastrous and cause brain damage or even death. Our whole body is vascularized because every corner of our body, every cell, must be nourished with nutrients, building blocks (amino acids), and oxygen and because waste materials must be transported away to be broken down and excreted. Therefore, the capillaries, which allow the flow of substances between blood and tissues, perform one of the most vital functions in the body.

The lymph is a faintly yellow fluid consisting of 95 percent water (lymph plasma) in which we find lymphocytes and other so-called plasma proteins that exist only in the lymph. Lymph forms a key part in our defense and immune system. The lymph originates from the flowing of fluid from the blood through the capillaries into the tissues, or into the intercellular spaces, where the fluid part of the blood, the blood's plasma, is being "sucked up" by the lymph vessels. Eventually, the plasma is returned to the blood via the lymph nodes. In addition to draining off excess tissue fluid and returning it to the blood, the lymphatic capillaries transport waste products as well as dead blood cells, pathogenic organisms in case of infection, and malignant cells from cancerous growths. In the lymph nodes, invading bacteria are filtered and destroyed by the lymphocytes.

The lymph and blood systems function in a dynamic and highly complex interplay. A change in one factor results in far-reaching consequences. A reduced vein tone triggers a slowdown of circulation with a simultaneous increase in pressure on the capillary level. There, the capillary membrane may succumb and become weak and more permeable. The surrounding tissue is saturated with excessive fluid and the tiny lymphatic capillaries are overburdened. This inundation results in local edema, also called lymphedema. A failure of lymphatic drainage, in turn, causes fibrosis, a pathogenic growth of connective tissue, which may eventually result in thrombosis. This shows the importance of dissolving a venous-lymphatic congestion as early as possible. Even if it originates at the capillary level, it quickly affects the entire circulatory environment and should therefore be eradicated at the root. The effects of a distorted venolymphatic system are not always life threatening, but they genuinely bother millions and millions of people. When left unattended, venolymphatic disturbances such as high blood pressure may eventually upset the heart muscle, resulting in angina pectoris, cardiac arrest, or heart failure.

The healthy interplay among all parts of the vascular system is compromised by stress of a nutritional nature, by stress of a physical nature, and of course by a combination of both. Nutritional stress consists of more than overloading the vascular system in a way that obstructs and immobilizes; deficiencies in essential nutrients are just as much part of nutritional stress because they can lead to malfunction, decay, and degeneration. A lack of vitamin C and OPCs combined with a lack of antioxidants puts great stress on the cardiovascular system. Stress can be caused by the overwhelming presence of something as well as by the overwhelming absence of something. The reason many people fall ill at the beginning of their retirement is simply that they have an absence of work.

The physical stress that burdens your vascular system may also not be what you think. Physical simply means things like pressure, mobility, speed, volume, and gravity — the push and pull in the circulatory system. Because most of the blood is situated beneath the level of the heart and lungs, the major physical problem encountered by the cardiovascular system is gravity. Gravity is overcome by the heart's power, the resilience of the vascular wall, the tone of the veins, the condition of the veins' valves, and the level of activity of the veins' surrounding muscles, which help to "squeeze" the blood through the valves in an upward movement. Therefore, a lack or an absence of movement creates much more physical stress on the circulatory system than does physical activity. Cycling, walking, jogging, stretching, or any other form of sports or activity greatly assists the vascular system in its task to bring the blood back to the heart and lungs.

Varicose veins are the most visible result of nutritional and physical stress on the vascular system. The valves in the veins prevent the blood from flowing back. If the valves of the veins slacken or if there is insufficient movement, congestion takes place. The blood saturated with waste products and CO_2 stagnates in what may become varicose veins. In particular, for people who have to stand for hours on end, sit immobilized for long periods (on long flights, on long drives, or in long meetings at the office) or who walk only short distances, as applies to salespersons, these factors come into play. Feeling tired after not having done much stems from this lack of real movement and real physical activity. A special case is pregnant women. Their blood circulation is physically impaired because the backflow, in fact the "upflow," is impeded by the fetus. They frequently suffer from edema in their feet and ankles and from heavy legs, a phenomenon that occurs especially in the evening and that is reported by as many as 50 percent of all women. Women are obviously significantly more affected by problems of blood upflow than men, and they suffer from varicose veins much more than men, partly because female hormones tend to disturb the vascular wall.

Varicose veins are seriously swollen, distended, and knotted veins, visible especially in the legs. People develop varicose veins when the valves and walls of the vascular veins are weakened. In situations of prolonged immobility, the sheer weight of the blood puts a strain on the valves and vascular wall, causing the veins to widen and lose their elasticity. At the place of widening, the valves no longer function efficiently and the problem spreads. Apart from the fact that varicose veins are unattractive, the so-called functional symptoms of varicose veins can be unpleasant and very painful. Varicose veins cause heavy legs, redness, and painful swellings and stings. At night, such stings are the cause for frequent awakenings, leading to sleepless nights and fatigue. People suffering from these symptoms cannot stand still for more than a few minutes without feeling discomfort. Neither can they walk long distances. OPCs can be of tremendous help because they strengthen the vascular wall and improve the flow of blood. In France, the oldest and most used application of OPCs is for the functional symptoms of varicose veins.

The French medicines containing OPCs as their active ingredient focus specifically on the improvement if peripheral circulation. Peripheral circulation takes place in the circulatory system, distal to the heart, in the veins and arteries. Peripheral circulation goes from the heart, moves through the arteries, passes the capillaries and then goes back to heart. All capillaries together have an enormous total length of several miles. Because they are the narrowest and most fragile section of the circulatory system, their structure and function play an important role in the total peripheral circulation. OPCs may prevent and dissolve peripheral congestion because they keep the narrowest part of the circulatory system in good condition. Because they keep the vessel wall in good condition, OPCs make peripheral circulation less prone to accidents and problems. Once an accident takes place, damage is sometimes irreversible. For instance, people with clearly visible varicoses must not expect that these destroyed veins will completely disappear when they take OPCs. In most cases, the structural damage is irreversible. But taking OPCs will most certainly cause the accompanying "functional" symptoms to be mitigated, if not to completely disappear. Because a varicosis itself will react less violently, there will be a significant cosmetic improvement in many cases.

The increased permeability of the hair vessels and the impairment of the veins may also result in the development of a particularly unpleasant type of varicose veins: hemorrhoids. While women suffer from edema and varicose veins more frequently, a relatively larger number of men are bothered by hemorrhoids. One origin of hemorrhoids, which are varicose veins at the anus, is long periods spent in a sitting position and living a sedentary life. People who spend long days sitting in their office chair, take frequent flights, or travel long distances by car are often affected. The problem is aggravated by a diet low in roughage. The veins in the lower intestinal area expand, itching occurs, and in the worst case, the veins even burst. Bowel movement is painful, and blood is excreted. Because of the risk of infection, this condition is harmful and may require medical treatment, possibly even surgical intervention.

For all these vascular ailments, OPCs turn out to be a potent remedy as both prevention and cure. In addition to the previously mentioned clinical tests performed during the 1960s with Flavan, numerous systematic clinical trials followed during the 1970s. They were performed with the OPCs that were the result of the newer production patent filed by Masquelier in 1970, allowing the production of OPCs from plant materials other than pine bark. Finally, in 1978, the French company Labaz came out with a remedy called Endotélon. When Labaz began the registration process for Endotélon, governmental regulations for drug admission had become tighter and more complicated. In Masquelier's recollection, Labaz had to submit about 2,000 case studies. The clinical studies for Endotélon were performed in hospitals all over France, in Paris, Lyon, Strasburg, Nancy, and Toulouse.

During the Flavan trials, patients suffering from a variety of vascular problems were treated with OPCs. In the Endotélon studies, scientists proceeded from one specific problem and tested a large number of patients all suffering from identical symptoms. The specific problems selected for the Endotélon tests were veinolymphatic insufficiencies, especially circulatory problems in the eyes and legs. Later, Endotélon would also be successfully tested in post-surgery breast cancer patients. By the end of the 1980s, the result of what Masquelier had begun in an ill-equipped laboratory during the years after World War II formed the basis for three reputable vasoprotectors frequently and broadly prescribed by French physicians until today. Unintendedly, the intense use of OPCs as a vasoprotector by the French pharmaceutical industry and medical profession confirmed the fact that OPCs are the vitamin with the "P" effect. But the vitamin side of this scientific progress went unnoticed, mostly because all these scientific developments took place in France and not in the Anglo-Saxon world, but surely also because they took place in the field of medicine and not in the field of nutrition. Yet, Masquelier, his colleagues, and his students were convinced that they had unraveled the secrets of vitamin P. Unfortunately, vitamin P had become so bashed and trodden on that it was impossible to resurrect.

After all those decades of discoveries, research, and development, OPCs' general acceptance filled Masquelier with pride. But as Masquelier explains, his positive feelings were tempered because the successes did have a counterproductive effect. OPCs experienced the destiny of a talented actor who records great success with a specific role and who is then restricted to play such roles for the rest of his life. Once the French pharmaceutical industry had categorized OPCs as vasoprotector, it did not consider any other applications, be it for reasons of routine or lack of curiosity. There also existed an administrative reason for this restriction. Once a medicine has been assigned to a specific disease, in France, the medical indication cannot be changed any more or even expanded to cover an additional indication. In the words of Masquelier, "If somebody in France found that Aspirin cured AIDS, we would still not be allowed to officially use it as a remedy for AIDS since Aspirin was once and for all registered as a medicine against headache. My products are the most effective vasoprotectors, and their fast as well as lasting efficacy has been thoroughly explored. But I knew that OPCs had a potential which by far exceeded their vasoprotective properties." And that is what Masquelier succeeded in proving in the further course of his research.

16 OPCs' PLACE IN NUTRITION

The fact that the manufacturers of Resivit, Flavan, and Endotélon presented OPCs in the form of medicinal products does not turn OPCs into a drug. At the time, the commercial choice was made to market OPCs in France under medicinal indications, so it happened that OPCs were blessed with this medicinal status only because of their medicinal use, not so much because OPCs are a medicine per se. In comparison, even though scurvy is a disease, using vitamin C to prevent it doesn't turn vitamin C into a medicine. The phytonutrient OPCs prevents and cures numerous vascular and other conditions. Because OPCs are nutrients, it would be logical to conclude that these vascular conditions are caused by a nutritional deficiency, just as scurvy is caused by a deficiency in vitamin C. If scurvy is a deficiency disease that does not exist when there is sufficient vitamin C in the diet, why wouldn't we also call the conditions that do not exist in the presence of sufficient amounts of dietary OPCs deficiency diseases?

In his patent of 1965, Masquelier clearly listed a wide variety of vascular disorders that could result from a deficiency in OPCs, which he referred to as vitamin P factor. In this context, he described vitamin P's position in nutrition as follows: "OPCs are found in nature, in the natural state, in fruits and vegetables in particular. A normal diet should therefore provide an adequate amount of P factors to avoid any deficiency. However, these constituents [Masquelier meant OPCs] are usually located in the bark, teguments, cuticles, and woody parts of plants, so that they are eliminated when we eat fruits and vegetables. It is therefore hardly surprising that there are individuals who suffer from problems indicative of factor P deficiency, in spite of having a healthy, balanced diet. In addition, numerous bioflavonoids are very poorly soluble or even insoluble in water; we assume they will have little activity when absorbed with our food."

Seeing today's abundance of vitamin supplements in pharmacies, drugstores, health food stores, and supermarkets, we must conclude that Masquelier was a real nutritional pioneer when during the mid-1960s he wrote about a nutritional deficiency of OPCs. At that time, he had not only conclusively brought to light many of the health benefits of OPCs, but he had also squarely placed these health benefits within the framework of the modern, western diet, which is prone to be deficient in OPCs. Thus, he announced in 1965 the notion of taking OPCs as a vitamin, as a dietary supplement. Masquelier attributed all the conditions he described in his French, British, and American Flavan patents to a nutritional deficiency in OPCs, thus acknowledging OPCs' essential status of phytonutrient.

Yet, it is entirely consistent with Masquelier's thinking that OPCs are being sold as medicines as well as dietary supplements. The same feelings of satisfaction that he experienced when the French OPCs medicines rose to fame now fill his mind as he sees MASQUELIER's Original OPCs products being taken as a dietary supplement by millions of consumers around the world. Many of these consumers do not suffer from the health problems researched in the framework of the French vascular medicines. Yet they do supplement their diets with OPCs because they see it as a way of staying healthy and fit. When Masquelier wrote his 1965 Flavan patent, dietary supplements as they exist today were practically unknown. But since the late 1970s, people have become increasingly aware of the fact that dietary supplements play a prominent role in their health. Although the early history of OPCs products determined that OPCs began their voyage on the marketplace as a medicine in France, the more recent history of OPCs has confirmed what Masquelier and his colleagues have been telling us since the beginning of their research: OPCs are vitamin P. OPCs are essential nutrients, and OPCs products belong in the group of vitamin supplements that are freely sold without medical indications. Masquelier sees the simultaneous marketing of his OPCs products, as a medicine and as a dietary supplement, as a rewarding acknowledgement of the many facets of his work and research.

In earlier centuries, when people didn't know about the relationship between food and health and often had no food anyway, nutritional deficiency symptoms (such as scurvy) were people's persistent companion. Humans were not yet aware that they needed to consume certain foods or their ingredients. Even those who reflected on this issue were fishing in troubled waters. In 1850, the English had found that the intake of lemon could prevent scurvy in sailors. But this insight resulted in some grotesque conclusions. The healing effect was attributed to the acid in the lemons. Since lemons were relatively expensive some captains thought up a cheaper solution: They gave to their men a solution of sulfuric acid! The acid, of course, had disastrous effects on the poor guys. Even people who could afford a varied diet were not spared. Louis the Holy, King of France, suffered from scurvy during a crusade. Insufficient nutrition caused him to lose all his teeth; in fact, the toothless denture of this king from the 12th century is in the treasury of Notre Dame in Paris.

Unfortunately, it still is true today that insufficient nutrition keeps many people in a state of sub-scurvy or sub-health. The early stage of vitamin C deficiency is still much more common than generally assumed. Cardiovascular and other degenerative diseases are the result of a deficiency in vitamin C, OPCs, and other essential nutrients. The cardiovascular and cancer mortality rates are proof that in all their affluence, the western societies still suffer from a suboptimal supply of vitamin C and OPCs. To put it in no uncertain terms, many of us still suffer from scurvy, be it that this form of scurvy manifests itself, for instance, in the form of vascular diseases. The abundance of food products and our bulging refrigerators give the false impression that food cannot be the cause of disease because there's plenty of it. In turn, this idea leads to the rather mediaeval thinking that disease is a curse that can be cured only by physicians who wear white coats and scribble prescriptions that may be deciphered only by pharmacists who then deliver us drugs with fancy names and side effects to which we must subject ourselves to drive out the curse. At best, physicians advise us to stop eating eggs and to quit smoking.

The human body does not produce OPCs, vitamin C, or any other vitamins, minerals, or phytonutrients. For these things, it is entirely dependent on food. In the case of OPCs, this is not all that simple. Vitamin C is contained in many fruits and vegetables, and even in meat. The likelihood that you will consume some milligrams each day is great. But OPCs, which exist in a large number of plants, are found primarily in the bark, shell, woody parts, and skin; that is, in those parts that we most often dispose of before consuming the fruit or vegetable. In grapes, the major quantity of OPCs is contained in the seeds. If we swallow the seeds unchewed, hardly any OPCs can unfold their effects in the body. Chewed grapes seeds, on the other hand, are not particularly tasty.

Moreover, many people do not like fresh fruit. Fear of environmental contamination causes people to peel their fruit. Thus, they try to avoid consuming heavy metals and chemicals that may be present in or on the outer leaves or skin. Unfortunately, these are the very parts in which most OPCs are located.

When I once visited the United States, I found that a prominent natural foods store in California sold seedless grapes — very convenient because customers don't have to spit out or chew the seeds. But the seeds are the most nutritional parts of the grapes! Grapes without seeds contain mostly water, sugar, some fibers, vitamins, and minerals. They are not completely "empty calories," but they are devoid of the proteins, oils, and OPCs contained in the seeds. It shows that even health-conscious retailers and growers of fruits and vegetables cannot always avoid the dictates of consumers' wish for convenience. It also shows that even people who set great store by healthy nutrition may well be affected by a vitamin P deficiency. The situation Masquelier had described in his 1965 patent turned out to be stunningly true even in today's health-conscious environment. It is even more stunningly true in the world of greasy burgers and processed food. In a January 2003 *Newsweek* article titled "The Deadly Noodle," authors Stefan Theil and Dana Thomas report, "No part of the world is immune from empty calories." They cite an official of the World Health Organization, who explains how places as remote as the Fiji Islands have fallen victim to empty foods: "Where in the past they produced their own fruits and vegetables, now they're swamped with canned soda and mutton fat imported from New Zealand. Call it the Coca-Colafication of the Pacific Islands."

Insufficient intake of OPCs through fruit is caused by industrial processing, which deprives fruit of its vital ingredients. A well-known example is canned food, but even fresh fruit that is served in our households may contain few OPCs because the fruit has not completely matured. OPCs are found primarily in completely ripe fruit, with only a minor amount present in unripe fruit. Today's produce, especially the fruit that goes into mass distribution, is frequently picked before it is ripe. The long chains of distribution to bring the fruit to the consumer take time. To prevent the fruit from rotting before reaching the consumer, growers pick it prematurely and allow it "to ripen" during transport. This is not meant to be a critique of those who have mastered the art of mass-distributing delicate fruits and vegetables, but consumers must be aware that not all fruits and vegetables that look alike automatically contain the same amounts of OPCs. Try to buy normally ripened fruits and full-grown vegetables. Consume the skin and seeds of certain fruit such as apples. If you are afraid of chemical contamination try to purchase uncontaminated organic fruit as is offered by farmers adhering to the requirements for organically grown food. You may have your own garden where you can plant fruit. Worm-eaten apples should not be a source of annoyance but encouragement.

The safest method to supply the body with adequate amounts of OPCs is in their regular, daily intake in the form of a dietary supplement. The safest way to make sure that you're getting the researched and qualified OPCs is to take

MASQUELIER's Original OPCs. Apart from the fact that OPCs provide the full range of vitamin P effects, they are also tremendously strong and safe antioxidants, an aspect discussed in greater detail in *chapter 28: OPCs, the Mightiest Scavengers of Free Radicals.* Their superior antioxidative power makes MASQUELIER's Original OPCs (ANTHOGENOL) and MASQUELIER's French Pine Bark Complex extremely fit for daily use as a dietary antioxidant. As antioxidants, OPCs are recommended, for instance, in the event of regular intake of vegetable oils, which are rich in polyunsaturated fatty acids (PUFAs). Polyunsaturated fatty acids have become an important ingredient of today's diet, especially the diet that is officially recommended to reduce the risk of cardiovascular diseases. Unfortunately, unsaturated fatty acids are the preferred target of the free radicals.

The free radicals that bother us most are radical forms of oxygen that indiscriminately "burn holes" in practically everything our body contains and is made of. Not only are fatty acids turned ineffective by free radicals, but they initiate a process generating huge quantities of even more poisonous new free radicals. Consuming unsaturated fatty acids in an isolated manner, without balancing the diet with antioxidants, means exposing oneself to a biological risk. This is an aspect untold by the food multinationals that offer us their vegetable oils, margarines, mayonnaises, and salad dressings that contain PUFAs, but the risk is there nevertheless. It is vital to combine the consumption of unsaturated fatty acids with the intake of an effective radical scavenger. As shown by good old Mother Nature, the very reason plants produce OPCs and other antioxidants is to protect the sensitive substances such as fatty acids from oxidation. Large-scale industrial manufacturing of vegetable oils destroys the antioxidants or separates them from the oils contained in the raw materials. Cold pressed oils from first pressings of olives, linseeds, grape seeds, and other sources still contain the naturally occurring antioxidants, but these are not the oils used in the margarines we find on the mass markets' shelves.

When it comes to protecting themselves against free radicals, elderly people are especially at risk. Certain enzymes that the body produces — such as peroxidase, catalase, and superoxide dismutase (SOD) — provide natural, innate protection against free radicals and oxidative accidents in our body. But the older we grow, the less effective these free radical scavenging enzymes become. This means that when we need the enzymatic protection most, during the second half of our lives, we become exposed to exponentially growing health risks. To defuse the situation, we should take dietary antioxidants to put the brakes on the oxidants that speed up the aging process. Some additional conditions may also overload and overwhelm the body with free radicals. These conditions concern:

- o People who are exposed to increased radiation of the sun or live at high altitudes.
- o People who regularly take medication on the basis of synthetic, polycyclic substances.
- o People who smoke. In heavy smokers, nicotine destroys vitamin C and thus deprives the body of an important natural antioxidant. OPCs balance this deficiency and, thanks to their protective effect, succeed in reinforcing the vitamin C.
- o People who regularly consume "royal" quantities of alcohol. This habit requires an antioxidant counterbal-

ance. The example of alcohol consumers convincingly illustrates the significance of such prevention; after all, liver degeneration is caused by an excess of free radicals. Those who regularly consume considerable quantities of alcohol should be taking OPCs. The relationship between alcohol and OPCs is discussed further in *chapter 31: Red Wine Drinkers Live Happier and Longer* and following chapters.

17 ARE OPCs VITAMINS?

A vitamin is a substance the body cannot make. Although we need vitamins in small quantities only, we cannot live without them. When our food lacks vitamins, we invariably develop serious and life-threatening diseases, such as scurvy. By establishing a direct link between the absence of a specific substance and the specific condition that develops as a result of the deficiency, one can demonstrate that such a substance has a vitamin effect. Assuming that scurvy is caused by the lack of both vitamin C and OPCs, one should be able to cause scurvy symptoms by administering vitamin C while completely excluding OPCs. That would prove that OPCs are a vitamin.

In the days of Szent-Györgyi, a deficiency in what was then called vitamin P could not be produced under experimental conditions because there still was insufficient knowledge of OPCs. A vitamin P deficiency could not be produced with bioflavonoids (Citrin). According to Masquelier, the food administered to Szent-Györgyi's laboratory guinea pigs was most likely very deficient in flavonoids but not necessarily deficient in OPCs. Although Szent-Györgyi made sure that the test food did not contain bioflavonoids, the OPCs stayed in undetected and escaped deletion. This is how the guinea pigs received OPCs, perhaps in trace quantities, and this is how the OPCs disturbed the tests. Logically enough, the permeability of the test animals' capillaries was thus not affected by the lack of citrus-bioflavonoids, to which Szent-Györgyi had mistakenly attributed the name vitamin P. Invisibly, OPCs did what the bioflavonoids were supposed to do, and that's why no vitamin P could be observed.

In Masquelier's opinion, if that experiment were conducted today and a vitamin P deficiency could be produced, it would be successful provided that the term vitamin P refer to OPCs instead of bioflavonoids. The discoverer of OPCs would give two groups of guinea pigs identical food containing a suboptimal supply of vitamin C but completely devoid of OPCs. A suboptimal supply of vitamin C would be the daily amount that could not prevent symptoms of scurvy. One of the two groups would then be given a daily supply of OPCs, while the other group followed a diet that contains no OPCs at all. Sooner or later, the animals of the second group would suffer from scurvy because their vitamin C resources would be gradually depleted. Masquelier is absolutely convinced that the OPCs group would healthily survive. This would then prove that OPCs play an essential role in the prevention of scurvy and that scurvy can be prevented by a combination of an insufficient dosage of Vitamin C and OPCs and not just by Vitamin C alone.

I could envision a somewhat different approach that would prove the same thing. It is based on the fact that the body is able to store a limited amount of vitamin C to overcome temporary shortages. Normally, this Vitamin C supply is replenished every day, but in case of a severe deficiency and in the absence of OPCs, the stored Vitamin C is depleted within several weeks. Under this somewhat different research scenario, two groups of guinea pigs would be on a diet that would contain sufficient Vitamin C but would be completely devoid of OPCs. Under these conditions, the guinea pigs would build up a certain stock of Vitamin C. If researchers then completely eliminate the Vitamin C from the food of both groups and at the same time begin to feed one group a sufficient daily dosage of OPCs, scurvy would manifest itself in the group that would have no Vitamin C and no OPCs within several weeks. I doubt if the guinea pigs that would get OPCs would show severe symptoms of scurvy, but if at all, the onset of these symptoms would be very much delayed. The OPCs would recharge the vitamin C supplies built up in the body during regular vitamin C intake. Thus proof could be furnished that OPCs is an essential nutrient.

In fact, Masquelier did perform a somewhat similar vitamin test that clearly illustrates the role of OPCs in recharging vitamin C molecules. The ultimate proof that OPCs were the long-sought cofactor of vitamin C was furnished by a test performed in 1976 by Masquelier and his two colleagues, Laparra and Michaud. The experiment, which could never have been performed by someone without a profound knowledge of OPCs, was simple but ingenuous, and it produced a milestone scientific result. I stress the element of simplicity once more because people often think that simple experiments cannot lead to milestone discoveries and completely new insights. This is not true. Masquelier's scientific work is proof that simplicity can lead to great results.

Guinea pigs belong to one of the four animal species that, similar to humans, are not able to synthesize vitamin C. Therefore, next to people, guinea pigs are the perfect species to test the effects of vitamin C. Masquelier divided a number of guinea pigs into five lots and furnished them with no or varying quantities of vitamin C. The higher the daily dosage of vitamin C, the more vigorous the animals were and the longer they lived. Animals with an optimal vitamin C supply — that is, those that were given 20 mg of vitamin C per kilogram of body weight — presented the reference group (Lot 1). Lot 2 did not get any vitamin C. These animals succumbed after five weeks. Lot 3 was given vitamin C (5 mg per kilogram of body weight), but this quantity was insufficient for them to survive. These animals lived twice as long as Lot 2. Lot 4 was administered a somewhat higher but still insufficient quantity of vitamin C: 10 mg per kilogram of body weight. This group lived for 14 weeks, but then the animals succumbed.

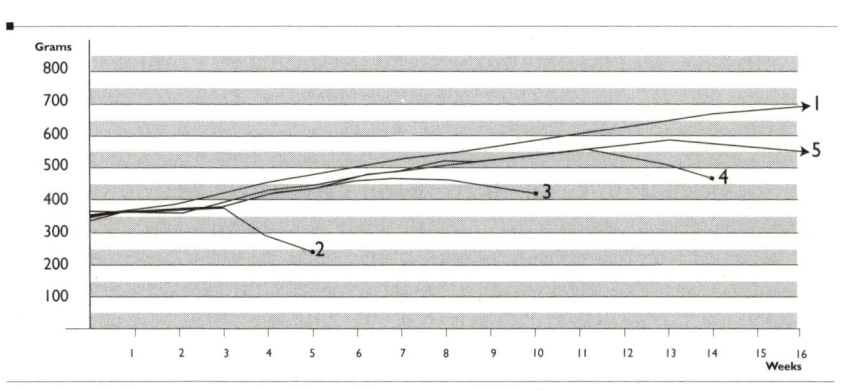

Lot 1 = Reference animals - 20 mg / kg vitamin C / daily
Lot 2 = Animals totally deprived of vitamin C - 0mg / daily
Lot 3 = Animals deficiently fed - 5 mg / kg vitamin C / daily
Lot 4 = Animals deficiently fed - 10 mg / kg vitamin C / daily
Lot 5 = Animals deficiently fed - 5 mg / kg vitamin C / daily & 20 mg / kg OPCs/daily

The fifth lot was given only 5 mg of vitamin C, same as Lot 3, but the guinea pigs received an additional 20 mg of OPCs per kilogram of body weight. Although these animals were fed the quantity of vitamin C that turned out to be insufficient for the animals of Lot 3, they lived as long as the animals of the reference group (Lot 1) that had received a normal dosage of vitamin C. Thus the evidence was furnished that the presence of OPCs drastically boosts the efficacy of vitamin C. Food containing OPCs ensures that greater quantities of vitamin C are available to the body. As a vitamin C enhancer, OPCs can safeguard survival even if the body is supplied with insufficient quantities of vitamin C. Further studies showed that the administration of OPCs reduces vitamin C requirements to as little as one-tenth. In Masquelier's view, it would even be beneficial to accompany every intake of Vitamin C, whether in the form of normal food or in the form of a supplement, with a daily dosage of OPCs. Doing so would increase vitamin C's effect tenfold. In *chapter 39: OPCs, Vitamin C, and the Facts of e-life,* the intimate relationship between vitamin C and OPCs is explored in greater depth.

The well-known vitamin C researcher Linus Pauling, who was awarded the Nobel Prize twice, calculated the quantity of vitamin C necessary for a human being. In doing so, he proceeded from the production of ascorbic acid in animals and deduced that

Linus Pauling

people, depending on height and weight, should consume a maximum dosage of 18 grams of vitamin C per day. This exceeds the official guidelines by far, but who cares? Pauling, who took the megadosages of vitamin C every day, lived to be 93 years old in good health, so he was certainly not wrong with his high regard for vitamin C, which performs numerous important protective functions for the body. With all due respect to the Nobel Prize winner, he might have taken a little bit less, had he known Masquelier's research and OPCs. Pauling could have achieved a possibly better effect with a significantly lower dosage if he had simultaneously taken OPCs.

I do not have to stress the manifold virtues of vitamin C. Ample evidence has been furnished for its numerous protective effects. I sum up a few benefits of vitamin C's relationship with OPCs:

- Vitamin C is required for the making of collagen, which exists everywhere in the body as a kind of glue: in the bones, skin, tendons, sinews, cartilage, and connective tissue. It keeps these structures elastic and healthy and thus favors mobility and motion.
- Vitamin C promotes wound healing.
- Vitamin C keeps blood vessels intact.
- Vitamin C is an indispensable ingredient in the production and/or activation of defense cells, blood corpuscles, folic acid, and hormones.
- Vitamin C plays a major part in transporting iron in the bloodstream and in providing cells with oxygen.
- Vitamin C has anticarcinogenic effect because it absorbs nitrates and nitrites.
- Vitamin C is one of the important antioxidants that prevent free radicals from destroying body cells. It also protects other vitamins against oxidation.

Consumers are faced with the question of how to consume vitamin C appropriately. Like millionaires who can live well off the interest generated by their assets, consumers who take their daily dosage of vitamin C may think that large amounts of vitamin C may be the most effective. But as millionaires know, quantity isn't everything. As history shows, certain conditions do not respond to vitamin C alone, not even when it is taken in large quantities. In addition, not all consumers like to swallow several grams of vitamin C every day, and such a high dosage cannot be provided by the healthiest diet full of fruits and vegetables. Moreover, the workings of vitamin C and OPCs are synergistic *and* complementary. One cannot fulfill all the tasks of the other. Do what Mother Nature does and make sure that you get optimal daily amounts of vitamin C and OPCs.

18 OPCs AND BIOFLAVONOIDS: THE ESSENTIAL DIFFERENCES

During the many years of Masquelier's research, one of his most important and recurring issues was demonstrating the differences between OPCs and bioflavonoids, especially between OPCs and the better known bioflavonoids rutin and hesperidin. This meant that Masquelier and his colleagues were up against vested scientific opinions and also against vested economical interests. Without yet realizing the full extent of his words, Masquelier mentioned one of the differences between OPCs and bioflavonoids in 1948 in his doctoral thesis as he explained how tannins (the bigger proanthocyanidins) could be characterized by their propensity to fix to proteins. OPCs, being the smaller proanthocyanidins, show that same affinity for proteins, though in a more delicate way because the strength of the affinity increases with the size of the proanthocyanidin. Bioflavonoids completely lack this affinity for proteins. They lack the astringency that is so typical for OPCs and tannins. This meant, for instance, that the way the leather industry used proteins such as hide powder and gelatin to detect tannins and determine their tanning quality of tannins had no relevance whatsoever in the field of bioflavonoids. Its affinity for proteins such as collagen is one of the major reasons OPCs perform so well in maintaining vascular health. In turn, because all tissues are vascularized, OPCs play a key though indirect role in the health of all our tissues and organs.

There is another equally fundamental biological difference between OPCs and bioflavonoids: their bioavailability. A substance is bioavailable when, after it is swallowed, it passes through the stomach intact, can be absorbed by the blood from the intestines, and is then transported throughout the body. One doesn't have to be a genius to understand that when it comes to judging the biological value of essential food components, establishing their degree of bioavailability is a prerequisite one may not skip. A food component may do well in a laboratory test, but it may not do equally well in the body for the simple reason that it either ends up in the toilet or is destroyed in the stomach or intestines. The same is true for food components that are administered intravenously, by way of injection, bypassing the gastrointestinal tract. When it comes to testing bioavailability, Masquelier's research into the efficacy of OPCs and bioflavonoids is a classic and exemplary case.

In 1950, Masquelier and Tayeau did a comparative study to determine the vasculoprotective properties of intravenously applied OPCs and bioflavonoids (rutin and aesculin) *independent of their bioavailability*. They succeeded in proving that OPCs displayed significantly greater vasoprotective properties than did rutin and aesculin when injected directly into the bloodstream of the test animals. Tayeau and Masquelier found that after 24 hours, the capillary resistance had increased by 100 percent in those guinea pigs that had received OPCs. In the animals treated with aesculin, they observed an average increase of 44 percent, and in the guinea pigs that had been administered rutin, the increase in capillary resistance was 20 percent on average. This showed the superiority of OPCs over bioflavonoids in intravenous testing. The test confirmed the results of the test described by Masquelier in his doctoral thesis. Though less significant than the effects caused by OPCs, those from intravenously applied aesculin and rutin positively influenced capillary resistance. Now, Masquelier had to ascertain whether aesculin and rutin could deploy their vasoprotective effects when taken orally. If they were not bioavailable, the moderate vasoprotective effect they had in their injectable form would be of no avail to the consumer. They had to find out whether bioflavonoids would make it to the bloodstream and through the bloodstream to the vascular wall and the surrounding tissues. A quarter of a century was to pass before Masquelier managed to supply the relevant scientific results.

Although experiments with orally taken OPCs invariably produced very positive and consistent results, it had never been proven that these effects were directly attributable to OPCs. To laypeople, this may seem somewhat redundant. You take something and you see an effect. That should be sufficient proof. But for scientists like Masquelier, such proof is insufficient. They had to follow the OPCs from beginning to end, from mouth to tissue, as unambiguous proof of OPCs' bioavailability in the body. While setting up this test for OPCs, Masquelier and his colleagues decided to also test the bioavailability of rutin. This is how, with the help of radioactivity, he and his colleagues Jean Laparra, Jean Michaud, Marie-France Lesca, and Paul Blanquet showed the fundamental difference in bioavailability between OPCs and bioflavonoids.

This radioactive labeling technique enables researchers to trace the path of a radioactively marked substance in humans or test animals. In this way, the bioavailability of a substance can be tracked throughout the body after one has radioactively marked it. In the case of plant materials, radioactive marking takes place in an enclosed environment that is filled with radioactively marked CO_2, a normal constituent of the air. Warm-blooded animals, like humans, exhale CO_2, and plants inhale it. In reverse, we inhale oxygen while plants exhale it. When you radioactively mark CO_2 and bring it into the closed environment of a so-called phytotron, a plant growing in that phytotron inhales it and the carbon remains in the plant as radioactive carbon that can always be traced. Because OPCs are made with carbon, oxygen, and hydrogen, all OPCs made by a plant in a phytotron eventually become radioactive and photographically traceable.

Of course, it was not possible to radioactively mark in such a special device under laboratory conditions a large pine tree, the bark of which had always been the trustworthy provider of OPCs. There is no phytotron big enough to contain a pine tree. The Masquelier team needed a smaller plant and decided in favor of mini-vines of the Merlot and Cabernet varieties. In the laboratory, they grew these mini-vines that were about 12 to 16 inches (30 to 40 centimeters) in height until each bore green grapes. Then, for a period of 45 days, the full-grown vines were placed in the microphytotron and exposed to an atmosphere enriched with radioactively marked CO_2 ($14CO_2$). This is how, through the process of photosynthesis, all carbon-containing elements in the plant (including OPCs) exchanged their normal carbon against the radioactive carbon. Within 45 days, the grapes ripened. Finally, the seeds were removed from the grapes and eventually Masquelier's method was used to isolate the OPCs, which were now radioactive as well. Then the OPCs were given *orally* to mice.

With the help of a sensitive film, the radioactive OPCs, which had spread throughout a mouse's body beyond the stomach and the intestines, could be traced very well. A non-bioavailable substance would show up only in the intestinal tract because it could not have passed the intestinal wall and would not have been absorbed by the bloodstream. In the case of OPCs, however, it was immediately evident that the substance had spread throughout the entire animal. There was evidence of radioactive OPCs in practically all parts of the mouse's body, especially in those parts that have a higher density of collagen. In the skin, cartilage, lungs, heart, and blood vessels, where there was collagen, there were OPCs. At the same time Masquelier found OPCs in all areas where substances similar to mucopolysaccharides are secreted; that is, in the stomach, duodenum, and remaining intestines. This bioavailability test showed that OPCs had a particular affinity to proline-rich tissues in the body, which includes the connective tissue. The photo hereunder shows the OPCs found in various parts of the animal.

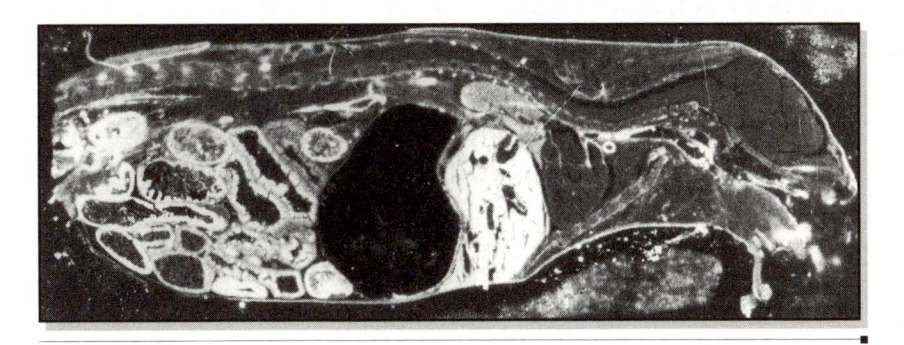

Knowing that something is bioavailable is meaningful, but knowing the speed of absorption and secretion is equally important. Having radioactive OPCs, these things could now be measured. The results were outstanding. Ten minutes after oral intake, OPCs can be traced in the blood, which means that OPCs pass immediately from the intestinal tract through the intestinal walls into the blood. After 45 minutes, the level of OPCs in the blood reaches its maximum level, and then it gradually drops. After seven hours, the level of OPCs is still above one-third of the maximum value. At five hours after oral intake, half of the ingested OPCs have been used or excreted while the remaining half is still there. In scientific terms, OPCs' half-life is five hours.

The researchers measured the excretion of OPCs by checking the radioactivity of the bile, which is the carrier of the substances that have been excreted by the liver. At 15-minute intervals, the radioactivity of the bile was measured for 12 hours. Also in this case, radioactivity could be determined after a few minutes. The bile-curve was comparable to that of radioactivity measured in the blood. After 11 hours, 14 percent of the administered OPCs had been excreted via the bile. Excretion of OPCs via the lungs and urine rarely occurs. Only after five hours is radioactive CO_2 encountered in the exhaled air.

When Masquelier and his coworkers tested OPCs for their bioavailability, they applied the same test to check the bioavailability of flavonoids, especially rutin. They orally administered radioactively marked rutin to mice and then made x-ray photographs. They observed rutin (see page 137) exclusively in the gastrointestinal tract. Outside the stomach and the intestines, there wasn't the slightest trace of rutin. Rutin passes from the mouth through the gastrointestinal tract and leaves the body without being absorbed. The test conclusively demonstrated that rutin is not bioavailable. One of the reasons for bioflavonoids' lack of bioavailability may well be that, while OPCs are easily soluble in water, flavonoids do not dissolve in water. This is another difference between OPCs and bioflavonoids, one that is used in analyzing the quality of OPCs.

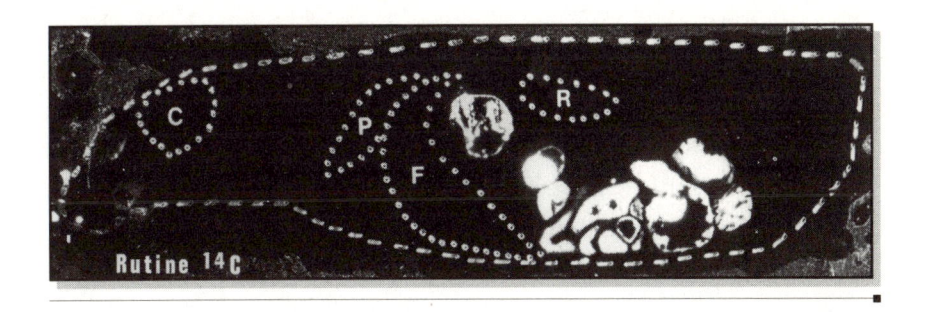

Masquelier's findings conclusively confirmed what was discussed in various other scientific publications of that period. In 1976, Joachim Kühnau stated in the *World Review of Nutrition and Dietetics* that a great deal of food flavonoids — among them the most widespread ones, such as luteolin, quercetin, and rutin — were largely subject to destruction by intestinal microorganisms and would therefore be absorbed only to a limited percentage as intact flavonoids. In 1993, the German Professor Dr. Bergner confirmed Kühnau's findings when he expressed in his Wine Compendium the following opinion in connection with the nutritional value of quercetin, a bioflavonoid found in wine: "Bioavailability appears to be low, since quercetin is destroyed in the intestines."

More recently, in September 2003, Dr. Mike Clifford of the University of Surrey in Guildford (England), while addressing the 51st yearly congress of the German Association for Research in Herbal Medicines held in Kiel, questioned the relevancy of in vitro studies performed with polyphenols such as flavonoids and "tannins." Yes indeed, Clifford said, in vitro things may work out fine, but one should draw no optimistic conclusions without checking the bioavailability of the tested polyphenols. A diet rich in fruit and vegetables, he continued, procures few bioavailable polyphenols that are able to cross the gastrointestinal barrier and reach the bloodstream. Of the approximately 500 mg of flavonoids that health-conscious consumers ingest with their daily diet, only 5 to 10 percent are absorbed by the small intestines. According to Clifford, 33 controlled in vivo studies showed that the antioxidant status of the blood hardly changes as a result of a diet "rich in polyphenols." The polyphenols that were found in small amounts in the blood of people who eat plenty of fruits and vegetables were isoflavones, anthocyanins, and flavanols.

Clifford's studies show that fruits and vegetables may contain lots of polyphenols, but most of them, including the flavonoids, are not bioavailable in significant quantities. The ones that are bioavailable, including the flavanols (catechins and OPCs), are not abundantly available in the diet — even in a healthy diet. Clifford's findings confirm what Masquelier has been saying since the 1960s when he first wrote: "OPCs are found in nature, in the natural state, in fruits and vegetables in particular. A normal diet should therefore provide an adequate amount of P factors to avoid any deficiency. However, these constituents [Masquelier meant OPCs] are usually located in the bark, teguments, cuticles, and woody parts of plants, so that they are eliminated when we eat fruits and vegetables. It is therefore hardly surprising that there are individuals who suffer from problems indicative of factor P deficiency in spite of having a healthy, balanced diet. In addition, numerous bioflavonoids are very poorly soluble or even insoluble in water; we assume they will have little activity when absorbed with our food."

The major differences between OPCs and bioflavonoids are as follows:

o OPCs are colorless; bioflavonoids are yellow.

- OPCs fix to proteins; bioflavonoids don't.
- OPCs are soluble in water; bioflavonoids are not.
- OPCs' bioavailability is excellent; bioflavonoids' bioavailability is poor.

19 NEW CLINICAL HIGHLIGHTS

Since Masquelier's earliest research, many human clinical studies have been published that provide evidence of the efficacy of OPCs in various fields, especially in vascular health. In all clinical trials done with patients suffering from vascular disorders, complaints significantly and rapidly subsided following the daily ingestion of an average of 150 mg of OPCs; to be precise, following the daily ingestion of 150 mg of OPCs that are in conformity with Masquelier's research and specifications. Especially in the case of elderly persons, increased capillary resistance and permeability could be confirmed, which manifested itself, among other things, in the reduction of liver spots (senile lentigo) and a reduction of burst blood vessels and small, usually spot-like subcutaneous bleeding. In patients suffering from liver cirrhosis, complications due to hemorrhage dropped following the daily ingestion of 300 mg of OPCs. Postoperative edema was reported to disappear more quickly after facelifts and surgery in the event of breast cancer. The following sections provide more detail.

Recommended Daily Dosage

Before highlighting some of the outstanding results of these clinical trials, let me say something about the recommended daily dosages. This information is especially relevant for those who want to use ANTHOGENOL (MASQUELIER's Original OPCs) under conditions similar to those for the trials described hereunder. It is important that you understand that OPCs work only in the researched quality and in the recommended daily dosages. As a rule, in case of illness, the recommended daily dosage ranges from 150 to 300 mg, depending on the severity of the condition and the "gear" into which you want to put the healing process. A severe condition that must rapidly heal requires 300 mg a day during the healing period. Preventive and maintenance dosages lie between 50 and 100 mg per day. Because of OPCs' efficacy, it will hardly ever be necessary to exceed the 300 mg-per-day level, although in crises such as an allergic attack, one may sometimes well overstep that level until the crisis has subsided.

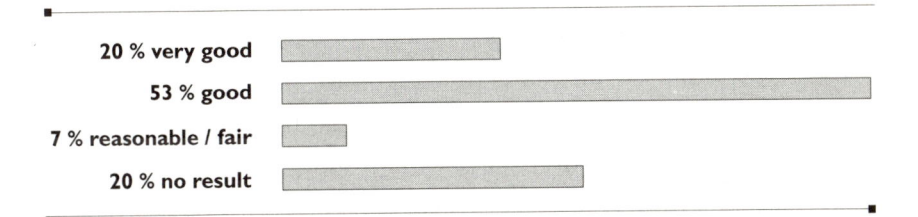

20 % very good	▬▬▬▬▬▬
53 % good	▬▬▬▬▬▬▬▬▬▬▬▬▬▬▬▬
7 % reasonable / fair	▬
20 % no result	▬▬▬▬▬▬

Capillary Resistance

In 1980, OPCs were tested double-blindly on a group of elderly people who, either spontaneously or as the result of taking one gram of acetylsalicylic acid per day, had a very low capillary resistance. For the whole group treated with 100 to 150 mg of OPCs per day, the results shown hereunder were obtained.

A "good" result means that patients had a noticeable improvement in capillary resistance after approximately two weeks. After about three weeks, the maximum attainable result was reached for all patients.

(Evolution de la résistance capillaire, spontanément ou artificiellement diminuée par l'action d'une substance capillaro-toxique chez des personnes âgées. G. Dubos, G. Durst et R. Hugonot. La Revue de la Gériatrie, Tome 5, no 6, septembre 1980.)

A similar study with elderly people also took place in 1980. Contrary to the group mentioned in the previous study, this group didn't suffer from pathological changes in the microcirculation. Maybe that's why the results were less pronounced than in the previously mentioned research. In 10 of the 21 cases, OPCs appeared to work efficiently. Nevertheless, the researchers concluded that they achieved improved capillary resistance and permeability in this group of elderly people by administering them 100 mg of OPCs per day.
(Résistance capillaire en gériatrie. Etude d'un microangioprotecteur = Endotélon. J.Y. Dartenuc, P. Marache et H. Choussat. Bordeaux Médical, 1980; 13: 903-7.)

In 1981, capillary resistance was tested in two groups of people averaging 46 years of age and suffering from high blood pressure and other problems. They took a recommended daily dosage of 150 mg of OPCs. In one of the groups, capillary resistance increased from 15.4 cm Hg to 18.1 cm Hg, and in the other (double-blind test) group, it increased from 14.8 cm Hg to 18 cm Hg.: See figure page 143. Blood pressure is determined by a number of factors, such as the strength of the contraction of the heart, the resistance produced by the smaller arteries, the blood volume and the volume of the extracellular fluids, the blood's viscosity, and the elasticity of the walls of the main arteries. The study underlines the protective role OPCs can play in cases of high blood pressure. OPCs play a central role in this interplay of factors that determine blood pressure.
(Etude des effets des oligomères du procyanidol sur la résistance capillaire dans l'hypertension artérielle et certaines néphropathies. G. Lagrue, F. Olivier-Martin, A. Grillot. Sem Hop Paris, 18-25 septembre, 1981.)

15,4 cm Hg	18,1 cm Hg	14,8 cm Hg	18 cm Hg
0 mg OPC	150 mg OPC	0 mg OPC	150 mg OPC
Group 1		Group 2, double-blind test	

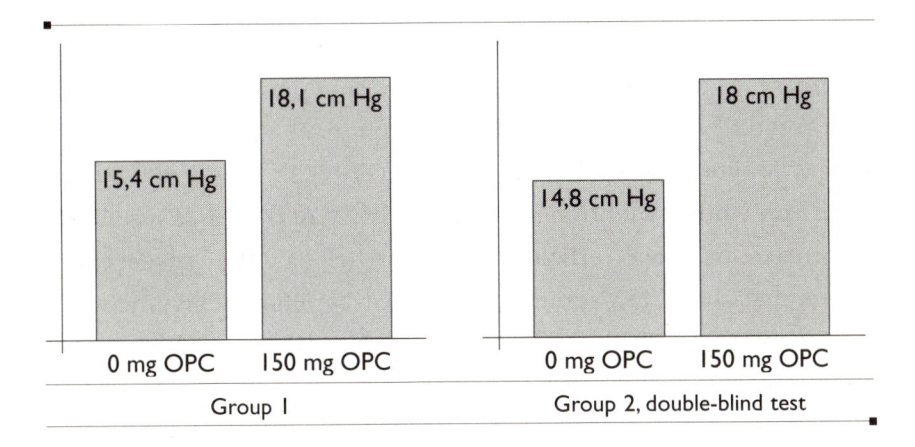

Cirrhosis of the Liver

Bleeding is one of the most serious and most frequent complications encountered in patients who suffer from cirrhosis of the liver. Therefore, the maintenance of good capillary resistance is of life-saving importance. The efficacy of OPCs in improving capillary resistance in patients suffering from cirrhosis of the liver was tested (double-blindly) in 1983. The researchers reported that with a dosage of 300 mg of OPC per day, they induced a significant improvement of capillary fragility.

(Effect de l'Endotélon sur l'indice de fragilité capillaire dans une population spécifique: les sujets cirrhotiques. F.X. Lesbre et J.D. Tigaud. Gaz. Med. de France - 90, no 24 du 24-VI-1983.)

Venous Problems in the Legs/Varicose Veins

Capillary problems manifest themselves mainly as a series of symptoms resulting from poor circulation in the legs. To reiterate briefly information that appears earlier in the book about Resivit, Flavan, and Endotélon, this complex of symptoms is classified under the term veinous insufficiency. Among these are obviously the varicose veins themselves, which may or may not be visibly deformed. In addition to these deformations of structure, most people complain about functional problems such as pain, swelling, itching, restlessness, and cramps that, in many cases, also can cause insomnia. All these functional problems are favorably influenced by OPCs. Although OPCs cannot make seriously deformed varicose veins disappear, they can decrease the extent to which they occur, often as the result of accompanying swelling. In the case of surgical removal of varicose veins, OPCs are a very useful means to support recovery.

In 1980, 78 patients with serious venous problems in the legs were tested with mg of OPC per day. The researchers described the results as favorable. They noted the results as shown in the figure hereunder.
(Essai thérapeutique d'un angioprotecteur périférique, l'Endotélon. C. Beylot et P. Bioulac. Gaz. Med. de France - 87, no 22 du 13-6-1980.)

22 very good
32 good
21 average
3 no result

The capilary fragility was in:

24 cases normalized
22 cases improved
13 cases improved considerably
13 cases unchanged
3 cases raised

In 1981, the effectiveness of OPCs with regard to functional venous problems in legs was tested on patients who didn't have deformed veins but who suffered nevertheless from the functional symptoms. The patients were tested with a placebo and subsequently with another medicine (Diosmine). In both cases, it appeared that a recommended daily dosage of 150 mg OPCs diminished the functional problems that can arise during impaired venous backflow: heavy legs, cramps, and swelling. The researchers point out the importance of recognizing these functional problems and treating them even before the varicose veins are visible.
(Abord Thérapeutique des troubles fonctionnels des membres inférieurs par un microangioprotecteur l'Endotélon. par L. Sarrat. Bordeaux Méd 1981; 11: 685-8.)

In 1981, OPCs were once again tested on 50 patients with functional disorders (chronic venous insufficiency). Also in this test, OPCs were compared with Diosmine. All functional symptoms appeared to have improved after 30 days following the intake of a recommended daily dosage of 150 mg OPCs. Both remedies appeared to be effective, but the researchers noted a significant advantage with OPCs in terms of speed and the duration of its effectiveness.
(Etude en double aveugle de l'Endotélon dans l'insuffisance veineuse chronique. P. Delacroix. La Revue de Médicine no 27-28 - 31 août - 7 sept. 1981.)

Venous insufficiency was again tested (in 1985) on 92 patients who took 300 mg of OPCs per day. This test also concerned functional disorders such as heavy legs, itching, nighttime cramps, and (subjective) edema. After four weeks, the

treatment turned out to be successful for 75 percent of the patients.
(Etude de l'Endotélon dans les manifestations fonctionelles de l'insuffisance veineuse périférique. Résultats d'une étude en double aveugle portant sur 92 patients. J.F. Thébaut, P. Thébaut et F. Vin. Gazette Médicale 1985, 92, no 12.)

Decreasing Vision

With advancing age, our bodily functions deteriorate. This process particularly affects vision, in part because of the ever-increasing influence of free radicals on the extremely delicate structures of the eye. But most certainly, today's eyes are also very much affected by uninterruptedly staring at computer and TV screens. People begin to notice their deteriorating eyesight not only when the images become less sharp, but also when they experience impairment of night vision. OPCs protect the eyes against excessive strain as well as against the consequences of too much or too little light. Too much light, such as with an unprotected glance at the sun, is as damaging to the eye as is the long-term exposure to insufficient light. This is the case for people who work or drive at night or in the dark.

A study conducted in France in 1988 showed that decreased vision in people driving at night or working at monitors was improved by up to 98 percent after OPCs had been taken for a period of four weeks. Otherwise healthy test subjects, not suffering from eye defects or eye disease, were tested for the effects of OPCs on their eyesight. These people were chosen from two groups: motorists/night drivers and screen watchers. They took 200 mg of OPCs per day. After four weeks, their resistance to blinding was measured, as was their eyesight in dim light.

Ninety-eight out of 100 people who participated in the test showed an improvement.

(Sens lumineux et circulation chiorétinienne. Etude de l'effet des O.P.C. (Endotélon). Ch. Corbé, J.P. Boissin, A. Siou. J. Fr. Ophtalmol. 1988, 11. 5. 453-460.)

The eye is particularly subject to vascular degeneration because the vascular system in the eye is not embedded in muscular fibers. When it comes to vascularization, the eye very much resembles the brain. Once the main artery has entered the eye, it gradually loses its elastic outer coating and muscular fibers. What remains of the vascular wall is its core structure, which consists of collagen fibers and the glucosaminoglycans. As in the brain, this makes the eye extremely sensitive to problems that affect the vascular structure. High blood pressure, free radicals, regular intake of aspirin (salicylates) and/or anti-inflammatory drugs (NSAIDs), overexposure to sunlight, and diabetes easily affect the eye's vascular system. The fact that the structure of the eye itself is extremely fragile makes it necessary that the nourishment of these fine structures takes place through an equally fine vascular structure. Add to this the precision that is required of the "instrument eye," and you'll understand what all those spectacles do on all those noses.

Retinopathy

Retinopathy is the decay of the retina, which is the inside "background screen" of the eye on which the lens projects it images. The term retinopathy covers many afflictions, which all relate to problems with this screen that actively translates the images it receives through the lens and transfers them to the optic nerve, which "wires" the pictures to the brain. The retina is an extremely precise and delicate tissue, rich in numerous very tiny capillaries, feeding the fine structures of the retina. Evidently, vascular problems compromise the retina's functioning and lead to vision impairment, which manifests itself strongly in diabetics. People suffering from diabetes are prone to increased vascular deterioration because the disturbed sugar metabolism has a negative effect on the vascular wall. This is why impaired vision in diabetics is called diabetic retinopathy. The processes leading to retinopathy occur throughout the body but become apparent especially in the extremities, such as the toes. In this respect, the vascular network of the retina is also considered to be an extremity, where the effects of diabetes are hard felt. In a worst-case scenario, diabetic retinopathy can lead to blindness.

Retinopathy and Diabetes

Retinopathy is especially a problem for people who suffer from diabetes. The long-term consequences of diabetes involve the decay of the entire vascular system. Degeneration of the coronary arteries can lead to heart attacks. Degeneration of the cerebral arteries can lead to stroke, and degeneration of the arteries in the legs can lead to gangrene. In some cases, toes and the lower parts of the legs need to be amputated. Further complicating cardiovascular health is the propensity of diabetics to develop atherosclerosis. On the level of capillary microcirculation, certain organs are especially afflicted. Kidneys may degenerate to the point of failure. Complications in the capillaries impair the function of the eyes, sometimes to the point of blindness. The 1997 *Miller-Keane Dictionary of Medicine, Nursing and Allied Health* estimates the number of diabetics in the United States at 16 million. In Europe, the disease is equally widespread. Because the decay of the vascular system is one of the major long-term effects of diabetes,

OPCs form the natural nutritional factor in the management of those vascular problems. OPCs do not play a role in the dietetic management aimed at keeping normal blood levels of sugar and fat. In that sense, OPCs do not replace insulin. In the case of diabetics, OPCs' role is confined to supporting the vascular system to resist the vascular effects of this condition. Because of their capacity to give dynamic support to the vascular system, OPCs were profoundly and successfully researched in cases of diabetic retinopathy.

The effects of a recommended daily dosage of OPCs were measured in 147 retinopathy patients (1978). The researchers concluded that OPC acts as a "trump card" in the treatment of all cases of exudations linked to ischemia that are of a diabetic, arteriosclerotic, inflammatory, degenerative, and myopic nature.
(Rétinopathies et O.P.C. par MM. Ph. Vérin, A. Vildy et J.F. Maurin. Bordeaux Médicale, 1978, 11, no 16, p. 1467.)

In 1981, the effects of OPCs were investigated again on 26 diabetic retinopathy patients. During 5 to 21 weeks (average 51 days), they took 100 mg of OPCs per day. The researchers concluded that, especially in cases of developing diabetic retinopathy, taking OPCs indisputably has a favorable effect, especially on unduly widened small blood vessels (microaneurysms) and deposits in the tissues of fluid containing proteins and cellular remains that has escaped from the blood (exudates).
(Les oligomères procyanidoliques dans le traitement de la fragilité capillaire et de la rétinopathie chez les diabètiques. A propos de 26 cas. par M. Froantin. Méd. Int. - Vol. 16 - no 11 - Novembre 1981 - pp. 432 à 434.)

Once again, in 1982, researchers observed 30 diabetic retinopathy patients who suffered from aneurysms, hemorrhages, exudation, and neovascularization after a period of insufficient oxygen supply caused by capillary failure. The recommended daily dosage was 3 x 50 mg of OPCs. The results were again significant: In 80 percent of the cases it was possible to stabilize lesions in the retina.
(Contribution à l'étude des oligomères procyanidoliques: Endotélon, dans la rétinopathie diabétique à propos de 30 observations. J.L. Arne. Gaz. Med. de France - 89, no 30 du 8-X-1982.)

Age-Related Macular Degeneration

Retinopathy manifests itself in hemorrhage and exudations in the tissue covering the background of the eye. The danger lies especially in the potential corrosion of the macula. The macula is an area in the middle of the retina that, owing to its special structure, is responsible for visual acuity. The macula is the control center that monitors the sharpness of the images received. In modern cameras, the middle of the screen often contains a small circle that permits the photographer to focus on a certain person, object or part of the scenery. The macula functions in an identical way.

Loss of macular function (macular degeneration) impairs the eye's capacity to focus, and what remains is an unsharp picture caught by the part of the retina that surrounds the macula. The textbooks speak of a loss of central vision. Most people who lose the center of what they see still retain the periphery, but the periphery doesn't function as sharply as the macula. Because we look at things by way of central vision, macular degeneration forms a great obstacle to creating a good entire picture of what we are supposed to see. Macular degeneration is a rapidly spreading condition that affects millions of people. The onset of the condition appears mostly in people 50 to 60 years of age. Some authors call macular degeneration the leading cause of irreversible blindness among people older than 65 years. This is why the problem is referred to as age-related macular degeneration (AMD). AMD is extremely hindering because it affects all our daily activities.

Normal vision Vision with AMD Late stage AMD

The retina is the three-layered light-sensitive screen that absorbs and transmits the incoming pictures to the optic nerve. The outer layer of the retina, which catches the incoming pictures, consists of rods and cones. The rods are active in dim light, and the cones are active in bright light. In the center of the macula, at the spot called the central fovea, the retina consists only of slim and elongated cones. These cones have a special structure that aids their detection of details in the visual image. Because the light falls directly on these cones and on nothing else, the center of the macula is the area where the retina has its clearest vision. AMD is a form of retinopathy in the sense that the macula and its central fovea form an integral part of the retina.

These "clearest vision" parts of the retina are as dependent on the retina's vascular system for nourishing and for carrying away waste products as are all the other parts.

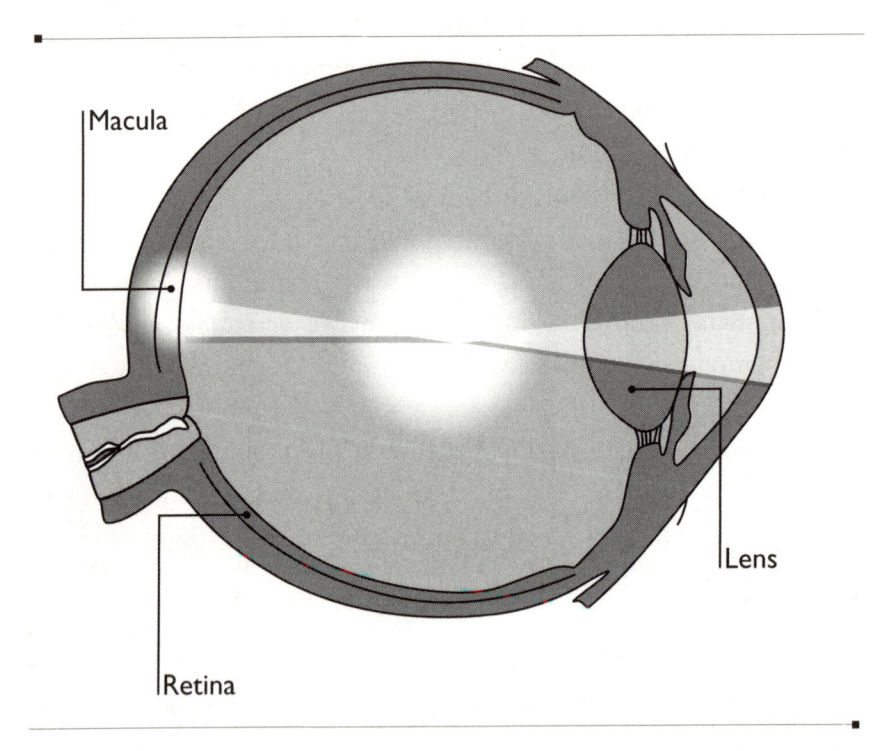

Macula

Lens

Retina

The diabetic retinopathy studies mentioned above all fully apply to AMD. This is confirmed by the fact that earlier, during the 1960s, the Flavan clinical trials, mentioned at the beginning of the book, had already brought us proof of the very beneficial effects of OPCs on impaired vision. Depending on their symptoms, patients were administered 160 and 240 mg of OPCs. This treatment produced favorable results in patients who suffered from rapid bleeding in the eyes, from Eales' disease, which is characterized by blocking of the retinal veins, from diabetic retinopathy, and from retinitis. I remind you of one of the

Flavan patients, a 76-year-old woman, who suffered from a macular lesion and inflammations of other parts of her right eye. Taking a modest daily dosage of 80 mg of Flavan (MASQUELIER's French Pine Bark Complex) during a period of three months, she satisfactorily improved her vision, and as a bonus, she got rid of her morning headaches.

Premenstrual Syndrome

When they are premenstrual, women can be confronted with a wide variety of psychological and physical symptoms classified as premenstrual syndrome (PMS). In general, scientists agree that these symptoms occur because of an increased sensitivity of the body to the normal physiological variations in the estrogen and progesterone levels. The most common premenstrual symptoms are painful, swollen breasts, a bloated stomach, a puffy face, undefined pelvic pain, weight gain, functional disturbances in the legs, irritation, depression, and headaches.

During 1987, the effect of a recommended daily dosage of 200 mg of OPCs was tested on 156 patients suffering from one or more PMS complaints during the second half of the menstrual cycle. In 60 percent of the women, the physical disorders disappeared after two cycles. In 80 percent of the women, the physical disorders disappeared after four cycles. Of the women suffering from psychological PMS symptoms, half reported that these problems had disappeared after the fourth cycle. In addition, OPCs appeared to be effective against menstrual problems (dysmenorrhea), which had disappeared in 66 percent of the women after the fourth cycle.

(Endotélon dans le traitement des troubles veino-lymphatiques du syndrome prémenstruel. Etude multicentrique sur 165 patientes.

M. Amsellem, J.M. Masson, B. Negui, F. Sailly, J. Sentenac, A. Siou, J.C. Tissot. Tempo Médical/no 282 - Novembre 1987.)

Sports Injuries

Most sport injuries result in edema. This usually involves ripped capillaries, which are the result of torn muscles, sprains, fractures, twisting, and whiplash injuries. Such an injury is painful and uncomfortable for anyone. However, the achievement-oriented athlete suffers most from this. For high-performance athletes and people who enthusiastically spend time and energy in sports activities, it is vital to quickly recover after an injury rather than stay away from training and competition for an extended period of time. Improvement of performance does not take place during the activity itself. Improvement is the result of the body's adaptation to the intensity of the training. This adaptation process occurs during the periods of rest and recovery between trainings, matches, and performances. Result-oriented sportspeople will therefore seek to alternate regular periods of activity with equally regular periods of rest and recovery. An interruption due to an injury rapidly spoils what was gained. The adaptation process is optimized when the body is supported with nutrients that prevent or help minimize the effects of injuries and stress, quench the free radicals created during intense activity, help the making and protecting of fresh collagen, and keep up circulation during rest and recovery periods. Therefore, professionals in the field of sports medicine show tremendous interest in researching the effects of preferably harmless, non-doping products that ensure rapid, thorough, and lasting improvement. In this respect, OPCs fulfill all requirements. OPCs repair not only damaged blood vessels but all structures containing collagen, including bones, skin, tendons, sinews, cartilage, and connective tissue.

In 1983, a French study performed in Nice reported the use of OPCs by injured soccer players. Most French are avid soccer fans, so the logic of testing Endotélon in this popular field led to this study. The effect of OPCs was measured for 10 days on 40 soccer players who had sustained an injury. Immediately after the injury, on the first day, they took 400 mg of OPCs. On days two through eight, they took 300 mg per day, and on the last two days, they took 200 mg per day. On the tenth day, edema appeared to a lesser extent in the OPCs group than in the control group that didn't receive OPCs. In some cases, the edema disappeared. The researchers also concluded that the overall physical condition of the OPCs group was better than that of the non-OPCs group.

(Les oedèmes post-traumatiques chez le sportif: essai contrôlé de l'Endotélon. J.J. Parienti et J. Parienti-Amsellem. Gaz. Med. de France - 90, No 3 du 21-1-1983.)

Edema After Facelift

Edema bothers not only bruised soccer players but also people who have undergone a facelift. "If you want to be beautiful, you must suffer," certainly applies during the aftermath of a facelift, which produces edema in practically all cases. The sooner one eliminates the edema, the better. To see if OPCs could be of help, 16 of 32 patients who were to have facelifts began taking a recommended daily dosage of 300 mg OPCs five days before the operation. After the operation, they continued taking the same dosage for another six days. The other 16 patients did not take OPCs. The facelifts were performed by the same surgeon, using the same surgical technique and the same kind of anesthesia. For each patient, researchers counted the number of days from the operation to the complete disappearance of the edema. The average number of days in the OPCs group was 11.4. It took the other 16 patients 15.8 days to fully recover from the edema. A difference of 4.4 days in this situation means a great deal to surgeon and patients.

(Effet de l'Endotélon dans les oedèmes post-chirurgicaux. Résultats d'une étude en double aveugle contre placebo sur trente-deux patientes. J. Baruch. Ann Chir Plast Esthét. 1984 - vol XXIX - no 4.)

Lymphedema After Removal of Breast Tissue

Mastectomy is the surgical removal of breast tissue, usually performed to remove breast tumors. Although breast-sparing operations are sometimes possible, the breast is completely removed in many cases. Apart from the psychological impact of this operation, lymphedema is a physical side effect that occurs especially when lymph nodes have been removed as well. The edema may be of a local nature, but it may also affect the entire arm. It is accompanied by pain, tension in the skin, and difficulties in shoulder and arm movements. Because stagnant lymph flow also inhibits the immune function of lymph, there is an increased risk of infection. The problem requires lymph drainage, special stockings, and exercise.

In 1989, French researchers reported that they had tested the effects of OPCs in cases of breast surgery. In a group of 63 women, 33 received OPCs and a control group of 30 received an inert placebo. During the first six weeks of the trial, the placebo was just as effective as OPCs, but after a longer period of time (six months in total), the placebo effect disappeared while it became evident that the positive effects of OPCs endured. The following figure compares the results obtained with OPCs and with a placebo after six months.

Symptom	OPCs improvement, in %	Placebo improvement in %
Skin tension	37.5	10.3
Suppleness	59.0	16.0
Pain	44.0	24.0
Burning, prickling	22.0	3.4

The speed of the lymph was improved with 0.5 cm per minute in the OPCs group. There was no change in speed in the placebo group.

(Oligomères procyanidoliques (ENDOTÉLON) dans le traitement des lymphoedèmes post-thérapeutiques des membres supérieurs. A. Pecking, J.P. Desprez-Curely, G. Megret. Symposium Satellite, Congrès International d'ANGIOLOGIE, Toulouse (France), 4-7 octobre 1989.)

20 STROKE, TRANSIENT ISCHEMIC ATTACK, AND ALZHEIMER's

The effect of OPCs in connection with age-related degeneration of brain cells can be attributed to two main factors:
- By strengthening the blood vessels and enhancing the capillary condition, OPCs help maintain and improve blood circulation in the brain.
- OPCs check free radicals that have a detrimental influence on the condition of collagen.

Moreover, as we will see later in this book, free radicals help create the bad type of cholesterol, which in turn has a negative influence on vascular and cardiovascular health. Free radicals not only attack the vascular wall, they also directly attack the gray matter. With age, they may cause a diminution of brain signals because free radicals "thin out" the brain's circuits. People suffering from diabetes, disturbed fat metabolism, or high blood pressure and people who smoke, drink too much, or take illegal drugs are at risk. Antioxidants have been found to positively influence brain health, which means that people whose diets are relatively deficient in antioxidants should consider themselves to be at risk.

The hair vessels in the brain are much less permeable than those in other areas of the body. Also, the arterioles (the endings of the arteries) are much stronger in the brain than elsewhere to prevent fluid from leaking into the brain, thus causing brain edema. Because the brain is surrounded by the skull and cannot expand outward, an edema will cause great harm and may even lead to coma and death. During strenuous exercise or in other situations that cause excessive circulatory activity leading to high blood pressure, the nervous system narrows the large and intermediate-sized arteries and prevents the raised blood pressure from reaching the capillaries in the brain. A failure in this system leads to stroke (cerebral infarct). In general, strokes occur when blood vessels break or become blocked by a blood clot (thrombosis), causing a lack of oxygen — and without oxygen, the brain cells die.

The problem is that many more cells are destroyed after a stroke, when the blood flow to the place of the stroke has been restored. This is because the blood's reentering of the stroke zone gives rise to free radicals, which kill the cells that were damaged but didn't die during the attack. This is the reason antioxidant prevention or immediate antioxidant intervention will salvage many of the cells that survived the stroke. A less violent form of a stroke is called transient ischemic attack (TIA). It is caused by the same factors, but with a TIA, the problems are handled in time so that there is no significant death of brain tissue. In case of a stroke, the lack of oxygen (ischemia) at the site of the stroke leads to permanent damage, especially because in the aftermath of the stroke, the free radicals increase the damage. A stroke causes permanent damage and can cause paralysis, dementia, blindness, or other serious brain disorders.

OPCs help the body to regulate disturbances in blood flow, which is especially relevant in cases of increased blood pressure. In 1983, the French researchers J. Cahn and M.G. Bourzeix tested this effect on artificially increased blood pressure and found that OPCs may increase the resistance of the capillaries, thus protecting the brain from the sudden rise of blood pressure.

During that same year, Cahn and Bourzeix also studied the effects of OPCs on artificially induced strokes (cerebral infarcts). For those who took preventive dosages of OPCs, compared with the control group that did not take OPCs, the seriousness of the induced stroke was significantly reduced. This second test showed that OPCs not only improve capillary resistance, but also help to reduce and restrain the effects of the stroke.

We need be concerned not only with too much blood flowing to and through the brain, but also with the type of degeneration that results from poor blood flow to and in the brain. Insufficient provision of oxygen and nutrients to the brain and the carrying off of waste materials leads to the degeneration of brain cells, which, in turn, can cause forgetfulness, lack of concentration, or learning disorders. Later in the book, we discuss how the membranes of cells can turn "rancid." This topic is of particular importance because the brain controls and monitors all functions of the body. It may not be expected that a rancid, corroded brain will be able to serve us well. The Alzheimer's brain is characterized by soft lumps of sticky proteins. How these lumps originate is still unknown. What is known is that Alzheimer's patients have higher than normal deposits of aluminum in the brain. Alzheimer's occurs in 50 to 70 percent of all people suffering from senile dementia. Improving healthy blood circulation comes to mind as a key protective factor. The role of OPCs in improving and maintaining peripheral circulation is well established. OPCs are the "vitamins" of the vascular system. They play a key role in nourishing the brain and carrying away waste materials.

Do OPCs have a direct positive effect in senile dementia? In Masquelier's American antioxidant patent, he claims a positive effect of OPCs in cases of cerebral involution troubles in aged people (U.S. Patent No. 4,698,360). With "involution," Masquelier meant the progressive degeneration occurring naturally with advancing age. Already in 1985, when he wrote the text of his '360 patent, he had the vision that in aged people, a lack of oxygen in the brain tissues could cause psychic and somatic problems, which are manifested in particular in cases of Alzheimer's disease. The lack of oxygen produces free radicals. So does the re-entry of blood after a cerebral incident. This blood re-entry problem, which is technically called reperfusion, also exists after heart surgery when the surgeon reopens the blood flow to the heart. Free radical reperfusion damage is a well-known complication in heart surgery. Free radicals, when they exceed the limits of the normal purifying scavenging enzymes, damage the cellular membrane walls. In the brain, free radicals damage the membranes of the nervous tissue, which leads to degeneration of the brain. Because of their superior scavenging power, OPCs help to prevent the effects of failure or inadequacy of the body's own scavenging enzymes when they are overwhelmed by free radicals.

Obviously, the Alzheimer's disease, its prevention, and the possible cures have been researched in ever-greater depths since Masquelier included this disease in his American antioxidant patent. In 1985, Alzheimer's lacked the notoriety it has gained in recent years. Alzheimer's is now known as a disorder caused by various factors. Oxidative stress has been identified to play a major role. Masquelier's French colleague, Professor Jean-Marc Orgogozo, even assumes a viral origin. In this context, he is conducting worldwide epidemiological examinations related to wine consumption and nutrition. So far, his results indicate that Alzheimer's disease is rarest in populations where people are used to consuming red wine as part of their daily food. Let's wait and see. At this point, there is sufficient reason to justify the preliminary conclusion that the antioxidative effect of OPCs so abundantly present in red wine might be one of the keys to solving the problem of Alzheimer's.

21 BEAUTY AND THE SIGNS OF AGING

Beauty has always been threatened by an invincible archenemy: aging. This genetically determined, unavoidable process affects all living matter. In fact, it also affects all inorganic matter, as you can witness when you see, for instance, the paint on your house crack or your garden hose become brittle and porous. With regard to the aging process in living matter, *chapter 30: Tumor Prevention and Cancer* describes in greater detail how the aging of the human body is somehow encoded in the "software" that controls the reproduction of cells and how it is accelerated by free radicals. Aging of the body is very different from aging of your car or the paint on your house, although most of the external factors that cause aging are similar. Any effort to resist the body's aging is rather ambitious. The anti-aging help offered to withering skins by the cosmetic industry thus falls on fertile ground.

The insight that free radicals play a major role in the process of physical aging has certainly had a revolutionary effect. Esthetic care seemed finally to have found a scientific answer, which in turn gave rise to the term anti-aging and to a multitude of anti-aging products. The industry and consumers began to realize that certain substances could protect the skin as well as all other living tissue against the attack of free radicals. To the extent that the cosmetic industry and the media turned their attention to free radicals and condemned them as coming from the sun and a polluted environment, they lost sight of the fact that the body itself produces oxygen radicals.

Oxygen radicals are a byproduct of normal energy production, and they also help us destroy intruding bacteria. The ambiguous role of oxygen has often prompted the use of the name of the Roman god Janus, who was known for having two faces looking in opposite directions. Almost 5 percent of intercellular oxygen is used for a meaningful purpose. The rest is neutralized by antioxidant enzymes, by food-borne antioxidants, and by antioxidants we take in the form of a dietary supplement. Overlooking this fact makes the use of a skin cream that contains antioxidants a somewhat wasted effort. The purely cosmetic fight against free radicals has led some of the companies to overshoot the mark by claiming that their topical (externally applied) products have great anti-aging potential. Provided that these cosmetic products contain significant amounts of significant antioxidants, they do protect the skin from free radical damage, but a far more sensible approach to the total problem of aging is to accompany the use of anti-aging creams and lotions with the oral intake of antioxidants such as OPCs.

Technically speaking, what we call "sunshine" is in fact the incoming flow of photons. Photons are tiny particles of electromagnetic radiation energy produced by the sun. Because of their high energy content, photons can easily destabilize the things they hit and thus cause free radicals, making the sun the major source of external free radicals. Other than the skin and the eyes' lens and retina, no organ of the body comes in direct contact with the light of the sun. Thus, no other organ of the body is more exposed to free radicals. Excessive exposure to the sun results in inflammation, collagen destruction, and acceleration of the skin's aging process. The extremely wrinkled skin of elderly people who have been constantly exposed sunshine — whether as sailors, sunbathers, or just residents of the sunnier parts of the world — bear witness to this process. Undeniably, antioxidant protection of the skin by way of creams and lotions will help inhibit its premature aging due to overexposure to sunlight.

In France, while probing the free radical scavenging effect of these OPCs, researchers of the Sanofi Research Center at Montpellier also tested the capacity of OPCs to protect the skin against the reddening effects of ultraviolet (UV) radiation. I must stress that OPCs do not act as a sun-block or provide a sun protection factor (SPF). OPCs act against free radicals, which are the result of UV radiation in the skin. With the naked eye, this effect can be seen as redness, also called erythema. The UV-relevant sections of the tests performed by researchers Barbier, Maffrand, Savi, Unkovic, and Vilain demonstrate that OPCs are potent protectors against the radical effects of UV radiation. OPCs provided an overall 34 percent reduction of the UV-caused redness, which is amazing considering that the cream used in the test contained a minute 0.03 percent of OPCs.

The method used by Barbier and his colleagues was actually quite simple. Two dorsal zones on the back of male albino guinea pigs were shaven, one on the left and one on the right. The zones were then both exposed to a lamp of which the radiance was filtered so as to deliver sunlight. The right and left zones both received a UV dose equal to four times the quantity of sunlight that causes reddening. Immediately after exposure and two hours later, the zone on the left side of the animals was massaged for 30 seconds with 300 mg of a cream containing OPCs in a concentration of 0.03 percent. Five hours after irradiation, the level of reddening was measured. The French researchers interpreted the 34 percent reduction of the reddening as a "moderate and significant reduction of the erythematic reaction in the various animals." Even to Masquelier, the fact that a cream that contained so little OPCs was so effective caused amazement. In a dermatological self-test, he had done on his arm with a free radical called dithranol (see *chapter 25: Regulating Inflammatory Affairs*), Masquelier had used a cream that contained 0.5 percent of OPCs. This is the dosage Masquelier had patented in his U.S. Patent 4,698,360. In that antioxidant patent, Masquelier describes a topical ointment containing 0.5 percent of OPCs. Such an ointment is protected under the '360 patent for its antioxidant (free radical scavenging) effect on the skin. According to Masquelier, a cream containing 0.5 percent of OPCs gives maximum protection against free radical damage.

Protecting the skin against radiation is obviously relevant for those on a holiday beach or at a ski resort. In addition, the radiation therapy that many cancer patients undergo blemishes the skin just as intense sunlight does. Skin injury as a result of radiation therapy can range from a mild sunburnlike reddening of the skin to blisters and ulcers. Like sunlight, radiation blows the skin's cells apart, and the skin reacts with an inflammation. In radiation therapy, it seems wise to use a cream that contains the patented dosage of 0.5 percent OPCs. In my opinion, the aggressive effect of x-rays and other radiation should also be mitigated by an appropriate ingestion of OPCs, and physicians should automatically administer OPCs, if not concurrently with the radiation treatment, then at least immediately after radiation to avoid radiation-induced damage in the healthy organs.

Paradoxically, what cancer patients want to avoid is what others try to produce by long hours of sunbathing, thinking that a suntanned face raises more esteem than an untanned one.

Through the late 1800s, people with fair skins were seen as upper class, and the parasol was a lady's antioxidant weapon when she had to go out. People with tanned skin were automatically thought to belong to the lower working classes. During the summer of 1823, the Dutch author Jacob van Lennep travelled through Holland by foot to better learn his country. In his historic diary of that journey, Van Lennep describes the problems he had making himself known as an upper-class person because the journey had tanned his otherwise fair face. In his day, being able to avoid the sun was a sign of wealth. On the other hand, the workers who lived in slums and worked long hours in factories never saw the sun, and they and their children developed rickets because of a deficiency in vitamin D. This was not the kind of fairness the rich strove for.

But the more people tan their skin by exposing it to the sun for that healthy and vigorous look, the greater the chance of wrinkles and premature aging. The cosmetic and dermatological indications of OPCs are obvious. In this context, the word cosmetic comes from old Greek kosmetos, which means well ordered or well arranged. Kosmetikos means skilled in ordering and arranging. Needless to say, OPCs is the number 1 kosmetikos because it is supremely skilled in keeping in order the connective tissue, the constructive element of the skin. OPCs are equally skilled in protecting and taking care of the vascular system. As with all organs, the skin must be nourished and waste materials must be carried away, which is why the corium, the dermis layer of the skin, contains a fine network of vascular vessels. OPCs positively affect skin disorders of the allergic type, disorders that result from vascular insufficiencies (rosacea, spider veins, etc.), or damage from sun exposure. OPCs' stimulating role in the biosynthesis and maintenance of healthy collagen make OPCs a prime constituent of skin-care products.

The skin has two major layers: an outer one, which is the epidermis, and an inner one, which is the dermis or corium. The surface of the epidermis consists of nonliving cells that serve as a defense against microorganisms and substances that could penetrate the body. The lower layers of the epidermis constantly supply new cells to the outer layer, which does not need blood supply. The underlying thicker part of the skin, the dermis, is made up of connective tissue (containing collagen and elastin) and contains blood vessels, hair follicles, and nerves. This is the part of the skin that is particularly sensitive to radiation (sunburn), heat (burn), and chemical influences (allergic reactions). This is where the OPCs work, especially when they are being applied from the inside and from the inside.

OPCs scavenge free radicals that are being formed in the dermis, especially under the influence of the sun. I must stress again that OPCs do not work as a sunblock, but they capture the free radicals that come into being when the sunlight's photons penetrate the skin. Another reason OPCs' antioxidant effect works so well in the skin is that OPCs impede the oxidation of lipids in the cell membranes. The cell's membrane is composed of combinations of polyunsaturated fatty acids (PUFAs) with phosphoric acid forming phospholipids. The cell's membrane consists of two layers of phospholipids. The phosphate end of the phospholipid is attracted to water. The fatty acid (lipid) end is repelled by water. Because the lipid sides of the layers also attract each other, the lipid sides of the layers face each other, and the phosphate sides that are attracted to water face the outside and the inside of the bilayer. The combination of water-friendly and water-resistant layers permits the control of the passing of water- and fat-soluble particles through the membrane. A special feature of the membrane is that it is a fluid and not a solid. Parts of the membrane can literally flow from one point to another along the surface. The membrane also contains cholesterol, which helps to determine the degree of permeability to water-soluble substances. The cholesterol also controls the fluidity of the membrane.

The fatty acids in the cell's membrane form a prime target for free radicals. This is especially relevant because the skin is the only organ of the body that is so often and so intensely exposed to free radicals, in this case by the free radicals caused by sunlight. Free radicals turn the flexible unsaturated fatty acids into hard saturated fats, which serve no function in the cell membrane. In fact, a hardened membrane suffocates the cell. The membrane must be fluid to facilitate the passage or transport of substances leaving or entering the cell. The membrane fulfills this function only in a liquid state because the phospholipids that facilitate the entrance and exit of selected molecules should have the capacity to change their form and change place in the fluid membrane. This is impossible when the membranes solidify, a process that is promoted by the free radicals that destroy polyunsaturated fatty acids (PUFAs). When the cell's membrane hardens under the influence of free radicals, it loses the capacity to let oxygen and nutrients into the cell. Likewise, carbon dioxide and waste materials cannot get out. The phospholipids work like small revolving doors. If they jam — for instance, because somebody forgot to give them a drop of oil — nothing can get in or out. In this context, good-quality plant oils resemble lubricating oil — inconspicuous but essential.

PUFAs are oils, which means that they are liquid. All plant oils consist mainly of PUFAs. Upon free radical impact, PUFAs harden, as when the olive oil in your kitchen seems to turn into butter, differentiating oils and fats. Beyond the implications for taste and cooking, the differences form a decisive factor in determining the health of all our cells and tissues, including the skin. PUFAs occur in our food. You won't find them in butter or in a T-bone steak, but only in vegetables, especially in good-quality vegetable oils. We don't produce PUFAs ourselves. Unsaturated fatty acids are broadly and intensely promoted as beneficial for heart and circulation. While most of the multinational food conglomerates are still massively filling consumers' preference for fatty, salty, sugary foods, their research departments are working on food products that contain vegetable oils and less salt and sugar. The importance of PUFAs is so great that they are also referred to as vitamin F. The problem is that PUFAs are defenseless against free radicals, so they need antioxidants such as vitamin E and OPCs for their protection. A diet that is rich in PUFAs requires the taking of antioxidants because when left unprotected, the PUFAs may do more harm than good under the influence of free radicals. When left unprotected against free radicals, PUFAs may even increase the risk of cancer.

Not only do free radicals cause the skin to age and wrinkle, they can also cause inflammatory and allergic reactions. As explained later in this book, the key factor in the allergies is histamine, which is released by free radicals as well as by substances to which a person is oversensitive. Pollen and animal fur, for example, can induce the release of histamine. Histamine induces the widening and increased permeability of the capillaries. OPCs can neutralize free radicals, counteracting the release of histamine, and regulate the permeability of the capillaries. When the skin shows rashes and reddening, we must not exclude the possibility that such skin problems may be a sign of detoxification. The skin also serves as an organ of excretion. In such cases, drinking water, taking detoxification supplements, and taking enemas form part of the solution.

To manage the problems of aging, one needs to fight against both exogenous free radicals (induced by the sun, for instance) and endogenous free radicals of metabolic origin (alcohol clearance, byproducts of energy production, etc.). The ideal scavenger, then, should act through both external and internal (oral) applications, which requires that it be bioavailable and totally harmless. This is why cosmetology has been using OPCs since 1988, incorporating them in a wide range of creams and lotions. OPCs are also recommended in the form of dietary supplements. When used externally and internally, OPCs produce a "double whammy."

22 COLLAGEN

Practically all diseases are caused by a nutritional deficiency or imbalance . When we correct this deficiency or imbalance in time, the body is able to heal itself, even when the disease has progressed to a severe stage. This is exactly what happened to the members of Cartier's group who were on the brink of dying from scurvy. Without fresh food, they were lacking vitamin C, and their bodies were no longer able to renew their collagen supplies. Everywhere in the body where collagen normally exercised its supportive function, a collapse occurred. The gums bled, and the men lost their teeth. Without the surrounding collagen fibers, their joints hurt terribly. Disorders due to capillary permeability such as edema manifested themselves. Circulatory problems appeared because the veins also owe their elasticity to collagen and elastin. When the sailors drank the broth made from the needles and the bark of the Anneda tree, the deficiency symptoms of collagen degeneration receded. The men recovered within a relatively short period of time, which proves that the body has the capacity to make significant amounts of collagen after only one to two weeks.

From Cartier's reports about the rapid healing of his crew, some may think that the sailors consumed both vitamin C and OPCs. Vitamin C came from the needles of the Anneda tree, OPCs from its bark. Like the Maritime Pines from the Les Landes region, the Anneda tree has a thick bark. Its content of OPCs is sufficient to prepare a tea for healing scurvy. Historically, whenever people suffered from a lack of fresh fruit and vegetables, especially in their raw form, they have been marked by scurvy and sought ways to avoid it. Tradition has the story of the first French circumnavigator of the world, Louis Antoine de Bougainville, who explored primarily the South Pacific during the second half of the 18th century. Although he got lost during his last voyage, what remains of his endeavors, other than a couple of French islands in the Pacific Ocean, is the following story. De Bougainville's sailors were suffering from scurvy and there was no food left aboard. Hunger caused the weakened men to catch and eat rats, plenty of which were dwelling in the "tween decks." Not only did the sailors survive thanks to this unsavory diet, but they even recovered from scurvy. Why?

The man who introduced Linus Pauling to vitamin C was Irwin Stone. In 1976, Stone wrote a book called *The Healing Factor: Vitamin C Against Disease,* in which he explained how abundant vitamin C is in nature. "We can surmise that the production of ascorbic acid (vitamin C) was an early accomplishment of the life process because of its wide distribution in nearly all present-day living organisms. It is produced in comparatively large amounts in the simplest plants and the most complex; it is synthesized in the most primitive animal species as well as in the most highly organized. Except possibly for a few microorganisms, those species of animals that cannot make their own ascorbic acid are the exceptions and require it in their food if they are to survive. Without it, life cannot exist." Other than humans, only four mammals are dependent on food for their vitamin C intake. They also lack the capacity to synthesize vitamin C. By eating rats, which make their own ascorbic acid, de Bougainville's men unwittingly obtained the required vitamin C, and as a result, their bodies continued the production of collagen.

Collagen is part of the connective tissue that holds all the cells of the body in place. According to its name (French colle = glue), collagen acts like a glue for our cells. Quite literally, collagen keeps us in shape. At the same time, collagen allows flexibility, motion, and mobility. In that sense, collagen allows life because without motion, we die. In the vascular system, collagen and elastin hold the form of the vessels and provide flexibility, strength, and resilience. Collagen is found abundantly in the skin as well as in cartilage, bones, and tendons. It could be described as a sort of wrapping material, comparable to the paper that a salesperson might use for wrapping up a fragile article you just purchased.

OPCs recognize collagen and attach to its constitutive amino acids so that the collagen matures, maintaining its elasticity and strength. While OPCs directly protect collagen in this manner, they are only indirectly involved in the continuous creation of fresh collagen. The making (biosynthesis) of collagen takes place under the influence of only one unique substance: vitamin C. Without sufficient vitamin C, no collagen synthesis will take place. Because OPCs protect vitamin C, they contribute indirectly to collagen synthesis, showing in an impressive manner that Szent-Györgyi was right in recognizing vitamin C and vitamin P as co-factors. It is only under their joint effect that the body is able to fully unfold its capacity to produce fresh collagen. OPCs and vitamin C meet at a biological crossing from which they pursue the identical objective, the building, maturation, protection, and maintenance of collagen. In *Chapter 39: OPCs, Vitamin C and the Facts of e-life* you will see in greater detail the intense relationship between Vitamin C and OPCs.

Collagen is structured like a winding ladder in that it possesses parallel poles connected by regular cross-links or rungs. The lateral parts consist of protein chains, or polypeptides that are intertwined.

In fresh collagen, the lateral poles and the rungs that link them are very regularly positioned. The rungs are placed at equal distances, thus keeping the poles regularly spaced. People who are familiar with carpentry and ladders know that only ladders that have regular rungs and that poles are flexible and do not break without warning. Ladders that have misplaced, irregular, and oblique rungs are not flexible and will rapidly break. The same is true for collagen. Only regular collagen is flexible; collagen that is irregular will break. In addition to the normal wear and tear that destroys collagen, free radicals disturb the making of collagen and impair existing collagen. Free radicals cause the misplacement of the crosslinks, the rungs, and as a result, the connective tissue becomes weak and brittle.

When this takes place in the capillaries, fluid will leak into the surrounding tissue. Further up in the circulatory system, the vascular walls of the veins and the valves weaken into varicoses. If these collagen and elastin problems are not solved, an inflammation will manifest itself after a certain period of time. If you do not counteract these processes, the affected arteries and veins will suffer to such a degree that new connections between arterioles and veins are formed. But these naturally formed bypasses cannot fully replace the circulatory capacity that was lost. Eventually, the process results in sclerosis. In the skin, we can see this broken collagen as wrinkles! The problem is that once you have them, they won't go away. Inside the body, the impact of broken collagen on our health is devastating. It will lead to impaired blood flow, loss of internal mobility, the storing of toxins, inflammatory processes, strokes, and eventually, all the degenerative diseases we fear so much.

Our body is subject to a continuous aging process, and all parts of the body, including bones, have a finite life span. In 10 years, you will be the same person, but you will not have the same collagen or the same bones you have today. Radioscopy would reveal no difference, but the individual components of your body will not be the same. Every second of the day, the body produces fresh collagen with the help of vitamin C. Our pool of connective tissue is being ceaselessly replenished to replace worn-out collagen, which is easily bruised and used and easily upset by free radicals. We need it as fresh, unused, and intact as possible. No wonder the body has developed a system to handle a fast "turnover" of collagen — first in, first out.

To get rid of worn-out collagen, the body uses enzymes called collagenases. They break down the ruins of collagen so that the remains can be excreted. The collagenase enzymes do not remove the collagen ruins we call wrinkles. If the body could break down wrinkles, we might be able to enjoy eternal youth because we would have an everlasting pool of fresh collagen that could replace the wrinkled collagen. Some people suffer from a collagen disease that is characterized by too much collagenase activity. This results in excessively weak collagen as the patients suffer from scurvylike symptoms, such as bruises. Scientific research showed that when they take OPCs, the OPCs attach

Protection of Collagen and Elastin by OPCs against degrading enzymes

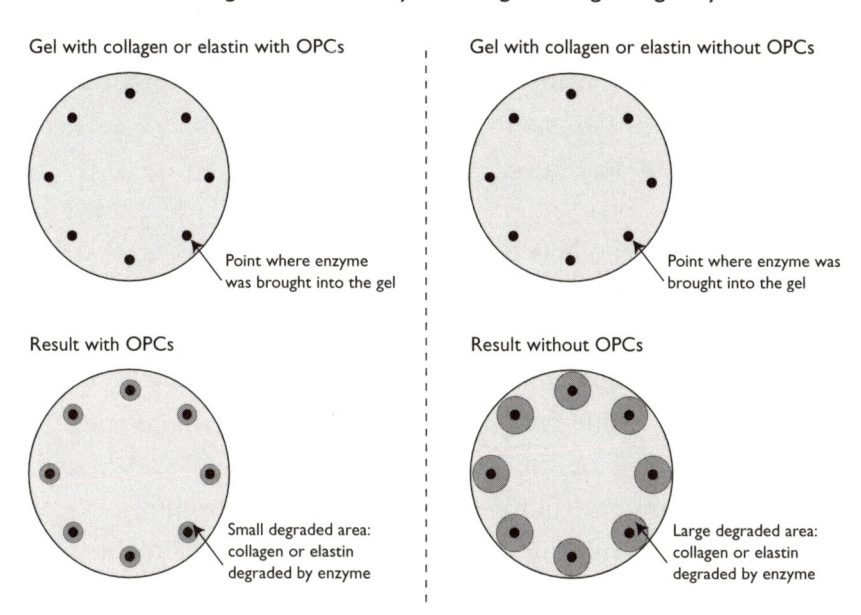

Gel with collagen or elastin with OPCs — Point where enzyme was brought into the gel

Gel with collagen or elastin without OPCs — Point where enzyme was brought into the gel

Result with OPCs — Small degraded area: collagen or elastin degraded by enzyme

Result without OPCs — Large degraded area: collagen or elastin degraded by enzyme

This simple experiment shows that OPCs, when mixed with a gel that contains collagen or elastin, protect the collagen or elastin against degrading enzymes. The dishes on the left contain gel + collagen or elastin + OPCs. The dishes on the right contain only gel + collagen or elastin. The degradation is visible as the dark grey area that surrounds the points where the enzymes were put into the gel.

themselves to their collagen in such a way that the collagen-splitting enzymes cannot get in touch with the collagen. Thus OPCs have a triple effect: They promote collagen production by helping vitamin C, they inhibit collagen destruction with the collagenase enzymes, and they protect collagen against the onslaught of free radicals.

With reference to the *chapter 21: Beauty and the Signs of Aging*, there is an interesting message for "smokers under the sun." The British medical journal The Lancet reported in its 24 March 2003 issue that smoking significantly contributes to the formation of wrinkles because smokers have 30 percent more of another enzyme, one that degrades collagen. It is called matrix metalloproteinase, or MMP. In turn, MMP is monitored by yet another enzyme called tissue inhibitor of metalloproteinase (TIMP), which inhibits MMP's activity. When the balance between MMP and TIMP is tipped in favor of MMP, more collagen is destroyed. As a result the skin will become weaker and lined. In vitro studies had shown that sunshine tips the MMP-TIMP balance in favor of MMP, but the researchers wanted to find out if this process takes place also in the human skin. Two groups of volunteers, one group that smoked and the other that didn't, had their buttocks irradiated regularly by UV light. All volunteers received the same quantity and intensity of UV light, sufficient to make sure that the irradiation itself could not be the cause of individual variations. Then, the researchers examined the activity of MMP and TIMP in tiny pieces of skin taken from all the tanned buttocks. All smokers had 30 percent more MMP than the non-smokers. According to this study, smoking has a very negative impact on the skin's collagen. Smoking in the sun is your skin's worst nightmare.

In the beginning of this book, I told you that simplicity played a major role in Masquelier's research. This fact is impressively illustrated by the Hot Water Test he and his colleagues used in 1981 to prove the protective effect of OPCs on collagen. When collagen is immersed in hot water, it immediately shrinks. However, if the collagen has been saturated with OPCs beforehand, it shrinks much less and more slowly. This simple test was performed with five different collagen strips. One reference strip was not pretreated; the others were pretreated with bioflavonoids, catechins, tannins, and OPCs, respectively. Whereas the untreated reference strip contracted in hot water within 10 seconds, the OPCs strip took 210 seconds to contract. The tannin strip needed 70 seconds, and the catechin strip, 45 seconds. The strip pretreated with bioflavonoids contracted as quickly as the untreated reference strip. This confirms that bioflavonoids (the yellow pigments) have no affinity for collagen, which is one of the essential differences between OPCs and bioflavonoids.

When the force of contraction was measured, it was found that the speed of contraction correlated with its force. When the maximum initial contraction force of the untreated strip was set at 100, the OPCs strip recorded a value of 4.76. The OPCs strip hardly contracted. The tannin strip recorded a contraction of 14.28 and the catechin strip, 22.1. The strip that had been impregnated with bioflavonoids contracted with just as much force as the reference strip; that is, with the strength that was marked as 100. This simple test provided simple but irrefutable evidence of the exceptional properties of OPCs as protector of collagen against a physical attack.

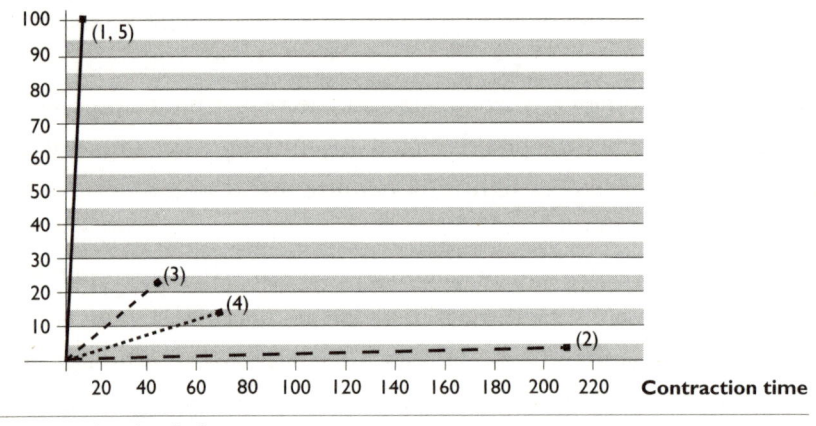

Contraction force

[Graph showing contraction force vs contraction time with the following lots:
- Lot 1 = Reference (point at (1, 5), near vertical line)
- Lot 2 = OPC (dashed line, point (2) near 200)
- Lot 3 = Catechin (point (3) near 60)
- Lot 4 = Tannin (point (4) near 80)
- Lot 5 = Bioflavanoids (same as Lot 1)]

———— Lot 1 = Reference
– – – Lot 2 = OPC
- - - - - Lot 3 = Catechin
············ Lot 4 = Tannin
———— Lot 5 = Bioflavanoids

In 1984, a completely different experimental approach made by other scientists proved again the tremendous efficacy of OPCs for vascular protection. A substance called 3'aminopropionitril fumarate causes serious changes in the vascular walls. In simple terms, 3'aminopropionitril makes a person very sick. The changes produced in vascular tissue are visible even to the naked eye. Laboratory animals that had taken OPCs for a certain period of time did not respond at all to being exposed to 3'aminopropionitril. Despite the exposure, their vessels remained unaffected and similar to those of untreated healthy animals from a reference group. This test provided proof that OPCs help collagen to withstand chemical attack. Our blood vessels form an enormous network of broad highways and narrow mountain paths. The entire length extends over about 125 miles. Maintaining such a network is not an easy job, especially when the owner doesn't seem to care. Even those who do care have a hard time.

The breakdown of collagen and the resulting leakage of the capillary system due to increased fragility do not cause acute diseases that strike as lightning coming out of the blue. It takes time to undermine the capillary system to the point of collapse. Take, for example, cardiovascular disease. Some people may think that one is "struck" by a heart attack as one is hit by a bus. Although the heart attack itself is indeed an acute problem, it is only the last step in a long process that lasted many years. In light of the fact that the body is quite good at the effort of self-healing, it is not difficult to deduce that the counter-effort to undermine it must be considerable. Certainly, the natural process of aging is a counter-effort that seems to be programmed beyond our control. But the body is subject to not just the aging process.

Dietary habits form a major influence that can either support the body's efforts to repair and maintain health or impair those efforts by undermining and/or overwhelming them. The nutritional component in these matters has been accepted by the scientific community as well as by the general public. Nevertheless, when it comes to advising the public about the intake of vitamins and minerals, scientific consensus recommends daily allowances, which are negligible when it comes to satisfying the body's requirements. While orthodox medicine wants us to believe that 60 mg of vitamin C per day is enough to meet all our needs, Pauling and other orthomolecular-oriented scientists recommend at least several grams per day.

OPCs bridge the abyss between those conflicting views in that they may help boost suboptimal dosages of vitamin C to the megalevel proposed by Pauling. Masquelier once said, "In a way, Pauling was right about his high doses of vitamin C. Not knowing about OPCs, he had no other options. But I am convinced that if Linus Pauling had known OPCs, he would not have prescribed 18 grams of vitamin C, but a small amount of vitamin C and a small amount of OPCs. Most certainly I feel that I would have been able to convince him."

In an otherwise healthy person, insufficient production of collagen is caused by a deficiency in vitamin C and OPCs. No matter how much officialdom disagrees, when you accept cardiovascular disease as a form of scurvy that is caused by nutritional deficiencies, you gain more control of your life. By all scientific means, the breakdown of collagen stands for scurvy. The branch of medical science called etiology occupies itself with the causes and origins of disease. When logically, truthfully, and scientifically applied, etiology can only confirm the causal relationship between insufficient collagen production and a deficiency in vitamin C and OPCs. It may seem an impossible leap to label cardiovascular disease a kind of scurvy, but *chapter 23: The No. 1 Killer, OPCs, and Cholesterol* shows that the equation is not as mind-boggling as it appears.

23 THE NO. 1 KILLER, OPCs, AND CHOLESTEROL

The vascular conditions that respond so well to OPCs are unpleasant, painful, debilitating, and frustrating. Yet, varicose veins or visual deficiencies are not life-threatening diseases with potentially fatal consequences. In the purely vascular context, OPCs repair a troubled area rather than perform a life-saving action. In comparison, if some faucets in the house are leaking or if some drainpipes are jammed, the situation is awkward but does not turn the entire house into an uninhabitable ruin. A plumber can correct the problem so that the house returns to a properly functioning state. However, when left unattended, such small problems may eventually cause the collapse of the whole structure. Likewise, vascular disorders may take on a life-threatening character, especially when vascular disorders turn into *cardio*vascular disorders.

The heart and the vascular system are intimately related; the heart muscle cannot function without an adequate vascular system that supports its functions. Any obstruction in blood circulation will make the task of the heart tougher because it will have to work harder and because blood pressure may rise. Obstructions in blood circulation, loss of elasticity of the vascular walls, weakened capillaries, inflamed blood vessels, and similar vascular conditions cause high blood pressure. In men and women alike, high blood pressure reduces life expectancy because it increases the risk of cardiovascular disease and cerebral infarction.

Compared with the number of people who suffer from cardiovascular disease, the number of people who have a pure heart problem unrelated to conditions of the vascular system is very small. Such conditions include heart deformations and heart rhythm problems, which can usually be solved by surgery or placement of a pacemaker. A much larger group of people is afflicted by the almost epidemic cardiovascular degeneration caused by stress, genetic disposition, lifestyle (poor diet, smoking, alcohol, lack of exercise, etc.), high blood pressure, or obesity. In the industrialized countries, almost half of all deaths are a result of cardiovascular failure. Cardiovascular incidents are the number 1 killer in Western societies. Recent American statistics confirm that more women now die of heart disease than of all cancers combined.

Can OPCs thwart danger in the case of vascular problems that may take a fatal course? Yes. The phenomenon known as the French Paradox, described in *chapter 31: Red Wine Drinkers Live Happier and Longer* shows that the OPCs contained in red wine drastically reduce cardiovascular mortality, even if the lifestyle actually includes a number of elements that promote cardiovascular degeneration. OPCs can reduce the risk of succumbing to failure of the cardiovascular system. To put it in a positive way, OPCs can save and prolong life. Masquelier repeatedly received such reports from physicians who had prescribed OPCs (Resivit, Flavan, or Endotélon) as vasoprotectors. They reported to him the beneficial effects OPCs had on factors involved with cardiovascular health. What especially drew their attention was that their patients' cholesterol levels at the end of treatment were lower than at the beginning. This is how Masquelier learned that OPCs that were recommended for heavy legs, hematoma, hemorrhage, retinopathy, and so on also influenced cardiovascular health.

Masquelier was not really surprised by these insights because during the early stages of his research, he had already explored the connection between red wine consumption and normal cholesterol levels. Knowing that red wine contains OPCs, Masquelier had assumed that the cholesterol-controlling properties of red wine should be attributed to OPCs. As early as 1961, he had presented the relationship between red wine consumption and normal cholesterol levels at an International Medical Conference in Bordeaux. In the audience was the dean of the medical faculty of the University of California in Los Angeles (UCLA), Milton Silverman. When Masquelier had finished his speech, Silverman got up and said, "Dear Professor, please come to us and deliver this lecture at UCLA. I am convinced it would be a huge success because at the moment there are two things that Americans fear most of all: communism and cholesterol." The fear of communism has been replaced by fears of the forces that brought the Americans "9/11." Contrary to communism, cholesterol still scores high on the list of most feared things.

Encouraged by this transatlantic support, Masquelier decided to take a closer look at cholesterol and OPCs. He found that in 1957, a scientist by the name of A. Fay Morgan reported that animals that had been given red wine did not have increased cholesterol values even though they had been fed a cholesterol-rich diet. The total amount of fats in their blood was even lower than that of a control group that had lived on nothing but bread and water. A third group was given some alcohol diluted in water so that the scientists could check the results obtained with the wine group. If alcoholic water did not produce the same results as wine, the cholesterol-lowering effect of the wine was to be attributed to something other than its alcohol content. In fact, the animals that were given alcoholic water recorded much higher cholesterol levels than the animals that received red wine. This finding justifies the conclusion that alcohol itself isn't a cholesterol manager.

When Masquelier learned of Morgan's study, he immediately figured out that the OPCs contained in wine must be the cholesterol-managing factor. In the years that followed, his hunch was confirmed by various examinations done with OPCs by other scientists. With the rates of vascular and cardiovascular disorders steadily on the rise, these were far-reaching discoveries. In 1966, the German pharmaceutical company E. Merck even filed a patent describing OPCs as cholesterol regulating and, more in particular, as cholesterol-reducing substances. Almost two decades later, studies conducted at the University of Paris by Dr. J. Wegrowski and his colleagues confirmed that in the presence of OPCs, considerably less cholesterol is being deposited in the vascular wall.

In 1984, Wegrowski showed that much less cholesterol was deposited on the elastin tissue in the vascular wall (of the aorta) in the presence of OPCs than in the absence of OPCs. More specifically, Wegrowski and his colleagues reported that although the level of penetration of cholesterol in the aorta was not reduced by OPCs, significantly lower amounts of cholesterol were bound to elastin in the aorta. The animals in this test were hypercholesteremic rabbits, which means that they suffered from an excessive amount of cholesterol. Yet OPCs positively interfered by inhibiting the fixation of cholesterol to the arterial wall. Even when excessive amounts of cholesterol exist and penetrate the vascular wall, OPCs somehow protect the vascular wall against cholesterol deposits.

Another piece of the puzzle that Masquelier was putting together was provided by the Czech scientist E. Ginter. Ginter had studied the body's elimination of cholesterol in conditions of a vitamin C deficiency. Normally, the elimination of cholesterol takes place under the influence of enzymes, which transform cholesterol into bile salts in the liver. In the form of bile salts, cholesterol is then unloaded via the intestines. This enzymatic process requires the presence of vitamin C, which makes cholesterol elimination vitamin C dependent, as was proven by Ginter.

Ginter examined two groups of guinea pigs. In the course of 24 hours, the first group was fed a diet containing hardly any vitamin C (0.5 mg), while the second group was given 10 mg of vitamin C. In the course of that day, the latter group transformed 23.6 mg of cholesterol into eliminable bile salts. The first group transformed only 16.6 mg of cholesterol per day, which is equivalent to a 30 percent difference. The cholesterol level in the blood of the guinea pigs that had been taking vitamin C was at 126 mg per 100g. The cholesterol level of the animals suffering from a vitamin C deficiency was at 218 mg per 100 g — almost twice as high. On the basis of Ginter's experiment, we can now also look at cholesterol in the context of a vitamin C deficiency, of scurvy, although of course vitamin C is not the unique factor that guarantees faultless cholesterol management.

Diet of guinea pigs	Vitamin C Mg / 100 g Liver	Vitamin C Mg / 100 g Bile	Cholestorol Mg / 100 g Blood	Cholestorol Mg / 100 g Liver	Cholestorol transformed into bile salts mg / 24h / kg.
Normal 10 mg Vitamin C / 24h	8,2	21,6	126	359	23,6
Deficient 0,5 mg Vitamin C / 24h	1,6	4,7	218	443	16,6

For decades, we have been told to fear "cholesterol" more than we fear the devil. The very word "cholesterol" causes people to imagine clouds of danger and imminent death. In the United States, two anticholesterol drugs are on the list of the top 10 prescription drugs. Under pressure of all the propaganda and warnings, people seem to have forgotten that cholesterol is not a poison but a vital substance that is essential for survival. This is why the body itself produces cholesterol, so that it is not dependent on food-borne sources. Why lower the level of a substance that plays a vital role in the human body? Why send cholesterol to damnation by demonizing it as very dangerous? We need to take a closer and more open-minded look at the mechanisms that control and monitor the way cholesterol is transported, deposited, and eliminated. Doing so will allow us to realistically determine what we need to do to live with cholesterol as a companion and not as an enemy.

Cholesterol is a fatty substance that is produced internally by the liver in the amount of roughly 1 g per day. To produce cholesterol, the liver uses the saturated (animal) fats we ingest through our food. These fats actually induce the liver to make cholesterol. Our food, predominantly the food of animal origin, supplies not only fats but also cholesterol. Contrary to what most people have been conditioned to believe, the cholesterol we ingest with our food only slightly contributes to an increase of cholesterol in the blood. The liver responds to an increase of external, food-borne cholesterol by switching off or lowering its own cholesterol production. External cholesterol does not produce variations in the blood level of cholesterol greater than 15 percent, upward or downward.

However, eating lots of animal fat can cause an increase of cholesterol of up to 25 percent. Therefore, if you want to keep down your cholesterol level, it is wiser to watch the intake of fats than to watch the intake of cholesterol. It is even wiser to take unsaturated fatty acids (plant and fish oils) instead of animal fats because PUFAs seem to slightly push down the level of cholesterol in the blood. Even if you eat a cholesterol-free diet, your body will use saturated fats to make all the cholesterol it needs.

As the textbooks on medical physiology explain, the body uses as much as 80 percent of all of its cholesterol to make cholic acid in the liver. In turn, cholic acid is combined with other substances to form the so-called bile salts (gall). Ginter found that this process depends on the presence of sufficient amounts of vitamin C. Sub-optimal levels of vitamin C suppress the elimination of cholesterol. When there's sufficient vitamin C, the major part of the body's cholesterol is constantly being eliminated through the intestinal tract in the form of gall. Gall is first stored in the gall bladder and is then led into the small intestine, where it helps the digestion and absorption of fats. Of the remaining 20 percent of cholesterol that is not being used to make of gall, part is stored in the corneum, the outer layer of the skin. Together with other fats, cholesterol makes the skin highly resistant to external water-soluble substances and the action of many chemical agents. The cholesterol in the skin prohibits excess evaporation of internal water through the skin.

The remainder of the body's cholesterol plays a vital role in the formation of the membranes of the cells. Together with the phospholipids, cholesterol determines the fluidity of the cell's membrane. The integrity of the membranes of all cells throughout the body is based mainly on phospholipids and cholesterol. The cell's membrane is like a film made up of revolving doors that control what goes in and out of the cell. Cholesterol forms part of that system of revolving doors. A very small amount of the body's cholesterol is used by the adrenal glands to form certain hormones. Cholesterol-based hormones are progesterone and estrogen (formed in the ovaries) and testosterone (formed in the testes). These glands can also synthesize their own cholesterol. The quantities they take from the body's cholesterol stock are zero to minute.

Like fats, cholesterol cannot be transported by the bloodstream as a pure free-floating particle because, like fats, cholesterol is not water soluble. The blood is not a suitable medium to transport such insoluble particles. To transport cholesterol from the liver to the cells, the body uses water-soluble carriers called lipoproteins. A lipoprotein is a combination of a lipid (fat) and a protein. Lipoproteins were discovered in 1929 by Michel Macheboeuf who worked at the Pasteur Institute in Paris. Macheboeuf was an older colleague of Masquelier's university professor Tayeau. Macheboeuf found a water-soluble lipoprotein that we now recognize as high density lipoprotein (HDL). In 1946, American researchers found more lipoproteins, one of them now accepted as low density lipoprotein (LDL). During the 1960s, more became known about the role of various lipoproteins in the distribution of fats and cholesterol.

The lipoproteins make it possible to transport fatty substances via the blood. In the liver, a specific lipoprotein loads up three substances that are not soluble in water:
- Large quantities of fats (triglycerides)

- Much smaller quantities of cholesterol
- Phospholipids

On their first rounds through the body, the lipoproteins that do the pick-up in the liver first offload the fats in the tissues where fat is used for energy or stored. These lipoproteins that contain fats, cholesterol, and phospholipids are called very low density lipoproteins (VLDLs). After the fats have been delivered to fatty tissue, LDLs remain. The only things that LDL still carries around are cholesterol and phospholipids. In that form, LDL and its fatty cargo are recognized by the cell membranes, which then attract and "swallow" the entire LDL+cholesterol+phospholipids. Inside the cell, the LDL+*cargo* is dismantled and the cholesterol and phospholipids are offloaded and used. As long as the LDL is in the blood, it does not offload its cholesterol.

The reason people fear cholesterol is not that the body uses it for hormone production, that it helps digestion, or that it protects us from dehydration. People fear cholesterol because they are convinced that it forms deposits on the vascular wall. A closer look at how cholesterol is transported reveals, however, that no free cholesterol sticks to the vascular wall. The idea that pure, greasy, sticky cholesterol is the direct cause of a simple plumbing problem is antique and oversimplistic. For instance, it does not take into account that fact that cholesterol can penetrate only the lining and the underlying connective tissue of the vessel walls as LDL's cargo and not as pure cholesterol. For that reason alone, we should no longer speak of cholesterol but rather of LDL. As stated by Robert E. Olson of the Department of Pediatrics of the University of South Florida during a 1997 symposium called *Evolution of Ideas About the Nutritional Value of*

Dietary Fat, "Cholesterol per se is not the agent because LDL, which contains cholesterol, is pro-atherogenic, whereas HDL, which also contains cholesterol, is anti-atherogenic."

So it's LDL and it isn't cholesterol. Does this change bring us any closer to what really happens? The obsolete explanation still tells us that "cholesterol deposits" in the vascular wall occur because too much LDL-cholesterol is floating around in the bloodstream. According to the promoters of this theory, atherosclerosis remains a matter of quantity. The idea is that the LDL "trucks" will seek a place to "park" when there are too many LDLs "on the road." Along the highways of blood circulation, the vascular wall is the most accessible "parking lot" for LDL. It's all a matter of trucks backing up on an inert and passive parking lot. All this then leads to an atheroma, or plaque. After a while, the plaque hardens. The full sequence of events is known as atherosclerosis. The solution is simple: less cargo = fewer trucks = less plaque.

Let's assume that the issue *is* a matter of quantity and that plaque comes about when people overload the body with an excess of cholesterol coming from butter, cheese, gravy, cream, milk, sauces, meat, eggs, and other fatty or animal-fat-containing products. The liver will automatically reduce its own self-determined cholesterol production when too much external cholesterol is ingested. In reverse, when we sparingly eat animal fats and cholesterol, the liver will increase its production of cholesterol. The body's own production of cholesterol is regulated by what it needs and by the amount of animal fats in the diet. An excess of saturated fats in the diet poses a much greater risk than an overconsumption of cholesterol. This is because the liver will react by stepping up its own cholesterol production when it gets too much fat delivered. This changes the cholesterol problem into a fat problem. But a fat problem can be solved without cholesterol-suppressing or fat-lowering drugs: eat less animal (saturated) fat.

Those who want to deal with the cholesterol problem by counting numbers should in any case not overlook the fact that they may subtract the cholesterol they eliminate from the cholesterol the body makes and ingests. Although this topic is rarely addressed in the anticholesterol publications, people should be able to eliminate 80 percent of the cholesterol they ingest and the cholesterol the body produces. There is an important condition that will make this happen: a sufficient daily dosage of vitamin C. With that, the body will be able to properly eliminate the bulk of all its cholesterol in the form of gall. Therefore, those who reduce the problem of atherosclerosis to counting cholesterol should at the very least take vitamin C to stimulate cholesterol elimination. A more balanced approach would be a combination of watching the intake of animal fats *and* taking sufficient vitamin C every day.

The most balanced approach would be to watch dietary intake of fats, take vitamin C, and take OPCs. This is the natural way to maintain a good balance between incoming and self-produced cholesterol and outgoing cholesterol. According to Masquelier, OPCs boost the activity of vitamin C, and as a consequence, the process of eliminating cholesterol via the gall is stimulated. Comforting as this may be, the question remains whether taking vitamin C to boost cholesterol elimination will prevent plaque formation. Before addressing that question, we need to discuss another lipoprotein that is also involved in the transportation of cholesterol: high-density lipoprotein (HDL). Although less is known about HDL than about LDL, we do know that HDL is specifically active in picking up cholesterol from the cells to transport it to the liver. Under normal circumstances, LDL works as the courier that delivers cholesterol from the liver to the cells, and HDL picks up the cholesterol from the cells to take it back to the liver. What could interfere with this process and cause cardiovascular disease?

The widely promoted and infinitely repeated theory rests on a rather simple equation. When too much LDL is delivering too much cholesterol to the cells in the vascular wall, the HDL cannot pick up all the cholesterol, so a certain amount of cholesterol remains "in the depot." This depot may become a plaque so thick that it protrudes into the bloodstream and reduces or even stops blood flow. Supposedly, all this is caused by one single factor: excess of cholesterol in a "passive" vascular wall that remains without response. This theory assumes that the HDL is not picking up the excess of deposited cholesterol. This may be the case, but if the vascular tissue undergoes all this passively and without taking action, an overloading of the vascular wall might just be a temporary problem. It could be resolved when the level of cholesterol diminishes and the HDL returns another day to pick up the cholesterol.

Unfortunately, people who have perfectly healthy levels of cholesterol and lipoproteins can still develop plaque and cardiovascular disease. The textbooks attribute this impossibility to two extraordinary factors: diabetes and smoking. We know that diabetes has a weakening influence on the vascular wall, so it is no wonder that a diabetic patient may develop vascular abnormalities that lead to plaque formation. We have seen how prone diabetics are to circulatory problems in the periphery of the vascular system and how these problems may lead to impaired vision and even to gangrene. It is the second commonly accepted factor that Masquelier saw as the definitive support for the explanation that the essential cause of plaque formation is free radicals.

This more balanced explanation of atherosclerosis revolves around the fact that there may be a natural reason the LDL backup forms plaque. This explanation tells us that a backup consisting of normal, intact LDLs doesn't turn into plaque all by itself, only because there are too many of them, but that something happens beforehand. Initially, while they are still on the road in the blood or backed up in the vascular wall, LDLs and their unprotected cargo are easy targets for free radicals. For a free radical, an LDL with its cargo is a sitting duck. Think of LDL as a truck that must take its cargo through a war zone filled with free radicals. When the truck is left unprotected, free radicals shoot its "tires" out and make its cargo (fats and cholesterol) go rancid.

This explanation further says that plaque formation begins because the vascular wall does not recognize the LDL and cargo after they have been oxidized, deformed, and wrecked by free radicals. Plaque formation, according to this theory, begins when the LDL is wrecked and its cargo turns rancid. Then the vascular wall actively attempts to neutralize what it no longer recognizes as safe and beneficial. In fact, the reaction of the vascular wall is the normal inflammatory response of any tissue that is confronted by what it perceives as an invader. In the case of the vascular wall, the wrecked LDL must be kept from re-entering circulation. It must be kept in the parking lot where it ended up after it was hit by free radicals. It must be neutralized.

The following points sum up:
- When too many free radicals get in touch with too many unprotected LDLs, the free radicals will wreck the LDL and make its cholesterol turn rancid. In turn, rancid fats behave as free radicals in a chain reaction. Because cholesterol is a fatty substance, they can turn it rancid just as they can make oils and butter "go bad." Radical fats change normal fats. That's how rancidity spreads through butter, from the outside to the inside.
- The rancid cholesterol is no longer recognized by the HDL as something it must take to the liver. Bereaved, HDL remains without cholesterol. In the meantime, the vascular wall has taken action.
- Once struck by a free radical, the LDL and cholesterol cargo drives the vascular wall into an inflammatory frenzy. It considers the wrecked LDL an unwanted particle, an intruder that must be seriously dealt with, so it calls for help. From the blood, the vascular wall attracts white blood cells, also known as leukocytes or monocytes. White blood cells act by moving through the vascular wall to reach a site of injury or to scavenge intruders or unknown particles.
- Before moving through the wall, the white blood cells that have descended into the vascular wall must first mature into macrophages. When called to arms, these macrophages vacuum the wrecked LDL to clean up the area.

- Vacuuming an excess of wrecked LDL, the macrophages become so laden with LDL's fatty remainders that they become "foamy." These fat-inflated foamcells get company from another white blood cell called a T-lymphocyte.
- This nightmare that began with free-radical-damaged LDL has now turned into an uncontrollable mess in which the wall's muscle cells try to overgrow the mess by capping it with a matrix of strong collagen fibers. Underneath the cap, the plaque may harden and go into "stenosis," making the vascular wall inflexible.
- The collagen cap may break as the result of inflammation, and the inflammatory process weakens collagen. Collagen may become brittle and break as a result of free radical attack.
- An open, uncapped plaque will then cause the release of clotting factors in the blood as well as in the plaque itself. When the blood clot stops the flow of blood in the heart muscle, a person feels pressure and tightness under the breastbone. When the clot persists, heart muscle tissue will remain without blood too long and it will acidify.
- In an acid environment, the red blood cells will stiffen and can no longer pass through the capillaries. This spreads the lack of oxygen, causing a person to feel the acidity in the heart muscle as angina pectoris.
- Eventually, muscle cells may suffocate and die, releasing lysosomes, which are enzymes that destroy cells. What remains is a scar in the heart muscle. Too much scar tissue may stop the heart from functioning normally. In the worst case, the heart stops.

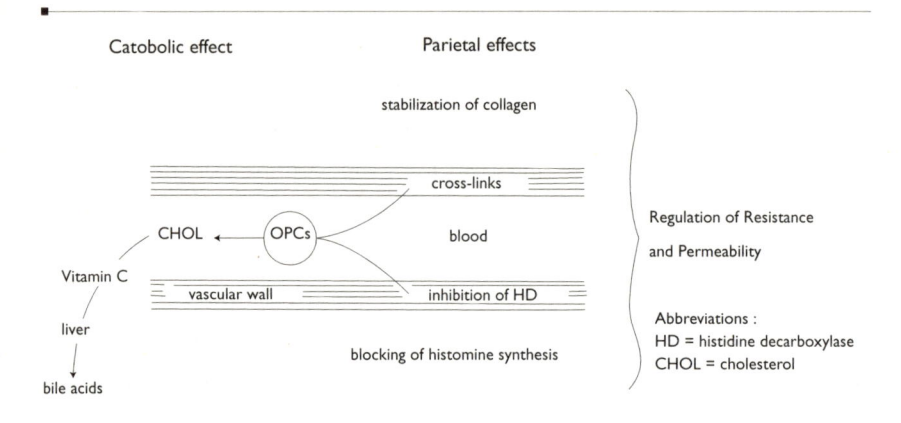

```
                Catobolic effect              Parietal effects

                                          stabilization of collagen
                                                                              ⎫
                                ═══════════════════════════════════           ⎬
                                ═══════════════ cross-links ════════          ⎭
                           CHOL ←──── OPCs            blood                Regulation of Resistance
                 Vitamin C       ╱         ╲                               and Permeability
                          ╱      ═══ vascular wall ═══ inhibition of HD ═══
                     liver                                                 Abbreviations :
                       ↓                   blocking of histomine synthesis HD = histidine decarboxylase
                  bile acids                                               CHOL = cholesterol
```

In this illustration, Masquelier explains how OPCs play a central role in vascular health. OPCs help produce the vascular wall's collagen and stabilize it by protecting it from free radicals and collagen-splitting enzymes. OPCs also inhibit histamine formation by interfering with the histidine decarboxylase enzyme, which makes histamine. OPCs protect cholesterol against free radical damage and help vitamin C in the excretion of cholesterol via the liver. When this takes place at the level of the capillaries, OPCs regulate capillary resistance and permeability.

Amazingly, an outline of this cascade of events was proposed by Masquelier in the 1970s. As recently as in the May 2002 issue of the *Scientific American*, Dr. Peter Libby, a Professor at Harvard Medical School who also practices cardiovascular medicine, wonderfully explained "the new view" on atherosclerosis. Although Dr. Libby is likely unfamiliar with the works of Masquelier, his well-illustrated article contains many similarities. The Harvard professor explains in great detail the inflammatory aspects of atherosclerosis. The sequence of events listed above is probably closest to the truth. It explains that 85 percent of all heart attacks are not due to a completely clogged artery that blocks the blood's access to the heart It talks about why heart attacks occur when plaques expand outward instead of inward, leaving blood flow unhampered for many years. It explains why stents or bypasses often fail to resolve the problem and prevent future heart attacks.

It also explains why it is inaccurate to call cholesterol in LDL bad and cholesterol in HDL good in view of the "new" views on the origin of heart disease. We need LDL to transport cholesterol to the tissues. The level of LDL in our blood is constantly in direct response to the intake of fats, which is perfectly normal. We cannot blame LDL for doing the job it was intended for. HDL has the capacity to pick up excess normal cholesterol from the cells. It is beyond reproach. Those who want to use the terms bad and good with respect to cholesterol can use "bad" to describe the rancid cholesterol in wrecked LDLs and "good" to describe normal cholesterol.

Do OPCs defend LDL and cholesterol against oxidation by free radicals? Yes! During 1993, Dr. Edwin Frankel of the Department of Food Science and Technology of the University of California found that the phenolic substances found in red wine inhibit the oxidation of LDL. He even found that wine that was diluted 1,000-fold inhibited the oxidation of LDL significantly more than did vitamin E. Frankel concluded, "Our findings show that the nonalcoholic components of red wine have potent antioxidant properties toward oxidation of human LDL." Together with his French colleague Pierre-Louis Teissedre, Frankel undertook the effort to check the level of one such nonalcoholic component (catechin) in the blood of people who had consumed red wine. The relatively modest amount of 300 ml of red wine containing 80 mg of catechin resulted in a significant presence of catechin in the blood as shown on the next page.

These findings are important not only because of the antioxidative effect of OPCs, but certainly also because OPCs do much more to prevent cardiovascular disease. On June 22, 1993,

Catechin concentration in plasma of 4 volunteers following catechin-free diet, after drinking 300 ml of red wine.

Catechin concentration in µmol/l

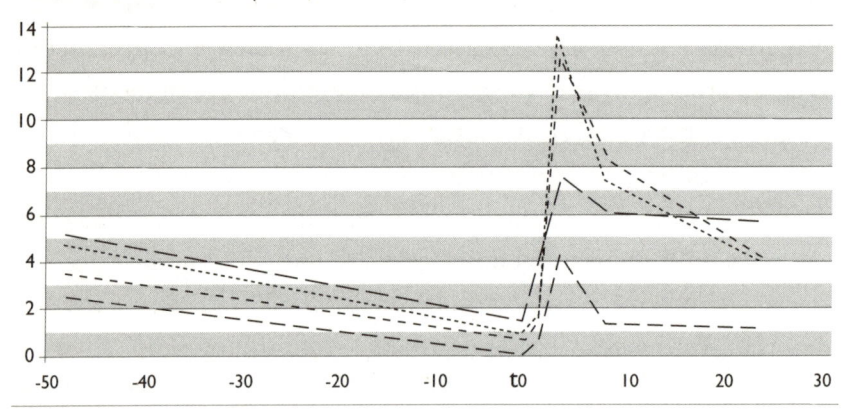

This illustration shows the level of catechin in the blood of 4 volunteers who began following a catechin-free diet 50 hours (-50) before intake of 300ml of red wine. The moment of taking the wine is marked as t0. There are marked peaks at approximately 5 hours after wine intake. In vitro tests showed that 2 µmol/l of catechin produces an 80 percent inhibition of oxidation of human LDL. In 3 of the volunteers' blood the level of catechin coming from 300 ml of red wine still ranges between 4 and 6 after 24 hours. In the blood of the 4th volunteer, catechin dropped to slightly above 1.

Masquelier attended a scientific symposium in Bordeaux for which Edwin Frankel had been invited as a speaker. He not only spoke of his research on the protection of LDL-cholesterol, but also mentioned how phenolic flavonoids had been reported to inhibit substances that play a role in inflammations and thrombosis. By "down-regulating" these substances, "phenolic flavonoids in wine and grapes may reduce the thrombotic tendencies and inflammatory reactions in the body," said Frankel. "We thus believe that the antioxidant activity of phenolic compounds in wine and grapes supports the epidemiological evidence that wine has a cardioprotective effect."

In view of the "new" views on atherosclerosis, the anti-inflammatory and antithrombotic effects combined with their outstanding free radical scavenging capacity and manyfold vascular properties make OPCs a nutrient that interferes with atherosclerosis at practically every essential stage of its development:
- Protection of LDL against free radical oxidation
- Inhibition of inflammatory responses at all stages
- Protection of the vascular wall
- Inhibition of blood clotting

In Bordeaux, Frankel referred to studies published by Masquelier's French colleague Serge Renaud. Dr. Renaud is known for his exploration of OPCs' role in inhibiting the rebound effect, which is the increased clotting of blood after the drinking of alcohol. Renaud researched many aspects of the influence of alcohol and red wine on cardiovascular diseases. He found that the rebound effect does not take place in the presence of OPCs. (See *chapter 31: Red Wine Drinkers Live Happier and Longer.*) In 1990, he studied cholesterol content and plaque build-up in blood samples and tested the blood of three groups of people. One group had received diluted alcohol, a second group had received white wine, and the third group had taken red wine. It was found that only the red wine was able to reduce plaque build-up and increase HDL content. The diluted alcohol and the white wine had no effect.

Certainly, we should not overload the body with fats and we should avoid becoming overweight. But before singling out LDL and condemning it for doing its job, why not look at vitamin C status and boost the elimination of cholesterol by recommending vitamin C and OPCs? Why not protect LDL against free radicals by taking antioxidants? Before blaming eggs and butter, why not consider the condition of the vascular wall? Capillaries love vitamin C and OPCs. Why not help the vascular system to maintain its integrity by recommending vitamin C and OPCs? Why forbid and bluntly suppress a vital body ingredient instead of accepting a more elegant and more efficient solution? Why not inhibit the inflammatory processes that contribute to heart disease? We're no longer dealing with a plumbing problem caused by eating too many eggs or drinking too much milk. Today, we're looking at a combination of free radical damage and inflammatory response. Although the effects of this response are sometimes life threatening, the response itself is perfectly normal. Understanding the body's responses as normal also gives us the chance to prevent them in a perfectly natural way, which is in harmony with the body's systems. What's more, the modern insights that apply to cardiovascular disease also apply to cerebrovascular complications such as stroke and TIA. The efficacy of OPCs is equally relevant.

24 ARTERIOSCLEROSIS AND INFARCTIONS

Plaque formation must not be confused with another form of arteriosclerosis officially called medial calcific sclerosis. (Sclerosis means hardening.) In common language, this is what people call calcification, or hardening of the arteries. It is also a vascular disorder interfering with blood circulation and an equally important factor in the genesis of brain and heart infarction. Whereas the cholesterol sclerosis is actually a lipoprotein problem resulting from a dysfunction in cholesterol-related mechanics, the calcific sclerosis is a genuine tube problem. The vessels harden from deposits of fats and calcium. In both forms of arteriosclerosis, the vessels become rigid and the arteries lose the elasticity required for compensating and absorbing the increase in blood pressure caused by every contraction (beat) of the heart muscle. Therefore, arteriosclerosis is frequently accompanied by high blood pressure. Inversely, high blood pressure can be the cause of or accelerate calcific sclerosis. In the event of excessive pressure the blood injures the cells of the inner lining of the vessels, called the intima.

When a weak spot develops in the inner lining of the vessel, the middle layer, the media, is exposed to the blood. In the absence of the protective inner lining, the body tries to protect the media layer by fixing the "wound" in the intima by filling it with substances taken from the blood. Unfortunately, the substances that are readily available to form an emergency plaster are fats and calcium. By fixing the problem with them, the vessel handles an emergency but creates a long-term problem because this kind of calcification turns the arterial vessels into inflexible bonelike tubes. The afflicted blood vessels are no longer able to let sufficient blood pass because they no long widen with every beat of the heart. So less oxygen and fewer nutrients are going to the tissues, and less carbon dioxide and waste material are being taken away. Tissue with insufficient blood circulation may suffer from infarction. If a calcified vessel breaks, a blood clot forms, and this action will definitely prevent oxygen supply to a certain area. Anoxia, the technical term for insufficient blood supply, is the result of atherosclerosis (plaque) as well as of calcific sclerosis.

Complications of atherosclerosis include:
- Calcification of the atheromatous plaque
- Ulceration or rupture of plaque
- Thrombosis
- Hemorrhage into the plaque

Ulceration of a plaque promotes blood clotting (thrombus formation). Thrombosis occurring over a plaque, rupture of or hemorrhage into a plaque, may eventually result in occlusion of a blood vessel lumen. The blocking of an artery is called an embolism, and it leads to a deficiency of blood in the tissue surrounding the place of the embolism, causing an infarction.

Is lack of oxygen the only event that leads to infarction? Masquelier doesn't think so. In his opinion, another intimately related phenomenon immediately follows a period of anoxia. In Masquelier's opinion, an infarction is the result of anoxia that is accompanied by the arising of an excess of free radicals. In his U.S. Patent 4,698,360, he precisely described these events to support the claim that OPCs work in preventing cardiac or cerebral infarction for an additional reason. According to Masquelier, a lack of oxygen in the tissues of the brain causes psychic and somatic problems, which manifest themselves in their worst form as stroke, TIA, or Alzheimer's disease.

A lack of oxygen produces a chain reaction that eventually leads to the formation of free radicals. An excess of these free radicals cannot be kept in check by the body's own enzymes that scavenge free radicals. The free radicals then attack the cell membranes of the nervous tissue, leading to the phenomenon Masquelier describes as "cerebral involution." It is the progressive degeneration, the shriveling of the organs, that occurs naturally in the process of the aging of the body. Under the influence of an excess of free radicals, the body's involution takes place with increased speed, leading to the premature signs of aging and degeneration. In the brain, involution eventually means infarction (stroke or TIA). To assist the scavenging enzymes, we need to supply the brain with a potent antioxidant, which can halt the cerebral involution and help prevent the infarction. OPCs are the antioxidant of choice because they are bioavailable, extremely potent, and safe.

Almost the same phenomenon can be described for the process that leads to arteriosclerosis and infarction of the cardiac muscle. In many people, vascular aging begins at an early age, depending mostly on lifestyle and diet. Obviously, progressed forms of vascular aging lead to anoxia because the blood can no longer take oxygen to the surrounding tissues. As in a vicious circle, the lack of oxygen generates free radicals, which in turn cause the oxidation of fats, cholesterol, and lipoproteins. In this way, the process of free radical damage, which is the very cause of vascular aging and the ensuing hypoxia, is perpetuated in a self-stimulating process that will eventually also modify the blood-clotting particles, the platelets. Thus, blood clots (thrombi) are formed. The thrombi then close the capillaries and the hypoxia spreads to a larger area. When these events take place in the heart, this anoxious area becomes so large that an infarction occurs when part of the heart muscle dies and changes into scar tissue. To stop free radicals from speeding up this vicious cycle of events, OPCs are recommended as nutritional antioxidant support for the prevention of cardiac or cerebral infarction.

There is a related phenomenon that Masquelier always vividly explains. This has to do with the recovery phase after an infarction or period of hypoxia, when the inadequately supplied tissue begins to receive fresh blood and oxygen. Masquelier points out that the reintroduction of oxygen into previously bloodless or undernourished tissue triggers the release of an excessive number of free radicals. This reintroduction of oxygen into anoxious tissue is called reperfusion. It is also at this moment of reperfusion that the destructive effect of anoxia manifests itself in the cardiac muscle. It is a kind of free radical aftershock that is especially relevant when the heart has been without blood either because of infarction or a bypass or other heart operation. Introducing blood into the heart muscle after a period of anoxia causes an excess of free radicals. This is why the critical moment in heart operations is not during the operation but right after, at the time of reperfusion. A similar process can be observed in prematurely born children when they are accidentally supplied with excessive oxygen in an incubator. The result could be blindness or even death, which means that the oxidative stress in the cells is responsible for the fatal development. In the case of refilling the heart muscle with fresh blood, OPCs are able to keep the additional free radicals at bay, thus averting problems at a critical time.

How is it possible to determine whether somebody suffers from arterial degeneration and is in danger of infarction? High blood pressure is a clear indication. People who smoke, never exercise, are overweight, have high blood pressure must be on guard. This is particularly true if the body sends out signals, such as heartburn, a stabbing pain in the chest, or rapid tiring in the event of exertion. Personal lifestyle significantly affects the risk of cardiac infarction. Stress, lack of exercise, and careless nutrition are important factors in the genesis of this often-fatal disease. Because the changing roles of women in the last century have radically affected their lifestyle, women are increasingly affected by infarction, which used to afflict primarily men. Strangely, a woman has a 50 percent chance of dying from the first heart attack while a man has a 30 percent chance. Of the women who survive their first attack, 38 percent will die within a year. Of the men who survive their first attack, only 25 percent die within a year. A healthy lifestyle that follows these guidelines is essential to minimize the risks:

- Relax when you feel overstressed.
- Do not smoke.
- Avoid excessively fatty food.
- Exercise regularly.
- Take sufficient quantities of OPCs, vitamin C, and other essential nutrients.
- Avoid obesity and overweight.

25 REGULATING INFLAMMATORY AFFAIRS

Before further discussing the role of inflammatory mediators in vascular disease, let me briefly explain what causes the uncomfortable symptoms that are the signs of inflammation we can readily feel: redness, heat, pain, and swelling. The word inflame is well chosen. As discomforting as inflammation may be, it is the body's protective action against intruding harmful substances or particles as well as against injury or other destruction of tissue, which could be the result of an impact, strain, cut, or blow. It is not necessary that an impact or strain is major; a slight impact or repetitive movement, such as handling the mouse of a computer, can cause inflammation. Repetitive strain injury (RSI) is an inflammatory response of the hand and wrist that is feared by many who work on the computer. Tennis elbow is an equally bothersome form of RSI. Whether repetitive and slight or sudden and heavy, strain is always at the origin of inflammation. The great scientist Hans Selye called the ensemble of all these strains stressors.

Stressors aren't only of a mechanical impact nature, resulting in trauma, wound, bruise, or other injury (destruction of tissue). A stressor can also be physical, such as radiation from the sun (sunburn), x-rays, and radioactivity. Those who have ever received radiation treatment against cancer know that burns can be a nasty side effect. The strain can also be of a chemical nature (corrosive chemicals) or of an organic/biologic nature (fur of pets, pollen, and other allergens). In the final analysis, the body's reaction on every stressor is inflammatory, irrespective of whether the stressor is pollen, RSI, a kick against the leg during sports, or a strained ankle.

The universal inflammatory response expresses itself especially by drastically changing the vascular system. Inflammation widens the blood vessels and increases the permeability of the capillaries. The accelerated blood flow causes the symptoms of heat and redness, and the increased permeability leads to the swelling and the pain caused by fluid from the bloodstream flowing into the surrounding tissue. To produce these typically vascular reactions of the inflammatory process, the body uses substances that produce these reactions in the vascular system. They are called vasoactive mediators or go-betweens. One of the predominant and most well-known vasoactive mediators is a substance called histamine.

An inflammation develops to wall off a harmful agent (something dangerous or unwanted that penetrates the body) or injured tissue. Suppose you cut yourself with a dirty knife. Tissue is ruptured and the dirty particles that are on the knife penetrate the body. If you bruise yourself, tissue is destroyed and must be walled off to stop or delay the spreading of dirt, bacteria, or other toxic particles or debris that may appear in the damaged tissue. The "freezing of traffic" is intended to prevent blood and fluid from flowing out of the body and to prevent "rubbish," bacteria, and toxic substances from penetrating deeper into the body. The increased vascular permeability is necessary to allow large clotting agents and cells that scavenge intruding bacteria and other foreign particles (phagocytes) to enter the tissue. The clotting agents fence off the area while the phagocytes scavenge bacteria.

Let's now go back to the cardiovascular problems and imagine that there are no foreign intruders and no injured tissue that needs to be walled off. Yet we find an inflammatory response: a widening of the vascular system and an increase in permeability. This can happen only when the vascular wall itself is the injured tissue and the body recognizes the vascular area as a tissue that needs to be addressed by the inflammatory response. This can be better understood when we consider the vascular stressors discussed in the *chapter 23: The No. 1 Killer, OPCs, and Cholesterol* as the causes of the vascular injury that elicits the inflammatory response. Compare this phenomenon with the symptoms people exhibit when they strain and impair their voices. They try to speak louder to produce the same sound level to make themselves heard and thus strain their voices even more in a self-perpetuating cycle that results in more and more damage.

Likewise, the vascular wall, being the tissue that forms the major instrument in the inflammatory response, when injured itself, enters into a downward spiral of self-healing that worsens instead of improves its condition. Trying to protect itself, it helps destroy itself. The inflammatory mediators such as histamine make the vascular wall respond (widening and increased permeability) even though there is nothing outside the vascular system that needs to be sealed off or destroyed. Nevertheless, the spaces in the surrounding tissue, which is called the interstitium, are exposed to fluid that drains from the bloodstream. This results in edema (swelling) and the streaming out of the larger elements in the blood. Thus, the edema begins to act as a mechanical strain on the tissue and initiates an inflammatory response. The process perpetuates itself. Varicose veins are the most visible and sometimes very painful form of an inflamed vascular system. But the inflammatory process is also an active factor in the more dangerous but invisible cardiovascular and cerebrovascular disorders. The researchers Owens and Hollis were the first to demonstrate a direct relationship between atherosclerosis and histamine. In animals suffering from experimentally induced atherosclerosis, the researchers found an increased production of histamine in the wall of the aorta.

Imagine that the affected part of the vascular system is an intersection of roads. Under too much traffic stress (too many vehicles among which too many aggressive vehicles destroying the roads), the roads deteriorate, get bumpy, and begin to obstruct and damage the already dense traffic, leading to more traffic stress. The intersection then reaches the state of being injured and begins to lose its structure. The roads inflame and respond by widening themselves, which attracts more traffic. At the same time, the fences along the roads begin to show openings through which the traffic swells into the surrounding countryside (interstitium). There, certain traffic particles clot and immobilize the area. The result is a complete standstill that walls off the entire area.

Although histamine plays an important role in the cascade of events that lead to atherosclerosis, histamine is more commonly known as the dreaded mediator of allergic reactions and hypersensitivities. A special type of cell, called the mast cell, plays the key-role in these inflammatory events. The mast cell is a connective tissue cell that contains several inflammatory mediators in their inactive state. When mast cells are triggered, such as by free radicals or during an allergic reaction, they degranulate and release inflammatory mediators such as histamine, serotonin, and bradykinin. During degranulation, mast cells also release an enzyme called hyaluronidase. Its task in the mast cell is to activate histamine during the degranulation. Mast cells are present throughout the body, so at any given time and place they can instantly liberate their agents to initiate the inflammatory response.

Hyaluronidase splits hyaluronic acid, the cement material of connective tissues. Hyaluronic acid is found in the substances that lubricate the joints, in cartilage, blood vessels, skin, and the umbilical cord. Hyaluronidase dissolves hyaluronic acid and thus dissolves connective tissue. It is used by leeches, snakes, and various pathogenic bacteria (tetanus and streptococci) to dissolve connective tissue so that the body can be more easily penetrated and pervaded. Hyaluronidase is also used in medicine to assist easier penetration of drugs that are given through the skin. In intact mast cells, the hyaluronidase is in a dormant and inactive state. However, when the hyaluronidase is activated, it begins to dissolve the "bags" in which the mast cell keeps its histamine. This is the process that is known as degranulation. As long as the histamine is "in the bag," it is not active and does not exert any influence. Once released by the hyaluronidase, the histamine will provoke the inflammatory response, which then leads to all the well-known allergic reactions: redness, heat, pain, and swelling. Mast cells decompose under the influence of free radicals and so-called antibodies. Antibodies detect foreign particles. They are found on the surface of the mast cells. Such antibodies can trigger the degranulation of mast cells when they are being contacted by their foreign counterparts, the allergens. Pollen is such an allergen. When pollen meets with its antibody, the allergen-antibody cluster on the surface of the mast cell makes the cell explode, and the inflammatory response takes its course.

As early as 1948, Masquelier's research had drawn the special attention of his tutor, Professor Tayeau, to the inflammation-inhibiting effect of OPCs. Tayeau pursued this discovery. In 1956, subsequent to an experiment involving OPCs that he had conducted together with G. Lefevre, Tayeau arrived at the following conclusion: "We have demonstrated that leukocyanidol (the name used for OPCs at the time), the extract of peanut skins or pine bark, has antagonistic qualities in relation to hyaluronidase. From this viewpoint, it appears to be one of the most active vitamin P substances. This observation not only explains the effects of leukocyanidol on vascular resistance but also its anti-anaphylactic (anti-allergic) qualities."

Many years later, in 1985, Japanese biologists succeeded in furnishing more evidence that OPCs are antagonistic toward hyaluronidase, in fact that OPCs block the activation of hyaluronidase. The Japanese, who used an activator called 48/80, showed that OPCs interfere in the process at the exact moment when the activator is about to change the dormant form of hyaluronidase into active hyaluronidase. OPCs inhibit the activator because they lock onto the inert hyaluronidase precisely at the point when the activator must deploy its activity. Thus, OPCs keep the hyaluronidase "asleep" and inert. The Japanese scientists concluded: "These results suggest that many tannins may possess anti-inflammatory activity and anti-allergic activity." Although their use of the term "tannins" is not precise, the Japanese confirmed what Masquelier and Tayeau had found in France during the 1950s.

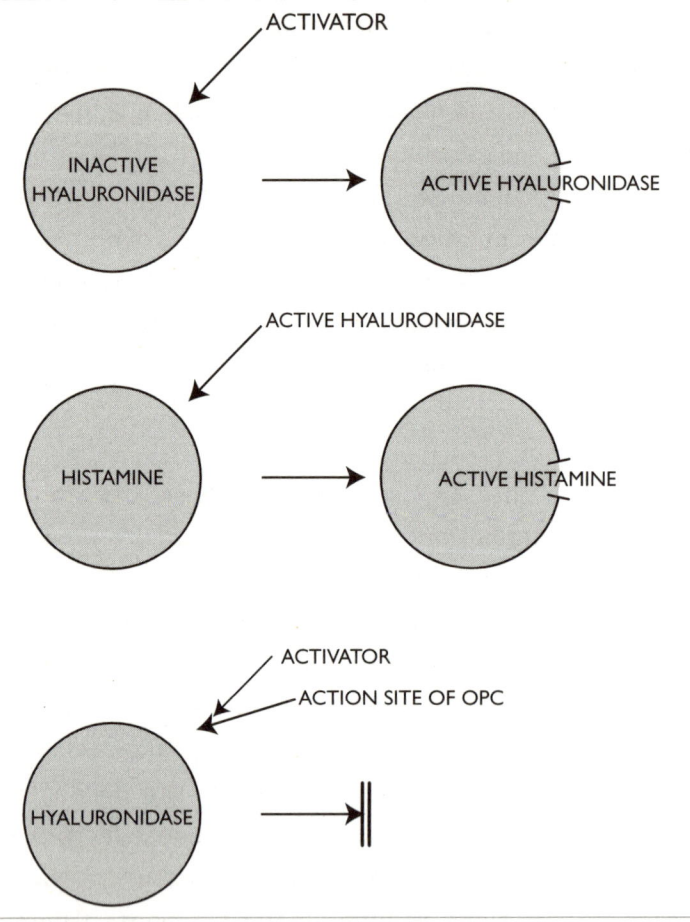

```
                    ACTIVATOR
                       ↓
    ( INACTIVE    ) ——→ ( ACTIVE HYALURONIDASE )
    ( HYALURONIDASE )

                ACTIVE HYALURONIDASE
                       ↓
    ( HISTAMINE ) ——→ ( ACTIVE HISTAMINE )

                    ACTIVATOR
                       ↓  ← ACTION SITE OF OPC
    ( HYALURONIDASE ) ——→||
```

The activator turns inactive hyaluronidase into its active form. Active hyaluronidase activates histamine. OPCs interfere at the site where the activator connects with inactive hyaluronidase, thus preventing the cascade of events.

The sword of free radicals has two very sharp sides that both trigger inflammatory responses. One side destroys normal substances, such as LDL and cholesterol. In their modified forms, these otherwise normal body substances trigger the inflammatory reaction because the body wants to dispose of them. The other side of the free radical sword directly triggers mast cells to degranulate. Masquelier made use of the fact that free radicals can immediately provoke a visible inflammatory reaction in the skin to show how enormously effective that OPCs exert their free radical scavenging and anti-inflammatory powers in the body. To visualize that OPCs act at the point where free radicals and inflammation meet, he put drops of diluted dithranol on two spots on his own lower arm. Dithranol produces a significant quantity of free radicals. When applied to the skin in small diluted dosages, it rapidly causes redness, pain, swelling, and lesions.

To show that OPCs neutralize these free radicals and reduce the inflammation, Masquelier prepared a cream with an OPCs content of 0.5 percent. After the dithranol evaporated, he covered one of the two spots with the OPCs cream. The other spot was left untreated. After 48 hours, a serious inflammation manifested itself on the untreated spot while the area covered with OPCs displayed a hardly visible response without edema. In the context of inflammations, this test deserves our detailed attention because it measures the inflammatory response of living tissue to a free radical. In other words, the test is based on the fact that free radicals can evoke an inflammatory response. There exists a great variety of histamine-releasing and histamine-producing substances, most of which come from outside the body. At the top of this list of substances rank the free radicals, which can immediately induce the release of histamine and evoke a strong inflammatory reaction, as shown in the dithranol test. By performing the dithranol test on his own arm, Masquelier showed how OPCs effectively counter both sides of the free radical sword. While the area treated with OPCs displayed hardly any response to the dithranol, the untreated region showed vehement irritation. Even today, some 13 years after Masquelier put the dithranol on his arm, the lesion of the untreated spot remains visible. It is a reminder of the enormous antioxidant and anti-inflammatory powers of OPCs.

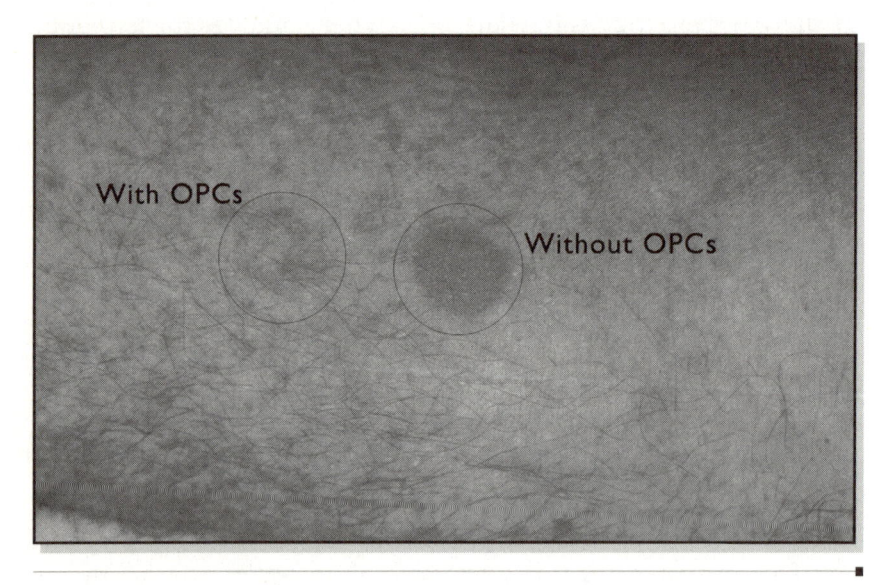

Inflammations, allergic reactions, and sensitivities can flare up anywhere in the body and result in numerous health problems and disorders. The inflammatory process manifests itself in skin diseases such as eczema, nettle rash, psoriasis, sunburn, and itching; in respiratory disorders including bronchitis, asthma, cough, and hay fever; in joint problems such as rheumatism; and in stomach ulcers and after hemorrhages. In all these events, the free radical scavenging effect of OPCs checks oxidative stress, which precedes and accompanies any inflammation.

Incidentally, the anti-inflammatory property of OPCs has been unknowingly used for centuries. As Masquelier explained to me, French people customarily treat an insect bite by picking and crushing the leaves of the three nearest plants and rubbing the mass on the painful spot. This custom is based on the experience that it helps to considerably reduce the redness, pain, and swelling triggered by the insect bite. What could be the explanation of this phenomenon? As unimportant and harmless as it may be, an insect's bite sets in motion the full spectrum of the inflammatory process, leading eventually to the degranulation of mast cells. Chances are relatively high that the leaves of three different plants contain enough OPCs to achieve a histamine-inhibiting effect.

26 HISTAMINE, STOMACH ULCERS, AND ALLERGIES

Histamine is an organic substance that contains nitrogen. Technically speaking, it is an "amine" that is made from the amino acid histidine — hence, hist-amine. Its functions include not only the vascular effects we have discussed above, but also, and most important, the increased stimulation of gastric juices. In the stomach, histamine contributes to heartburn as the stomach responds to improper eating, and this is why antihistamines are often prescribed when antacids are of no avail. Histamine may also accelerate the heart rate and the contraction of smooth muscle tissue. What effect histamine has on which tissue depends on the specificity of cellular receptors of histamine. Briefly, there are two kinds of receptors, called H1 and H2 receptors, that make this difference. Medicines that antagonize histamine reception are divided into two categories: H1 and H2 antagonists. Depending on the health problem, either one of these antagonists is prescribed.

We have seen that histamine can be released from the mast cells. But there is a more fundamental way that histamine is being produced. Chapter 25: *(Regulating Inflammatory Affairs)* described how the researchers Owens and Hollis had increased the production of histamine in the wall of the aorta by way of an experimentally induced atherosclerosis. They managed to normalize the situation by inhibiting the activity of an enzyme called histidine decarboxylase, or more simply, HD. The decarboxylase inhibitor used by Owens and Hollis interferes with a way of histamine production other than by releasing it from the mast cells. The histamine described in the experiment is the histamine that is being produced from histidine by the HD enzyme.

Histidine is an essential amino acid that is especially important for optimal growth of young children. Under the influence of the HD enzyme, histidine becomes histamine. The HD-produced histamine is found not only in the vascular wall but also in the inner lining of the stomach, where an excess may give rise to stomach ulcers and overproduction of gastric juices.

OPCs have been found to inhibit this specific histamine-producing enzyme (HD), which initiates processes as diverse as increasing the permeability of the vascular wall and forming stomach ulcers. OPCs are remarkably antagonistic to histamine because OPCs directly restrain the production of histamine from histidine as well as indirectly restrain the release of histamine from the mast cells. Because OPCs interfere at such a basic level with the production and release of histamine, they cover the field of both the H1 and the H2 antagonists. Evidence of this anti-HD effect was furnished in 1967 by the German scientists H.J. Reimann, W. Lorenz, and their colleagues. In one of their studies, published in 1977, Reimann et al. concluded: "Since histamine was suggested to be involved in the pathogenesis of stress ulcer disease, (+)-catechin, a rather specific inhibitor of histidine decarboxylase from rat stomach, was tested on immobilized rats. It prevented the formation of acute gastric lesions by 80 percent in seven series of experiments for half a year."

In other words, animal tests showed that, with their inflammation-inhibiting properties, catechins could prevent stomach ulcers and stomach hemorrhages *by 80 percent!* Admittedly, the test was done with catechins, but in Masquelier's mind, there is no doubt that his products, which contain catechins and OPCs, are just as effective as the pure catechins. By the way, the catechins used in the German studies were never used in medicine or in nutrition because catechins in their pure form are unstable and slightly toxic to the liver. It is a rather curious phenomenon that catechins, when extracted together with OPCs as in ANTHOGENOL, lose their toxicity and gain stability. In any case, to check his premises, Masquelier repeated Reimann and Lorenz's experiments with OPCs and arrived at the following conclusion: under the influence of MASQUELIER's Original OPCs (containing catechins and OPCs), the production of histamine was reduced by as much as 86 percent. This is a straightforward confirmation of the results obtained by Reimann and Lorenz.

Please note that Reimann and Lorenz produced an increase of gastric acid secretion in a very simple but efficient way. They immobilized the test animals. This shows how the stress of immobilization gives rise to an increase in histamine production, which is a yet-unexposed aspect of the "economy class syndrome." The theory is that immobilization during a long flight, the major part of which passengers are strapped to their seats, triggers a histaminic response that contributes to the deep vein thrombosis (DVT) problems discussed in newspapers lately. In that sense, OPCs' antagonism toward histamine may be a welcome side effect for long-flight passengers.

27 RHEUMATOID ARTHRITIS

The capacity for smooth and unhindered motion of the joints is provided by hyaluronic acid, which is the "glue" in the connective tissue. When hyaluronic acid is dissolved by hyaluronidase, the joint's capacity for motion dissolves. When the required motion is produced nevertheless, the joint's capacity is exerted and the strain that results sets the inflammatory process in motion. This may be a somewhat simple way to illustrate the onset of rheumatism, and in fact, the textbooks tell us that it is doubtful that there is one specific cause. Orthodox medicine speaks of "genetic disorder," of "infection, perhaps from an undefined virus or some other microorganism," of how the body is somehow triggered to produce an "autoimmune response," which means that the body suddenly deals with its own cells and tissues as foreign invaders. Whatever the cause, rheumatism begins with a proliferative inflammation of the synovial fluid. The result is rheumatoid arthritis, an articular ailment that bothers and even cripples millions of people. The disease is so widespread that nearly everybody knows how arthritis causes pain and disables people. In the United States, rheumatic diseases interfere with the daily activities of some 20 million people. Arthritis is the major cause of chronic disability. Curiously enough, three times as many women as men are afflicted by this disease.

Rheumatoid arthritis involves a broader spectrum of conditions than plain arthritis, but the terms rheumatism and arthritis are commonly used interchangeably by doctors and patients. Rheumatism ranges from morning stiffness to complete loss of function, immobilization, and even deformity of the joint. The onset of the inflammation marks the disease when the joints become swollen and painful. Most of the patients suffer from increasingly severe and frequent attacks. The official medical doctrine tells us that there is no cure for arthritis. The only thing that can be done is to alleviate the pain by way of pain killers and anti-inflammatory drugs such as indomethacin and ibuprofen. Gentle exercise may help to keep the joints flexible.

Rheumatoid arthritis is officially classified as a collagen disease that affects and, in some cases, destroys the joints of children as well as elderly people. That arthritis is a collagen disease automatically brings it under the influence of OPCs. Masquelier's American antioxidant patent (U.S. Patent 4,698,360) touches on this disease with the following words: "Similarly, alterations of the synovial fluid by depolymerisation of hyaluronic acid during articular diseases as well as collagen degradation during so-called collagen diseases (for instance, multiple sclerosis) spring from the action of free radicals and so enter into the therapeutic indications of proanthocyanidins."

The synovial fluid is the viscous substance in the joints that makes movement possible. Most of the freely moving joints are synovial joints in that the joints are surrounded by an articular capsule enclosing a space that is lined by the synovial membrane. The membrane holds hyaluronic acid as the fluid that lubricates the joints. The membrane has a capillary network that forms the connection between the synovial space and what is outside the membrane. Through this capillary network, the body is able to maintain the quality of the synovial fluid. In Masquelier's antioxidant patent, he described how free radicals can degrade hyaluronic acid. Obviously, when they are present in excess, free radicals can seep through the synovial membrane's capillary network, reach the synovial fluid, degrade it, and make the joint less flexible. This may then lead to the first stage of arthritis: the inflammation of the synovial membrane. In later stages, the inflammation may destroy cartilage, bone capsule, and parts of the muscle that control the joint. During the final stage of arthritis, fibrous tissue invades the joint, and eventually, this tissue may calcify and completely immobilize the joint.

At this point in the discussion of the inflammation called arthritis, remember how the many facets of OPCs' activity may interfere with many of the aspects that cause and perpetuate arthritis. I speak an optimistic word here, but I do so very cautiously because in the more severe forms of rheumatoid arthritis, much irreparable deformation has already taken place and some flexibility may be lost forever. Yet, OPCs' capacity to scavenge free radicals protects the hyaluronic acid against degradation. Additionally, the inhibition of hyaluronidase protects hyaluronic acid, and OPCs' vascular activity contributes to the maintenance of the capillary network in the synovial membrane. Then, OPCs' inhibition of the various inflammatory mediators (histamine) results in less pain and swelling. Readers who have reached this point of the book will begin to grasp why the effects of MASQUELIER's Original OPCs are so beneficial in diverse situations and conditions.

When it comes to fighting inflammatory symptoms, salicylates (aspirin) are prescribed by the common practitioner in many cases. So-called nonsteroidal anti-inflammatory drugs (NSAIDs) work the same way, and they are prescribed in all the other cases. Some well-known NSAIDs are Diclofenac, ibuprofen, Phenylbutazone, Napoxen, Aleve, Tylenol, and Advil. All these

NSAIDs are taken every day by millions of people to get rid of headaches, pain, inflammations, flu, and symptoms caused by rheumatoid arthritis. Like aspirin, NSAIDs upset the stomach and cause bleeding in 1 to 2 percent of users. Ibuprofen is even more apt to produce stomach problems than aspirin is. Studies performed on large numbers of patients in Great Britain and the United States tell us that 5 to 8 percent of these sometimes-acute stomach bleedings are lethal. A much larger number of people become seriously ill but eventually recover. In The Netherlands, the yearly death rate of rheumatoid patients who take NSAIDs is at 400 to 500. The problem did not escape the attention of the World Health Organization, which warned against the risks of NSAIDs. In an October 2003 report titled "Death by Medicine" written by American researcher Gary Null and his coworkers, NSAIDs are mentioned in the category of "drugs with the worst of side effects."

During 2001, the Dutch NIPO company conducted a survey of 460 rheumatic patients. Sixty percent of them said they suffered from pain every day and took anti-inflammatory drugs to kill or ease the pain. Half of the users said that they had not been able to understand from the product insert that drugs such as NSAIDs could have serious side effects. Thirty percent of the users had no idea that they should stop using NSAIDs in case of stomach problems. Aspirin and other salicylates interfere with the formation of substances that give rise to the inflammatory process, known by many as heat, redness, swelling, and pain. These inflammatory agents are prostaglandins. If aspirin inhibits prostaglandins, why then does the drug cause hemorrhagic lesions and ulcers in the stomach? In the regular textbooks, the prolonged bleeding time associated with aspirin is attributed to its interference with blood clotting, or platelet aggregation. The platelets are the blood particles that help the blood coagulate and clot so a person doesn't bleed to death through a ruptured blood vessel. Salicylates are therefore also prescribed in cases of cardiovascular disease to make the blood thinner so as to keep it flowing through an impaired circulatory system. However, making the blood thinner not only prolongs the bleeding time, but also allows the blood to escape more easily through the capillaries. Although aspirin and other salycilates do not increase capillary fragility, they decrease the relative capillary permeability because the thinner blood seeps through more easily. For this side effect, salicylates were once considered to be "capillarotoxic."

OPCs are extremely "capillaro friendly" and their anti-inflammatory properties are just as strong. In 1980, Hungarian researchers G. Blaszo and M. Gabor tested the influence of OPCs on the size of swelling they induced in rat paws with three inflammatory mediators: serotonin, carrageenan, and prostaglandin E1. In all cases, OPCs reduced the swelling to a "statistically significant extent." Blaszo and Gabor reported that in the case of the carrageenan-induced swelling, OPCs are "about twice as effective as phenylbutazone." Phenylbutazone is an NSAID used in the treatment of gout, rheumatoid arthritis, inflammation of the spine (spondilytis), and other rheumatoid conditions. Like all other NSAIDs, phenylbutazone may cause stomach bleedings and ulcers. Instead of attacking the stomach, OPCs perform their manyfold anti-inflammatory activities while also protecting the stomach by suppressing histamine production.

This book is not intended to give medical advice; the treatment of arthritis is best left to medical doctors and other qualified health professionals. However, OPCs play a safe and essential role in interrupting and reversing the many events that determine the inflammatory process. Also, where the use of Aspirin or NSAIDs is indicated, OPCs help prevent the negative effect these drugs have on relative capillary permeability. In the broader perspective of health, degeneration, and disease, OPCs' antioxidant capacity is probably its most dominant feature. It is the reason OPCs have a remedial effect on the many correlations between the factors that negatively influence our health, leading to such varying diseases as asthma, gastritis, and the inflammation of nerves and joints as well as other inflammatory disorders and allergies.

28 OPCs, THE MIGHTIEST SCAVENGERS OF FREE RADICALS

Hardly any other nutritional substance exerts such significant and immediate effects in so many seemingly unrelated disorders. The fact that OPCs are active in so many conditions may sound inconceivable. Those whose email boxes are full of spam about miracle drugs, cure-alls, and products that reverse aging may by now have developed a healthy skepticism, but MASQUELIER's Original OPCs product is far removed from the snake oil category of claptrap cure-alls. The explanation for this amazing phenomenon is obvious, and is certainly not a surprise to anyone who has read this far. OPCs manifest enormously strong and varied potential at a number of key intersections in the body, multiplying the beneficial effects in a great number of conditions. The following highlights an important intersection that makes OPCs of extreme relevance to the entire body.

The human body resembles a harlequin dress. It is patched up from 36 organs, 36 different forms of life, each of which functions in a unique manner. The organs complement each other's function and deliver their individual contribution to the functioning of the whole body. The cells that make up the organs can function only when their membranes are fully intact. Each cell's membrane is a double-layered, flexible, and very sensitive film of phospholipids. The lipid part of the phospholipids consists of the membrane's oils, the PUFAs. PUFAs are prone to oxidation by free radicals, which make the cell's membrane less flexible. Oxidized membranes starve and suffocate the cell.

The oxidation of lipids in the cells plays a dominant role in their aging. Consequently, it is also the root of tissue aging and the cause of the aging of the organs and of the whole body. In fact, the oxidation of unsaturated oils causes the onset of numerous different, seemingly unrelated disorders in various parts of the body. How the aging process expresses itself depends on people's individual genetic, psychological, and physiological make-up and on environmental and nutritional circumstances. But without exaggeration, it can be claimed that free radicals are the common factor in most degenerative diseases because they attack cell membranes in every organ. Therefore, the prevention of such unchecked oxidation processes is of outstanding importance. As a tremendously potent antioxidant, OPCs successfully fight against cell aging and disease on numerous levels.

Not too long ago, oxygen was considered to be always healthy and good, with no side effects. People went to the mountains or the sea to stock up on fresh oxygen, which was regarded as equivalent to life. It is true that without oxygen, we would not exist. It is indispensable for our metabolism and fulfills a number of vital functions in our organisms. Oxygen burns the fuel that provides the energy that keeps the body's temperature at 98.6 degrees (37°C). Oxygen assists the body's immune system to eliminate pathogenic bacteria and other intruders. It was only during the early 1980s that the damaging properties of oxygen burst into public awareness. Today, hardly anybody exists who hasn't heard of free radicals. Many people try to protect themselves against free radicals' dangerous oxidative attacks by taking antioxidants. Oxygen is now regarded as a Janus-faced substance, with a good side and a very dangerous one. It acts in a life-giving as well as in a destructive manner. The latter is the case when oxygen turns "radical."

What exactly are oxygen free radicals? They are molecules that can exert tremendous chemical activity with slight modifications in their structure. The oxygen that we inhale is a balanced molecule. However, when the balance is tipped, the "tipped" oxygen molecule and certain unstable combinations of oxygen and hydrogen gain enormously in oxidative power. One electron or one hydrogen can make that crucial difference. Oxygen-free radicals are unstable oxygen molecules that have either one electron too many or one too few. Thus, in a radical manner, they obsessively try to connect with other substances to violently rob them of what they need or get rid of what they have in excess to restore their own stability. This explains their highly reactive character. Free radicals are agents that amplify physical and chemical properties, both beneficial ones and damaging ones. They have a positive effect if they stimulate the defense cells of the immune system to fight pathogenic organisms.

The process of free radical formation is analogous to the game of billiards. Free radicals come into existence when a molecule is given an energetic shock, similar to the collision of two billiard balls. If one ball touches another one with sufficient energy, it changes the state of the touched ball from an immobile into a mobile condition. The oxygen molecule behaves like the ball that was pushed. It in turn pushes another molecule, possibly with even more power. The energy with which it was charged is not lost but triggers a chain reaction. A free radical can be generated by coincidental influences such as solar or cosmic rays, and it may then itself produce a new free radical, and so on. This snowball effect is the reason free radicals are extremely dangerous in the body.

In another analogy, imagine a flowerpot placed on a balcony railing on the fifth floor of a building. As long as the pot stays put, it is a harmless decoration and a pleasant sight to the occupants. But if it is pushed over the railing, it becomes life threatening. The flowerpot has a mass that contains the potential energy that could be unleashed by a seemingly trivial event.

You can perform a simple experiment to observe the formation of free radicals. Spread out a page of a newspaper on a table outside in the sunshine. Put a plate in the middle of the newspaper. Wait three hours to remove the plate, and what do you find? The area covered by the plate is the original color of the newspaper. The part that was exposed to the sun has turned yellow because the combination of sun and oxygen rapidly accelerated the aging of the newspaper. This experiment shows that the sun is one of the main origins of free radicals. It speeds up the aging process in everything it shines on, including your skin, the leaves of plants, the paint on your house, the tires of your car. It is a paradox. Without sunshine there would be no life on this planet. At the same time, the sun is the main exogenous source of premature aging. Taking OPCs and other antioxidants helps offset the negative side of these paradoxes of life on earth.

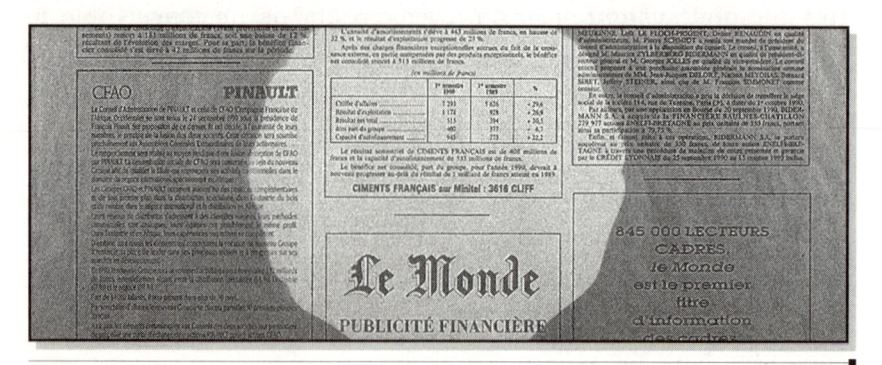

Because of the uncontrollably aggressive nature of oxygen radicals, it was unimaginable for a long time that they could exist at all in cellular tissues. Free radicals were known and used only in the chemical industry — for example, in plastic production. Nobody had thought that free radicals could exist in the human body. In 1969, however, the Americans J. Fridovich and J.M. MacCord succeeded in proving that radical oxygen has a place in cellular biochemistry. This discovery met with great response in medicine and biology. Since then, many antioxidant drugs and dietary supplements have been developed to counter the negative effects of these free radicals, and many nutrients have undergone tests to check their antioxidative capacity.

The effect of free radicals in our body is feared primarily because they may trigger chronic and degenerative diseases such as cardiovascular disorders, heart disease, cerebrovascular disorders, stroke, TIA, cancer, rheumatism, diabetes, hepatitis, renal failure, inflammations, allergies, high blood pressure, Down's syndrome, cataracts, Parkinson's and Alzheimer's diseases, immune deficiency, and exhaustion. Most of these chronic degenerative symptoms begin to manifest themselves after an individual turns 40 years of age. At midlife, the power of the immune system begins to weaken and is no longer able to provide sufficient resistance against free radicals in the body. The balance shifts in favor of the free radicals, thus enabling them to perform their destructive attack on body tissue and blood vessels in less and less controllable ways. Even though we do not notice this process until we see symptoms appear, free radicals constantly alter and/or damage the cell membranes, DNA and genes, lipids, and proteins. In this way, they negatively influence the condition of all the cells in the body.

Stress presents a favorable climate for free radicals. They can be produced as a result of stress, or conversely, they can generate stress themselves. An individual suffering from stress must have been in a rather poor biological condition to begin with. If stress occurs before the free radicals are produced, they develop as a consequence of the weakened organism. If, on the other hand, the free radicals themselves cause stress, the organism must have been in a poor and defenseless state from the start. In the case of acquired immune deficiency syndrome (AIDS), there is, for example, oxidative stress, which plays a major role in the symptoms related to this horrid condition.

The influence of stress is relevant not only to people who suffer from degenerative diseases, but also to healthy people who happily indulge in sports. It is undeniably true that the benefits of intense physical activity, exercise, and recreational sports far outweigh the potential disadvantages of injuries and free radical production. As reported during August 2003 by the Dutch TNO research institute, half an hour of physical activity every day reduces the chance of colon cancer by 40 percent. Even the risk of breast cancer is considerably reduced for those who exercise daily. Unfortunately, the more intensely and seriously one practices sports and exercise, the more one creates free radical stress in the body. Injuries always imply the release of free radicals. In addition, exercise involves an increase of the use of oxygen because more energy is needed and produced. To facilitate the intensifying energy production requires more radicals, and the risk that some of them will "fall by the wayside" increases. However, the solution is quite simple. Those who want to fully enjoy all the benefits of physical activity by limiting its free radical side effect must supplement their diet with antioxidants such as OPCs and the vitamins C and E. Refer also to the results of the sports injuries clinical trial mentioned in *chapter 19: New Clinical Highlights*. Apart from scavenging free radicals, OPCs shorten the healing time in case of injury.

Free radicals may be of other than oxygen origin. Cigarette smoke, nuclear radiation, exhaust fumes, the ultraviolet rays of the sun, nitrite and/or nitrate residues in food, medicines, and environmental pollutants can all behave as or cause free radicals. Nevertheless, oxygen plays the dominant role in the field of free radicals because the body uses a comparatively large amount of oxygen to produce energy. The problem is that the way the body uses oxygen differs from the way oxygen is used for burning other substances such as wood, oil, or natural gas. Such direct use of pure oxygen would create enormous damage if it took place in the body. To avoid such harm, the production of energy in the body takes place by way of a gradual, step-by-step process. Oxygen is cautiously transformed into water via various steps that must involve an oxygen radical (superoxide) and radical combinations of oxygen and hydrogen (hydrogen peroxide and hydroxyl). These intermediary radicals are necessary to make it possible to release energy in a gentle way. Even if we lived in a stress-free and perfectly clean environment, the body would need to produce oxygen free radicals to stay alive.

As gently as this energy production may take place, it does involve oxygen and oxygen-hydrogen free radicals. It is a paradox against which the body defends itself by producing enzymes that make these radicals harmless: superoxide dismutase (SOD), catalase, and glutathion peroxydase. However, as people age, this wall of enzymatic protection begins to show holes, and tissues become exposed to free radicals. Unfortunately, when taken as ingredients in our food or as dietary supplements, SOD, catalase, and glutathion are destroyed in the stomach and in the intestinal tract, so they cannot reach the tissues and cells intact. We can try to boost internal production of free radical scavenging enzymes, for instance by taking selenium, which is a constituent of glutathion peroxydase. The safest way, however, is to support the antioxidative enzymes by supplementing the diet with antioxidants such as OPCs and vitamins C and E.

The sum of the free radicals that escape the scavenging enzymes and the free radicals that are of external origin equals the cause of the dramatic increase in so-called civilization diseases. The air we breathe and the food we eat contain traces of hundreds if not thousands of chemical substances our bodies have not encountered before. This is especially so in the urban and industrial "civilized" areas of the world where people are exposed to exhaust fumes, cigarette smoke, preservatives, flavor enhancers, synthetic sweeteners, food additives, pesticides, fertilizers, heavy metals, and more. Poisonous and unknown substances test the limits of our immune systems, which are frequently depleted by an excess of free radicals and cannot prevent the body from falling ill.

I don't want to frighten the reader or sound like an anti-industry fanatic; I am not against industrial ways of food production. However, industrial processing of food does have serious side effects, especially in that it denaturizes food. People who consume nothing else are at risk because processed food often lacks the essential vitamins and enzymes found in fresh food. Pointing a finger at the food industry is a useless exercise in that it does not relieve people from their personal responsibilities. Lawyers attack McDonald's on behalf of people who could not control their appetite. Antiglobalism activists attack McDonald's for preparing the hamburgers that millions of people are willing to devour. Lawyers and activists gain the desired media attention, but it doesn't make one obese child less obese. It also doesn't change one iota of the fact that many of us do in our kitchens what the food industry does in its factories: denature food by cooking it.

One of the food industry's greatest problems is to stop products from going rancid. When fat turns rancid, the process starts at the surface where oxygen comes in contact with the fat. The oxygen does not attack in its usual form: regular O_2. Rather, the process is slowed down by cold and darkness whereas it is accelerated by heat and light. Thus it may be assumed that an initial input of energy (through heat or light) is required to set rancidity in motion. This energetic push kicks off free radical formation the way one billiard ball puts the other in motion. Without immediate intervention, the entire fat content in a jar will turn rancid. Free radical oxidation progresses fast, and once it is put into motion, it does not stop. The life span of free radicals is about a microsecond, and despite this flashy transience, they always manage to produce more free radicals before they succumb.

Can we liken the process that occurs when fat turns rancid to aging of the human organism? Etymologically and figuratively, the term "turn rancid" (French: rancir) means aging by losing one's properties. In this case, language professors and biochemists are in agreement. Our organism abundantly offers free

235

radicals their favorite targets: PUFAs. Can the body turn rancid? Yes, it can, and the rancidity will result in the many degenerative diseases that plague us. The problem is that we cannot see and smell the processes in the body as we do when we open a bottle of oil or a jar with old butter. We can only observe the results of the body's rancidity when the degenerative symptoms appear. The problem is also that we cannot protect our body from going rancid by sealing it off from oxygen and putting it in the refrigerator, as we do with oils and butter.

Rancidity is a word we would not normally use to describe the effects of free radicals on proteins. Nevertheless, connective tissue (collagen and elastin) are just as much under attack as fats and oils. Free radicals disturb the regular formation of collagen and interfere with the condition of the existing collagen. The result is irregular, brittle collagen that easily breaks. Thus, the aging process is accelerated and manifests itself in the loss of suppleness, resilience, and flexibility, which in turn lead to lack of motion and mobility. This kind of collagen degradation affects not only our oh-so-visible external appearance (sagging skin, wrinkles) but also our blood circulation, capillaries, arteries, veins, and lymphatic vessels — in fact, it affects every organ in the body because we find collagen everywhere. Another very delicate structure is DNA, the "hardware" on which our genetic program is stored. DNA consists of highly complex compounds called nucleic acids. These nucleic acids are easily disturbed by free radicals. Thus, free radicals are able to cause damage to DNA and thus compromise the functions of a cell, not in the least the function to produce an exact replica of the original healthy cell. *Chapter 30: Tumor Prevention and Cancer* covers the topic in more detail. Rancid DNA is regarded as one of the causes of cancer.

Also, numerous precarcinogenic molecules, harmless substances that have not yet assumed carcinogenic properties, turn dangerous under the influence of radicals and can clear the path for tumor development.

As a special category, some substances are not so much the target of free radicals but can be excreted by the body only by way of being converted into free radicals. These can be normal substances that are introduced into the body from outside through medication or food and cannot be excreted by the organism in the usual manner. They can be compared with poor fuel, such as moist wood, that can be ignited only through the addition of very dry wood (free radicals). An example of such substances is the synthesized organic molecules frequently employed in medical treatment. Another example is alcohol, which, if excessively consumed, generates an increased number of free radicals that act as alcohol-scavengers in the body cells. Alcohol belongs to the group of substances that require radical disposal. If it is consumed in moderate quantities, the liver puts an enzyme into action to perform the cleansing procedure. In the event of excessive alcohol consumption, this enzyme alone is no longer able to remove all the alcohol, and free radicals are called upon to rid the body of the excess. The majority of disorders and organic alterations attributed to alcohol are actually the consequence of the devastating effects of the free radicals that must dispose of the alcohol rather than of the alcohol itself.

29 SURVIVING THE RADICAL COMBAT ZONE

You may wonder how humans have managed to survive in this free radical combat zone. Fortunately, we have defenses to protect us against free radicals. Nature itself has taken several intelligent precautionary measures that enable us to live with the dangerous side of oxygen. First, it has endowed the body with the capacity to make enzymes that are capable of neutralizing free radicals: superoxide dismutase (SOD), catalase, and glutathione peroxydase. As we age, the body's capacity to produce these enzymes — and enzymes in general — weakens. Therefore, older people have less enzymatic protection than young ones, and eventually, the enzymatic wall of protection weathers and becomes less able to fulfill its task.

Hundreds of millions of years ago, life on this planet developed without oxygen. In those days, the first forms of life were bacteria, which were able to exist in the absence of oxygen. These anaerobic bacteria still exist today. They are still able to survive without oxygen. During evolution, in fact, they have come to fear oxygen as the toxic substance that will destroy them. When plants appeared on earth, production of oxygen began, and as a consequence, life forms gradually evolved that used oxygen to produce energy. Doing so, they developed the enzymatic system that today still protects our cells against the negative side effects of oxygen.

Nature has also endowed certain nutrients called antioxidants with the capacity to scavenge free radicals. Antioxidants complement the enzymatic defense system and help fight against oxidative stress. There is only one essential prerequisite humans must fulfill: make sure that the food they consume contains a sufficient amount of them. Among the most important antioxidants are OPCs, vitamin E (tocopherol), vitamin C (ascorbic acid), beta carotene, and the trace element selenium, which forms part of the scavenging enzyme glutathione peroxydase. In concert, food-borne antioxidants and free radical scavenging enzymes should help people get through the combat zone unscathed. A healthy diet containing low levels of oxidants and high levels of antioxidants is essential. In essence, such a diet should be composed of fresh ripe fruits, all vegetables that can be eaten uncooked, cereals (especially wheat and germs), whole-grain bread, fish, unprocessed first-pressing vegetable oils, nuts, beans, and sprouts. Butter, eggs, cooked vegetables, and meat can be eaten in moderation.

Even when you conscientiously strive for a healthy and balanced diet, a sufficient supply of antioxidants is not always guaranteed. This is not because there's something wrong with your dietary habits but because today's world imposes oxidative stress on your body. Because you may need more antioxidants than your diet can give you, you may wish to use food supplements containing complementary amounts of isolated, pure antioxidants. Such isolated antioxidants should fulfill the following set of requirements:

- They must be safe, even when taken over a lifetime.
- Their efficacy must be proven *in vitro* (in the laboratory) as well as *in vivo* (in the living organism).
- They must be potent so that you can take them in convenient daily dosages not exceeding several hundreds of milligrams.
- They must be readily bioavailable and biocompatible.

There are many substances that have antioxidant properties but have no place in the human organism because they are toxic or not bioavailable. One example is the oldest antioxidant used in food conservation: sulfur. Sulfur's antioxidant properties are the reason wine casks are sulfurized. Sulfur prevents the wine from oxidizing. It also effectively kills bacteria and parasites. Establishing the antioxidant properties of such products is fine, but it doesn't help us combat the aging of our tissues and cells. The use of salts of sulfur to preserve the freshness of salads, fruits, vegetables, wine, and beer has been seriously curtailed because sulfur can cause severe allergic reactions, especially in people suffering from asthma.

Of all the antioxidants that have been researched so far, OPCs royally fulfill the criteria set for human use. When Masquelier furnished proof of OPCs' antioxidative capacity in 1985, the safety, efficacy, and bioavailability of OPCs had been well established. But now it also came out that OPCs' efficacy as a scavenger of free radicals was far superior to that of other substances that were subjected to the same testing. This discovery is the absolute highlight of Masquelier's work. In 1948, he had succeeded in isolating OPCs. He had recognized and researched the vasoprotective properties of OPCs. During the decades that followed, OPCs were submitted to numerous tests. They became the active ingredient in various medicines. In 1965, Masquelier pointed out in one of his patents that disease might be the consequence of an OPCs deficiency, which confirmed the idea that OPCs are vitamin P. Then, in 1985, he discovered OPCs' superior antioxidant properties. Finally, as an antioxidative phytonutrient, OPCs became the principal ingredient in the ANTHOGENOL (MASQUELIER's Original OPCs) and MASQUELIER's French Pine Bark Complex products.

The free radical scavenging properties of a substance can be demonstrated in many ways. In 1985, Masquelier chose a test that is performed with a substance called nitroblue tetrazolium (NBT). The NBT-test makes use of the fact that under the influence of oxygen radicals, the otherwise colorless NBT turns blue. In the test set-up, enzymes that produce oxygen radicals are used to stimulate the blue pigmentation. The addition of an

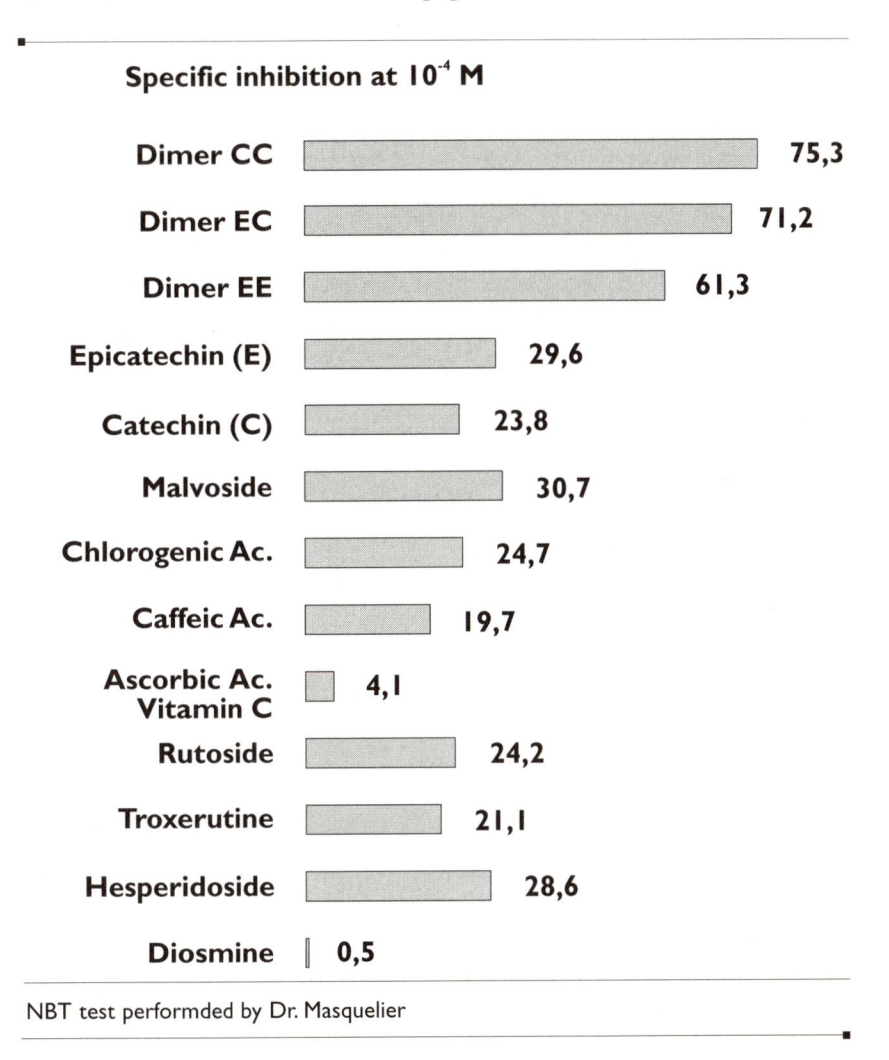

Specific inhibition at 10^{-4} M

Dimer CC	75,3
Dimer EC	71,2
Dimer EE	61,3
Epicatechin (E)	29,6
Catechin (C)	23,8
Malvoside	30,7
Chlorogenic Ac.	24,7
Caffeic Ac.	19,7
Ascorbic Ac. Vitamin C	4,1
Rutoside	24,2
Troxerutine	21,1
Hesperidoside	28,6
Diosmine	0,5

NBT test performded by Dr. Masquelier

antioxidant reduces the coloration. In 1984 and 1985, Masquelier conducted two NBT tests. On a scale of 0 (no effect) to 100 (blue coloring completely countered), the various substances he tested scored as follows. OPCs, of which three different dimers with slightly different molecular structures were tested, scored between 61.3 and 75.3 percent. They were followed at a significant distance by catechin monomers that ranged from 23.8 to 29.6 percent. The bioflavonoids also displayed an antioxidant strength of about a quarter, with hesperoside scoring 28.6 percent, rutoside 24.2 percent, and troxerutin 21.1 percent. Vitamin C, which hitherto had been considered one of the strongest antioxidants, ranked last at only 4.1 percent efficacy. The table that follows also shows chlorogenic acid, a compound that has received attention recently as a sunblock, slimming agent, and antioxidant. Compared with OPCs, chlorogenic acid is a weak antioxidant scoring 24.7 percent on the scale of 0 to 100.

During the second NBT test, Masquelier proceeded in a different manner to crosscheck the previous results. He calculat-

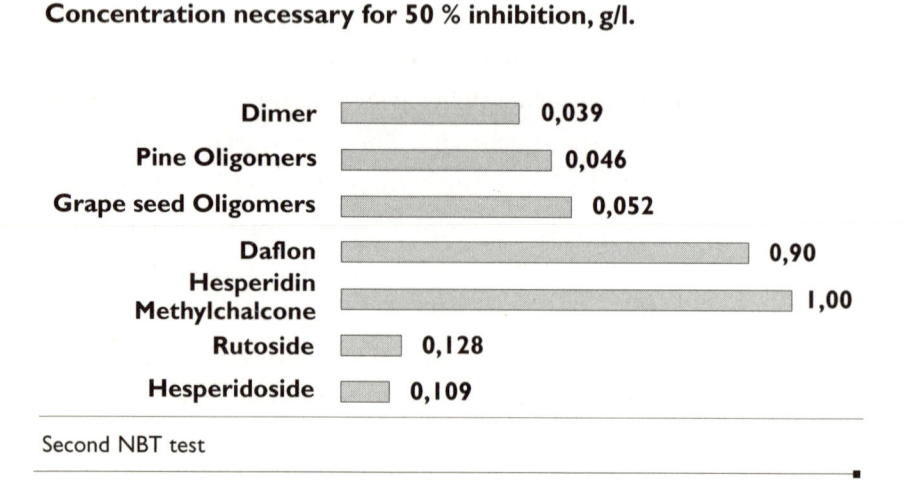

Concentration necessary for 50 % inhibition, g/l.

Dimer	0,039
Pine Oligomers	0,046
Grape seed Oligomers	0,052
Daflon	0,90
Hesperidin Methylchalcone	1,00
Rutoside	0,128
Hesperidoside	0,109

Second NBT test

ed and then tested the quantity of a substance needed to obtain exactly a 50 percent inhibition of the blue coloring. The substance of which the lowest quantity is required to obtain 50 percent inhibition is the best antioxidant. The results of this examination confirmed the first NBT test. ANTHOGENOL (MASQUELIER's Original OPCs) and Masquelier's French Pine Bark Complex came out as the best performing. The two products came out at values of 0.046 and 0.052 respectively. The citroflavonoid daflon recorded 0.90, and the bioflavonoid hesperidin scored 1.0.

These were fabulous results, which were amazing even to Masquelier. He had suspected that OPCs might be a strong free radical scavenger, but the fact that they turned out 18.4 times as strong as vitamin C was almost incredible considering the fact that the antioxidant efficacy of vitamin C was generally known and appreciated. Discovering a substance is one thing, but learning that the discovered substance scores almost 20 times better than vitamin C as an antioxidant was worth celebrating! Better news was still to come. A Japanese study done in 1987 at the University of Nagasaki by Shinji Ushida and colleagues showed that the antioxidant capacity of OPCs is 50 times stronger than that of vitamin E, which is also considered an outstanding antioxidant! Of course, Masquelier was delighted that his results were confirmed by other scientists. There was unambiguous and clear evidence that OPCs are the strongest antioxidant known so far. A comparative study performed by an American laboratory (ESA Laboratories) in 1997 confirmed that many years after Masquelier's discovery of OPCs' antioxidant properties, MASQUELIER's Original OPCs and MASQUELIER's French Pine Bark Complex were still unmatched in antioxidant performance.

Being aware of the importance of his invention, Masquelier laid his findings down in a patent application, which he filed on April 9, 1985, in the United States. On October 6, 1987, the U.S. Patent and Trademark Office granted Masquelier the patent No. 4,698,360. According to what has become known as the '360 patent, OPCs provide "a method for preventing and fighting the harmful biological effects of free radicals in the organism of warm-blooded animals and more especially in human beings; namely cerebral involution, hypoxia following atherosclerosis, cardiac or cerebral infarction, tumor promotion, inflammation, ischemia, alterations of the synovial liquid, and collagen degradation, among others."

According to Masquelier, "Until then, nobody believed that OPCs were an effective agent against free radicals. But you see, to me it was a logical thing since I had always been considering OPCs as an antioxidant from the beginning of my research. I have talked to you about the peanut, where OPCs protect the oily substances against rancidity. I've talked to you about the bark of the pine tree, where OPCs protect the terpenes. And I have spoken about the grape seeds, where OPCs protect the very fragile oils. In each of these cases, we find OPCs at the exterior in a pellicle, a bark, an envelope, protecting the oxidizable substances on the inside."

Always remember that the value of antioxidants such as OPCs can be measured and truly appreciated only in light of the amount of oxidative stress. In his '360 patent, Masquelier carefully explains this aspect as follows: "The radical scavenging effect (of OPCs) does not overcome aging, which is a biological process programmed in the genes, but it may prevent, attenuate, or inhibit different harmful effects of aging caused by an *excess of free radicals.*" We emphasize the word "excess" to explain that it is a matter of adding up all the factors of oxidative stress and then determining whether an excess remains when the body's scavenging enzymes and food-borne antioxidants have been depleted doing their work. When you see things from this perspective, you can place the word "free" in free radicals in a perspective that may make a biochemist frown but that may help you understand things. Think of a *free* radical as a radical that goes around undetected, unchecked, and unrestricted. It is free in that it escapes the body's enzymatic defense mechanisms or food-borne antioxidants. The free radicals are the ones that exist in excess of the purifying mechanisms. That's why they are the ones that must have our attention. They are like convicted criminals who are not behind bars — "free" criminals.

In the first claim that Masquelier makes in the '360 patent, he alludes again to the fact that we are concerned with balancing the oxidative and the anti-oxidative forces. Discussing "cerebral involution troubles in aged people," the inventor explains: "With aged people, hypoxia of the tissues causes psychic and somatic troubles which are manifested in particular by Alzheimer's illness. Hypoxia produces an accumulation of reduced substrates (flavins, coenzymes, etc.), whose auto-oxidation generates free radicals. These latter, *if they go beyond the limits of the normal purifying mechanisms which bring enzymes into play,* damage the cellular walls of the nervous tissue and lead to cerebral involution. To prevent the failure which is always possible of the purifying enzymes, it is then indicated to administer a medicament with radical scavenger effect, provided that it is bioavailable. Proanthocyanidins fulfill the conditions." (The emphasis is mine.)

Extending the effects of free radicals from the brain to the cardiovascular system, Masquelier discusses in his second claim how OPCs can counter the effects of hypoxia caused by atherosclerosis. "The atheromatous illness, which does not occur only in old people, well represents, however, the picture of vascular aging and causes progressive hypoxia of the adjacent tissues. This hypoxia, through the free radicals which it generates, increases the lipid peroxidation, itself implied in the pathogenesis of atherosclerosis. Through an identical mechanism, a modification of the platelet functions promoted by the free radicals causes the formation of thrombi, which are the basis of infarction. Proanthocyanidins are therefore indicated both for preventing the harmful effects of hypoxia following atheromatosis and also as agents for preventing cardiac or cerebral infarction."

OPCs work in many seemingly unrelated conditions because they scavenge an excess of free radicals. This is why the number of claims made by Masquelier could have been endless. Any condition resulting from the direct or indirect action of free (meaning excess) radicals responds to OPCs. In Masquelier's words, some of which I have again emphasized: "The free radicals, *when they escape from the biological and nutritional systems provided for eliminating them*, attack first of all the fragile architecture of the membrane. The alterations thus produced accelerate cellular aging, characterized by the collapse of the primordial functions of the membrane system. Inflammation and ischemia bring such mechanisms into play, and so treatment by proanthocyanidins is indicated. Similarly, alterations of the synovial liquid by depolymerization of hyaluronic acid during articular diseases as well as collagen degradation during so-called collagen diseases (for instance, multiple sclerosis) spring from the action of free radicals and so enter into the therapeutic indications of proanthocyanidins."

This is why Masquelier also makes the free radical claim for cancer. "Oxygen radicals," so claims Masquelier, "play an essential role in the tumour promotion process (in the promotion stage of carcinogenesis). Superoxide dismutase, tried as a protector, is a failure in this field for it is destroyed by the digestive enzymes and in any case does not clear the cellular barrier very well (KENSLER, T.W. et coll., SCIENCE, 1983, 221, 75-77). Similarly, lipid peroxidation is implied in the transformation of the aromatic hydrocarbons into carcinogens (in the metabolism of polycyclic aromatic hydrocarbon derivatives to ultimate carcinogens) (DIX, T.A., MARNETT, L.J., SCIENCE, 1983, 221, 77-79). By their high radical scavenging effect combined with their rapid diffusion in the connective tissue, proanthocyanidins are therefore indicated as protectors against risks of cancerization by chemical or physical (ionizing radiations) or biological (oncogens) agents."

30 TUMOR PREVENTION AND CANCER

Thirty years ago, Masquelier cooperated with the cancer prevention center in Bordeaux, the Centre anticancéreux Professeur Bergonié, a private institution involved in cancer diagnosis and research. At the time, researchers performed animal experiments using MASQUELIER's Original OPCs. These tests showed positive results that Masquelier, however, did not want to have published at the time. Cancer is too terrible a disease to precipitously feed what he then considered to be preliminary results to the media. The results certainly had a scientific value, but not being an oncologist, Masquelier felt that this application field of OPCs deserved more thorough examination and consideration. Later, especially in light of his discovery of OPCs' free radical scavenging effect, he began to better understand the role that OPCs could play in putting the brakes on the tumor-promotion process. He now feels more comfortable releasing the information he held back long ago. But being the prudent scientist he is, Masquelier warns readers to study his words very carefully and not jump to conclusions too hastily.

The free radical connection between OPCs and the cancer process is uncontroversial. In the genesis and initial development of tumors, free oxygen radicals play a major role. That's how Masquelier stated it in the '360 patent. Because of their unique free radical scavenging effect, OPCs inhibit the tumor promotion process. Does this mean that OPCs cure cancer? No! The treatment of cancer requires a lot more than taking OPCs. When people talk of cancer, they invariably refer to the last stage, when the degenerative process has finally erupted in a tumor, which disables or destroys the structure and function of one or more organs. Curing cancer at this late stage is not easy, and it would be a serious mistake to think that OPCs all by themselves could normalize such a completely derailed condition.

Whether patients choose alternative treatment, regular treatment, or a combination of both is up to them. It is not within the scope of this book to comment on or give advice as to what to do if cancer is diagnosed. Whatever the choice, treatment of what people call cancer always implies a combination of measures. No single substance or intervention can put final-stage cancer in remission. What Masquelier claimed in his '360 patent regarding cancer is something entirely different. OPCs will influence the tumor-promotion process because OPCs scavenge various forms of free radicals. OPCs are indicated as protectors against chemical, physical, or biological influences that increase the risk of developing cancer.

Are OPCs useless in the treatment of cancer? No, certainly not. Cancer spreads more quickly and metastases (i.e., the migration of tumor cells into still healthy tissue) develop with greater frequency when the organism is exhausted or stressed. In such a situation, OPCs will contribute to the overall condition of the patient and will help the body to boost resistance against cancer cells. Also, some types of cancer migrate to other areas of the body by forming metastases in unrelated organs. Cancer cells migrate by dissolving the substance that surrounds the cells of yet unaffected tissues. To penetrate healthy tissue, the cancer cells produce protein-splitting enzymes, proteases, which dissolve the substance that gives structure to the tissue. We know that OPCs protect water-soluble proteins in the blood serum against protease. Breast cancer is a type of cancer that spreads through metastases; that is, through the production of protease. Thus, it seems only logical for a patient to take OPCs as soon as breast cancer has been diagnosed to try to inhibit the migration of cancer cells to tissue that is still healthy.

As mentioned at the beginning of this chapter, in Bordeaux many years ago, Masquelier examined various stages of implanted tumors in mice. The animals were divided into three lots, each of which received catechins, OPCs, or tannins. The examinations were performed in two laboratories of the Bergonié Institute, which has facilities in Bordeaux and in Nantes. Masquelier performed the tests with one of his colleagues who had specialized in the anti-tumor effect of substances that were isolated from plants. Both Bergonié institutes arrived at identical results: OPCs prevent tumor expansion. OPCs turned out to be active, even though to a lesser extent than the larger tannins.

Masquelier concluded that OPCs can create this effect because they interfere with the work of the protein-splitting enzymes. In 1990, French Professor Chambon and his team identified a specific gene in lesions, meaning tissue that has lost function. A lesion could be any degraded tissue, including a wound, an ulcer, cataracts, or a tumor. The gene that was found by Chambon controls the production of a protease known as stromelysin 3. Stromelysin 3 plays a primary part in the invasive process of cancer as it facilitates the dissemination of metastases. Chambon and his colleagues assume that stromelysin 3 presents the primary target that must be aimed at in breast cancer therapy. Other proteases, especially collagenase, are known to play a role in this disease. It is hoped that OPCs, which have been confirmed to inhibit said enzymes, will soon be subject to more thorough examination with respect to this property.

Some other factors support the assumption that cancer cannot develop at all or develops more slowly when OPCs are active in the body. In this respect, Masquelier draws our attention to the fact that some viruses have been the subject of extensive studies to find out whether they could play a role in stopping or slowing down the cancer-promotion process. A virus consists of genetic material that is surrounded by a protein coating. Viruses can reproduce themselves only by injecting their content into a host cell. They then use the host cell's facilities to replicate. Research indicates that in this process, some viruses may be capable of interfering with cell reproduction by changing the genetic material. It is assumed that under the influence of certain viruses, a normal cell might become a malignant one. Supposedly, this effect is stronger when the immune system is deficient, and weak. OPCs help the immune system to make the body more resistant.

The origin of the degenerative cancer process that we eventually see emerge as a tumor is a change in the genes that control cell growth and cell reproduction. The genes are made of a double strand of DNA (deoxyribonucleic acid). Just before cell division, a group of proteins separates the DNA strands. Then each strand is exactly replicated and each of the new double strands forms the genes of each of the two new cells. What is special about DNA is that according to the sequence in which it is "stranded," it determines the exact structure of all the proteins and polypeptides made by the cell. Because all the enzymes in the cell are proteins, the DNA of that cell contains the codes and instructions for all of the biochemistry and structure of that cell. Simply put, everything that takes place in a cell, including its own reproduction, takes place under the control of the DNA in that cell. DNA holds the key to the making of every new cell.

Every year of life, the body forms many trillions of new cells. A week from now, your body will not the same body it is today. Millions of new cells will have copied themselves and taken the place of copied cells that have been removed. This makes the aging of living, organic things different from the aging of inorganic things, which age by erosion or deterioration. In the aging process of the human body, the newly formed cells are of a lower quality than the old cells that are being replaced. Some of the cells you produce today at this age are of a lower quality than the cells you produced a year ago. Unfortunately, with each year, more and more newly produced cells will be of a lower quality — as if each new cell is a copy of a copy of a copy on a photocopier. The last copy will be fainter than the original, no matter how precise the copying machine.

Our cells have an immensely precise mechanism to make copies of themselves; that is, of the strands of DNA that determine the functions of a cell. This precision is a fundamental requirement of survival in each species. The slightest mistake can have fatal consequences. Therefore, apart from having precise duplication mechanisms, the cell always does a quality check before it replicates itself. In this way, it can trace and repair abnormalities in the replication of each of the single DNA strands before it forms two new cells. Despite all this precision and precaution, accidents happen. The most serious of such accidents is a mutation in the genes that causes an entirely different protein biochemistry or "household" in a new cell. Such a mutated cell no longer contains the DNA of the surrounding normal cells of the tissue and will behave differently. A cancer cell is a mutated cell that will reproduce itself without limitation and in direct competition with normal body cells. It has lost the capacity to control its own replication.

Only a few cells that have mutated will eventually produce cancer. Many of them die. Many of them still have some feedback mechanism that will prevent excessive behavior. The body's immune system will trace the mutated cells because their protein household differs from that of the normal healthy cells. The immune system can thus find and destroy mutated cells before they get a chance to spread as cancer. In medicine, it is well known that people who have been on immune-suppressing drugs have a fivefold chance of developing cancer. People who suffer from a deficient immune system, as in AIDS, often die of cancer or pneumonia simply because their bodies lack the capacity to trace and destroy abnormal cells. This is why boosting the immune system must always form part of the treatment for people who have been diagnosed as having AIDS.

Cancer is rampant in our Western societies because of the presence of many carcinogens, those harmful substances that promote mutation. Radioactivity, radiation, and even ultraviolet light can interfere with the precision needed in replication. Most carcinogens we absorb are found in cigarette smoke, which is why one-quarter of all cancer deaths are caused by cigarette smoke. Cigarette smoking is the sole factor that has caused a rise in cancer deaths. If people did not smoke, the cancer mortality would show a downward trend instead of an upward one! If all smokers stopped smoking today, the overall cancer mortality rate would soon start trending downward. Viruses are another possible cause of cancer. Also, some physical irritants may cause cancer, especially in the intestinal tract. And oxygen free radicals strongly interfere with normal cell replication. Earlier, we referred to the world of free radicals as a combat zone. In other words, the body must deal with an overwhelming amount of psychological, physical, and chemical "noise" out there. Against the background of this noise, you will understand the relevance of Masquelier's '360 patent. By cutting the noise that constantly imposes itself on the immune system, you increase the probability that mutated cells are found and destroyed before they become the beginning of cancer.

Yet another condition that can induce cancer was described many years ago by the German scientist Otto Warburg. In the 1930s, around the time Szent-Györgyi discovered vitamin C, Warburg observed that in an anaerobic (anoxious/oxygenless) environment, otherwise-aerobic cells fell back into an anaerobic state. Normal cells seemed to regress to a prehistoric stage as if a spontaneous mutation took place. When the supply of oxygen is cut off, cells try to switch to an anaerobic method of energy production. However, anaerobic cells produce much less energy than aerobic cells. Anaerobic cells also produce lactic acid. During strenuous exercise, the skeletal muscles produce moderate amounts of lactic acid because, temporarily, there is a relative lack of oxygen. Lactic acid can be oxidized in the heart for energy production. According to the German medical doctor Johannes Kuhl, moderate levels of lactic acid are fine, but an excess of it induces tumor formation. However, when the respective area is provided with oxygen, the process can be reversed completely and cells can breathe normally again. By keeping the blood supply active, OPCs help provide oxygen and nutrients to the cells. In this way, OPCs help the tissues to breathe normally or recuperate from suffocation. This is how anoxia is a factor in not only cardiovascular diseases, but also in cancer.

More and more evidence confirms Masquelier's claim that OPCs inhibit tumor promotion. Not unexpectedly, some of this evidence emerges in the field of research that focuses on the healthy aspects of red wine. French red wine researcher Pierre-Louis Teissedre called attention to a study carried out in 1994 at the University of California at Davis by Professor Clifford and coworkers. The Clifford team "used transgenic mice carrying a human virus transactivating gene which induces cancer tumors. These mice," wrote Teissedre, "are predisposed to develop nerve tumors similar to those which appear in human neurofibromatosis." Neurofibromatosis is a genetic disorder characterized by tumor growth along various types of nerves. Bone, muscle, and skin may also be affected. The test animals received two different diets, both with an amino acid base but with one supplemented with red wine. According to Teissedre, "In the transgenic mice given the normal diet, the first tumor appeared after 55 days, but those given a diet supplemented with red wine did not manifest tumors until after 74 days."

Red wine's major antioxidative component is OPCs. Yet Masquelier always remains somewhat reluctant to discuss OPCs in the context of cancer. This reluctance immediately makes place for enthusiasm when Masquelier is invited to explain the beneficial effects of red wine in cardiovascular health and how it is that OPCs are the key to understanding the French paradox.

31 RED WINE DRINKERS LIVE HAPPIER AND LONGER

Some American readers may remember a TV program that created quite a reaction in 1991. During a broadcast of *60 Minutes*, French epidemiologist Serge Renaud made the following provocative statement: "Alcohol is one of the most effective remedies we have in order to reduce coronary mortality." Renaud explained that Americans ran a three times higher risk of dying of cardiac infarction than the French, although the French use considerable amounts of fat in their cuisine, exercise less or just as much as the Americans, and still smoke significantly more. Renaud also explained that the difference in cardiovascular mortality results not because Americans drink less alcohol than the French do — they don't.

So what is it that causes this French paradox? As you may have understood, the answer is that the majority of the French prefer to take their alcohol in the form of wine — red wine, to be precise. Although the French drink whiskey, vodka, gin, beer, and all of the other beverages that contain minor or major volumes of alcohol, the French accompany every meal with a couple of glasses of red wine. Even children drink red wine diluted with water. In 2003, wine still accounted for more than half of all the alcohol sold in France, with sales 60% higher than those for beer and more than 10 times those of spirits. In 1991, Renaud's statements may have been a novelty in the United States, but they weren't in France, where Masquelier had been exploring the benefits of red wine since the 1950s. What Renaud told the American public on national television, Masquelier had explained to American scientists who had visited France in 1961 to attend the conference at which California professor Milton

Silverman invited Masquelier to come to the United States to speak about cholesterol. It would take 25 years before Masquelier would give his speech in America. By then, the French paradox had already hit the media.

In 1979, the Welshman A.S. St. Leger had reported in the scientific magazine *The Lancet* that he had found a connection between wine consumption and longevity in industrialized nations. From a number of countries, St. Leger had collected the numbers of people between 55 and 64 years of age who had died of cardiovascular disease. He had then associated these cardiovascular mortality rates with the consumption of wine in the respective countries. The United States ranked last but one, the last one being Finland. France ranked first, followed by Italy and Switzerland. Since 1979, things have probably changed. More Americans have learned to appreciate the pleasure of drinking a glass of good red wine. California, Australia, and Chili, to name a few regions, have joined France as major producers of wine. Hundreds of articles have sung the praises of red wine. In France, the Ministry of Agriculture joined the cause and made wine the subject of more scientific research. Medical experts confirmed with increasing frequency that wine drinkers live healthier and longer, and they also expressed this opinion in the media. "If every American adult drank two glasses of wine per day, cardiovascular diseases, which account for almost half of the deaths in our population, would drop by 40 percent, and 40 billion U.S. dollars could be saved every year," claimed one of those experts in 1994.

In 1995, a study performed by the University of Copenhagen, and therefore called *The Copenhagen Study,* confirmed that regular wine consumption was the best protection against cardiac arrest and other fatal diseases. The risk of dying of cardiac or cerebral infarction was reported as being 60 percent lower in people who regularly consumed moderate amounts of wine. Another study that has become known as the *Monica Study* was commissioned by the World Health Organization. From 1985 to 1995, the *Monica* researchers had been systematically counting and comparing the numbers of coronary heart diseases in many countries around the world. When all the counting and comparing was completed, the *Monica Study* confirmed that in countries such as France, Spain, Italy, and Switzerland, where wine is being consumed as a normal part of the diet, the mortality rates for coronary heart diseases are lowest.

These results did not take Masquelier by surprise. What did surprise the good professor was that the healthy bond between humans and wine, which had already been documented at the beginning of the century, "hit the streets" at such a late stage. It seems to be Masquelier's fate that he is always ahead of his time. When it comes to wine and longevity, even more ahead of his time was Frenchman F. Dougnac. In the 1920s, Dougnac began studying medicine in his free time. In 1933, he completed his doctoral thesis on the subject "Wine and Longevity." He compared the geographic distribution of elderly people in France and found that the vast majority of people of high age lived in the Médoc wine district. Médoc is not far from Bordeaux, in the southwest of France.

Counting the numbers of people over 80, Dougnac found 88 percent more of them in the Médoc region than in the entire rest of France. Their advanced age could not be attributed exclusively to alcohol consumption because in the Normandy and Brittany provinces of France, where people drink alcoholic beverages made from apples such as cider and calvados, the numbers told a completely different story. In the Gironde, France's premier red wine district that includes Bordeaux and Médoc, 153 out of 1,000 inhabitants were between 80 and 100 years of age. But in the Calvados region, there lived not one single person of that age group. Much higher quantities of alcohol are, however, drunk in the Calvados area than elsewhere.

Long before the schoolteacher doctor Dougnac counted senior citizens in France, wine was known to be a companion of people in dire straits. In the times of scurvy, one seafaring nation seemed to be spared from this scourge: Portugal. While the English, the Dutch, and other seafarers were always haunted by this gruesome disease, it hardly ever affected Portuguese sailors. Yet, the Portuguese were just as handicapped when it came to preserving the freshness of the fruits and vegetables they had taken on board. What then made the difference in the sailors' diet? The Portuguese took sufficient amounts of red wine on their voyages. Every member of the crew was given his daily ration. Although red wine does not contain any vitamin C, the Portuguese sailors did not fall victim to scurvy.

Now that we better appreciate the boosting relationship between OPCs and vitamin C, we can understand why the Portuguese did not develop scurvy on their long journeys. When they set sail, they had sufficient supplies of vitamin C stored in their livers and adrenal glands. With their daily wine ration, they consumed enough OPCs to recharge the stored vitamin C required for collagen synthesis. The recharging effect of OPCs prevented excessive depletion of vitamin C, thus sparing the Portuguese seafarers the disease.

If it isn't the alcohol that helps people live longer, it must be something we find in red wine and don't find in other alcoholic beverages. In *chapter 23: The No. 1 Killer, OPCs, and Cholesterol,* we discussed the work of Dr. Edwin Frankel at the Department of Food Science and Technology of the University of California. He succeeded in furnishing evidence of the cardio-protective properties of red wine or rather of its nonalcoholic solid constituents. Frankel found that these red wine solids inhibit the oxidation of LDL. Later, he defined these active nonalcoholic constituents as phenolic flavonoids and he reported how they play a major role in inflammatory and thrombotic events. So, he reached the conclusion that phenolic compounds in wine and grapes support the epidemiological evidence that wine has a cardio-protective effect. In the broadest of terms, yes, the difference lies in red wine's "solids." With due respect to Frankel, in the narrowest of terms, the difference between alcoholic beverages and red wine boils down to OPCs.

Up to 1955, the existence of OPCs had never been mentioned in any oenological treatise or report (oenology is the study or knowledge of wine). Only tannins were discussed from time to time, mostly because tannins give wine its astringent taste. Until 1955, winemakers were convinced that tannins exist in wine because they let the wine mature in wooden casks. A couple of years after he had discovered OPCs, Masquelier developed an interest in searching for OPCs in red wine. His problem was that he would normally find OPCs by making them turn red. To identify colorless or red-colored OPCs in red wine seemed an impossible task.

Masquelier succeeded in solving this problem by means of electrophoresis. This method allows the motion of particles in a stationary liquid under the influence of an electric field. It is comparable to moving iron dust on a sheet of paper with the use of a magnet placed under the paper. In his experiment, the electric current separated the visible red wine pigment (anthocyanin) from the colorless OPCs and moved the two substances to different areas. Treating the colorless fraction with acid and heat, Masquelier then made the OPCs visible as they perfectly manifested themselves by the emergence of a second red area. This was the evidence that the colorless OPCs are a major component of red wine. It contains the identical OPCs molecules Masquelier had discovered in the red skin of the peanut and in the brown bark of the Pinus Maritima. All that was now left for him to do was to isolate OPCs from the wine and determine their concentration. This was done in 1956. Owing to this discovery, Masquelier managed to bring oenology up to date in the chemical field so that future wine studies were placed on a solid footing.

At this point, I must disappoint readers who prefer white wine to red wine. The health-enhancing and life-prolonging effects of red wine are not present in white wine. The difference has nothing to do with the color of the grapes; the color of wine is not necessarily related to the color of the grapes. Although red wine cannot be produced from white grapes, it is possible to make white wine from red grapes. Many varieties of champagne are actually made of red grapes. This is why a white wine made from white grapes is called a blanc de blanc (white from white), a name that does not fit a white wine that was made from red grapes. For the occasion, let me coin a white wine made from red grapes a blanc de rouge (white from red). The difference between red and white wines rests in the method of production. Winemakers produce white wine by pressing grapes, gathering the juice, and then letting the juice ferment. The seeds, skins, and little stems, altogether the "mash" or "marc," are separated from the juice at the pressing of the grapes. In white wine making, only the juice undergoes fermentation. The juice does not contain significant amounts of OPCs or other solid particles.

In the making of red wine, the first step is that the red grapes are crushed only. Mash and juice are not separated until the end of a two- to three-week fermentation period. Thus the OPCs contained in the seeds have plenty of time to dissolve from the mash into the juice, as do the red pigments (anthocyanin) that pass from the skins of the grapes into the juice to gradually lend the juice its red color. In the meantime, sugars ferment to alcohol, and with the gradual rise of the alcohol level, anthocyanin and OPCs dissolve better and better. With the rise of the alcohol content, the temperature also increases somewhat, creating a perfect alcohol/water environment for the natural extraction of OPCs from the mash. This is how considerable amounts of OPCs gently dissolve into the wine. It is nature's own way of extracting OPCs and presenting them to us in a palatable and healthy form. During white wine production, anthocyanins and OPCs have little or no opportunity to dissolve into the juice. Therefore, white wine contains 20 to 50 times less OPCs than does red wine.

Why is white wine produced the way it is, when with the same grapes and without much extra effort, one could make a much healthier OPCs-containing wine? After all, if winemakers treated white grapes the same way they treat red grapes, they

Red wine making

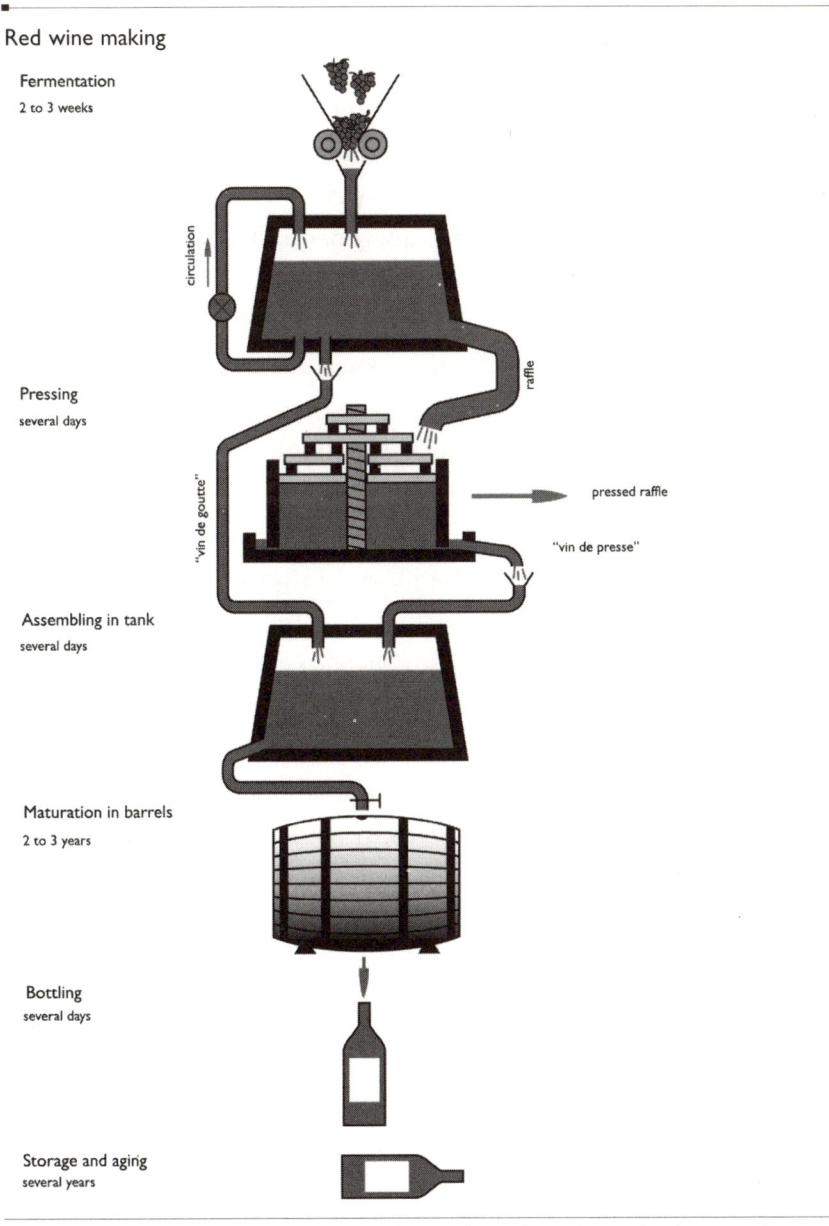

Fermentation
2 to 3 weeks

Pressing
several days

"vin de goutte"

raffle

pressed raffle

"vin de presse"

Assembling in tank
several days

Maturation in barrels
2 to 3 years

Bottling
several days

Storage and aging
several years

Martine Baspeyras, a student of Masquelier, explains the making of red wine in her doctoral thesis " PROPRIETES BENEFIQUES DES VINS ROUGES DU BORDELAIS". In the making of white wine, only the juice is used. There is no raffle, hence no OPCs.

would obtain a white wine with an OPCs content equivalent to that of red wine. In some parts of Eastern Europe, such white wines are produced and they do contain OPCs, which makes their taste very different from that of the regular white wines. The making of wine is a millennia-old tradition, and the notion that OPCs have a health-promoting effect is a very recent one. It was only in 1955 that Masquelier showed the presence of OPCs in wine, and it would take until the early 1990s before the French paradox hit the media. It made red wine makers happier, but it did not change their one and only yardstick to determine the quality of their products: taste. Health is a pleasant side effect, but if it isn't there, so be it. It all remains a matter of taste.

Everybody who has drunk regular white wine and red wine knows that there are significant differences in taste. Red wine contains not only pigments and OPCs but also tannins, considerable quantities of which are stored in the seeds. Tannins lend the red wine its characteristic slightly astringent, tannic taste, which is absent in white wine. This is the reason red wines go well with protein-rich foods of stronger taste, such as meat, while the white wines do better with protein-rich foods with a lighter taste, such as fish. When wine is drunk without food, white wines are often preferred because a white wine "drinks lighter" than a red wine. Many centuries ago, not knowing the chemistry of all of this, people just followed their taste buds to make these distinctions and choices. Knowing the health benefits of red wine, should we now completely abandon white wines? No! Both types provide enjoyment and a wide range of magnificent tastes. Therefore, I recommend that you regularly drink red wine for your health and white wine whenever you want to please your palate with a taste untouched by tannins.

The importance of red wine is undisputed in the scientific world. To Masquelier, there is no doubt that OPCs give the greatest contribution to the healthy aspect of red wine. Yet, he is well aware that many researchers continue to look for other beneficial solid components present in red wine. One of these components has recently had some good press. It is a substance called resveratrol, which supposedly has anticancer properties. Resveratrol appears in red wine in infinitely small quantities. The grape produces resveratrol in the skin toward the very end of the maturation period to protect itself against mold. The quantities of resveratrol that end up in red wine are so minute that, to reap their benefits, one would have to drink wine in ridiculously large dosages, or take resveratrol in isolated or highly concentrated form as a dietary supplement. Other phenolic compounds of red wine have been isolated and researched. Wine contains bioflavonoids, such as quercetin, but these flavonoids are of lesser value because they are destroyed in the gut.

> To get an idea of the concentrations of these solids in a bottle of red wine, look at the following figures:
> - Resveratrol: 1 mg
> - Quercetin: 10 mg
> - Catechin: 100 mg
> - OPCs: 1,000-2,000 mg

As you see, the concentration of OPCs is by far the greatest. As shown by Pierre-Louis Teissedre (see *chapter 30: Tumor Prevention and Cancer*), catechins are also present in red wine in bioavailable form.

There is still another reason to advocate drinking red wine with main courses. Tests done in Masquelier's laboratory confirmed a property of red wine that has been known and used in popular medicine for many centuries: its antiseptic effect. Louis Pasteur, the outstanding biologist and chemist of the 19th century, spoke these famous words: "Wine is the healthiest and most hygienic beverage." The bacteriological property of wine was of primary importance at Pasteur's time. Water, the poor man's drink, used to be unpurified, and it carried numerous germs that produced infections. Mixed with a small quantity of wine, it could be drunk without harm. Pasteur, who lost two children to typhus, was thus bound to appreciate wine primarily because of its antiseptic nature. Wine owes this property, which is achieved only after maturation, to its phenolic compounds. Fresh grape juice is ineffective. The substances responsible for wine's bactericidal effect develop only gradually. When we enjoy red wine with our food, this beverage provides efficient protection against the biological pollution of the food.

There is a story about four undertakers in Marseille who were not affected by the plague during the epidemic of 1790. They are on record as survivors, although they buried many victims. They are also on record as having drunk a potion made of red wine in which garlic had been soaked. Certainly, garlic is known for its bactericidal effects, but one may presume that the red wine in which the garlic was soaked made its own contribution to the undertakers' survival. The combination of garlic and red wine has survived until today. A typical French "pastoral bite" consists of a glass of red wine and a piece of bread rubbed with fresh garlic. Add to this the fish soup known as bouillabaisse and you're in the heart of the Mediterranean diet.

We have not yet mentioned another important wine-drinking country: Spain. Yet, it deserves a lot of credit, especially because it confirms what Pasteur said about wine some 150 years ago. A Spanish team of researchers found that wine drinkers suffer less from a viral infection we all know as the common cold. During 1998 and 1999, 4,287 faculty members and administrative staff of five Spanish universities responded to a questionnaire asking them about their drinking habits, tobacco use, lifestyle, and medical history. The findings of the study, which was published in 2002 in the *American Journal of Epidemiology*, tell us that there is an inverse or opposite relationship "between the consumption of wine, but not other alcoholic beverages, and the incidence of common cold. This inverse association persisted after adjustment for total alcohol intake, smoking, and known risk factors for common cold." Which means that beer, spirits, and other alcoholic beverages do not seem to affect the incidence of common cold. "Among those participants consuming both red and white wine, the association was even stronger among those consuming red wine exclusively," according to researchers Bahi Takkouche, Carlos Regueira-Méndez, Reina Garcia-Closas, Adolfo Figueiras, Juan Gestal-Otera, and Miguel Hernan.

32
OPCs AND THE REBOUND EFFECT

The previous chapter began with a provocative statement made by Serge Renaud on American television: "Alcohol is one of the most effective remedies we have in order to reduce coronary mortality." Indeed, there is clear scientific evidence that alcohol does have a beneficial cardiovascular effect. Although these and many earlier studies tout the health effects of alcohol, countless other studies demonstrate the bad effects of alcohol. However, many of these studies do not differentiate the various types of alcoholic beverages that supply the alcohol. This makes the drawing of conclusions a rather difficult operation. It would, for instance, be a serious mistake to consider red wine an ordinary alcoholic beverage for some political agenda just because it has the factor alcohol in common with beer, rum, cognac, and whiskey. From the viewpoint of traffic control, one may well advise against the use of alcohol. From the viewpoint of health control, one should stimulate the consumption of moderate amounts of red wine, even though it contains alcohol. Alcohol is by no means the only factor one must consider when discussing or evaluating alcoholic beverages.

Alcohol inhibits the sticking together (aggregation) of blood platelets. As a result, alcohol inhibits the clotting of the blood. Because of this "blood-diluting" effect, it reduces the risk of thrombosis, embolism, and infarction. Alcohol can lower the aggregation tendency of blood platelets by up to 70 percent, but this certainly does not mean that you can or must consume excessive quantities of alcohol in order to prevent heart disease. The alcohol-induced blood-diluting effect lasts for only a short period of time following alcohol intake. About 18 hours after intake, the so-called rebound effect manifests itself when the blood platelets "rebound" to an abnormally increased tendency to coagulate. They become even more coagulant than before the intake of alcohol, and thus the risk of blood clotting, of infarction, and of embolism is equally increased way beyond the level that existed before the first sip of alcohol. In some cases, the chance of platelet aggregation may even double. The rebound effect has been associated with increased risks of thrombosis, stroke, and sudden death, especially in binge drinkers who intentionally seek to achieve a state of drunkenness and then sleep themselves sober. At the onset of their sobriety, they run the greatest risk to be struck by the rebound effect. This is why the sudden stopping of a heavy drinking habit poses great danger.

Although reasonable consumption of alcoholic beverages cannot be compared to binge drinking, it should always be taken into consideration that the enjoyment of even moderate quantities of alcohol may have a down side in terms of the after-drinking rebound effect. The rebound effect has, of course, been the subject of numerous scientific studies. It turned out that this effect could not be found in French farmers, who tend to drink more red wine than other alcoholic beverages such as beer and spirits. Could it be that they warded off the rebound effect because of the protective properties of red wine, specifically because of its nonalcoholic constituents, OPCs? Could it be that these French farmers benefited from the cardiovascular protection that Masquelier's colleague Lavollay had observed in 1944 during the earliest tests performed with red wine? In that experiment, Lavollay succeeded in determining vascular stabilization in guinea pigs after he had given the animals red wine.

Dr. Serge Renaud at the French National Institute of Health and Medical Research performed an impressive experiment about the warding off and the occurrence of the rebound effect. To determine the possible cross-relationships of alcohol, OPCs, wine, and platelet aggregation, Renaud separated laboratory animals into five groups and provided them with different beverages as follows:

- Red wine
- White wine
- Water with 6 percent alcohol
- Water with 6 percent alcohol and 0.03 percent OPCs
- Pure water

The OPCs (MASQUELIER's Original OPCs) were provided by Centre d'Exploitation des Procyanidines (CEP). The quantity of OPCs used by Renaud in the water/alcohol mix corresponds to the average level of OPCs contained in red wine.

The figure on the next page shows the strength of blood platelet aggregation after intake of the drinks. The first bar, representing the intake of pure water, sets the mark of platelet aggregation at a randomly chosen 100. The drinking of water does not produce a change. The bar stays at 100. The second, third, and fourth bars show that water+alcohol (second bar), red wine (third bar), white wine (fourth bar) and water+alcohol+OPCs (fifth bar) produce a significant decrease in the ability of platelets to stick together. All four groups go down approximately 65 to 70 percent. To produce the rebound effect, all animals were then put on nothing but water, meaning that all of a sudden, they were being deprived of the benefits of alcohol.

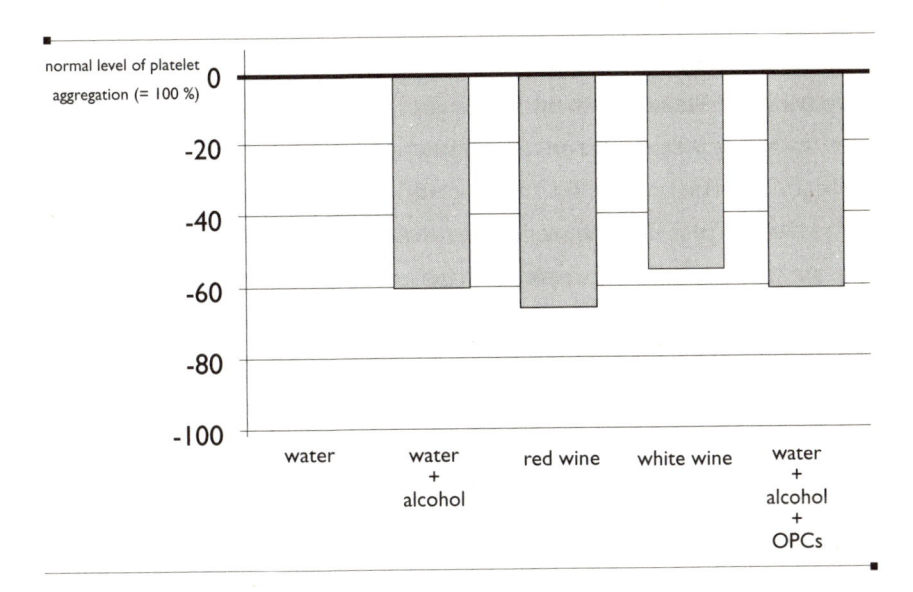

```
normal level of platelet     0
aggregation (= 100 %)
                           -20

                           -40

                           -60

                           -80

                          -100
                                  water      water      red wine   white wine   water
                                               +                                  +
                                            alcohol                            alcohol
                                                                                  +
                                                                                OPCs
```

The figure on the following page shows the devastating results of the rebound in the water+alcohol group. After having been without alcohol for 18 hours, the group that had received water and alcohol showed a highly increased propensity to platelet clotting. The rebound effect shoots platelet aggregation through the roof with 124 percent above the 0 (normal) level.

The animals that had consumed red wine, however, did not present any rebound effect when they were deprived of the red wine. The third bar shows that 18 hours of deprivation did not markedly change the level of platelet aggregation this group had reached right after the intake of red wine. The fourth bar shows that white wine produces a rebound of 49 percent rebound above the normal level of platelet aggregation. A total increase of approximately 115 percent. Somehow, red wine perpetuates the 59 percent reduction in blood clotting. The same continuation of reduced blood clotting was observed in the animals that had been administered water+alcohol+OPCs, showing that OPCs alone could perpetuate the reduction in blood clotting. Compared with the 124 percent increase produced by water+alcohol, the total difference in rebound between the water+alcohol group and the red wine and water+alcohol+OPCs group is an enormous 183 percent. The difference is almost double the original level of platelet aggregation (100). What you gain with water+alcohol, you doubly lose compared with the combination of alcohol and OPCs.

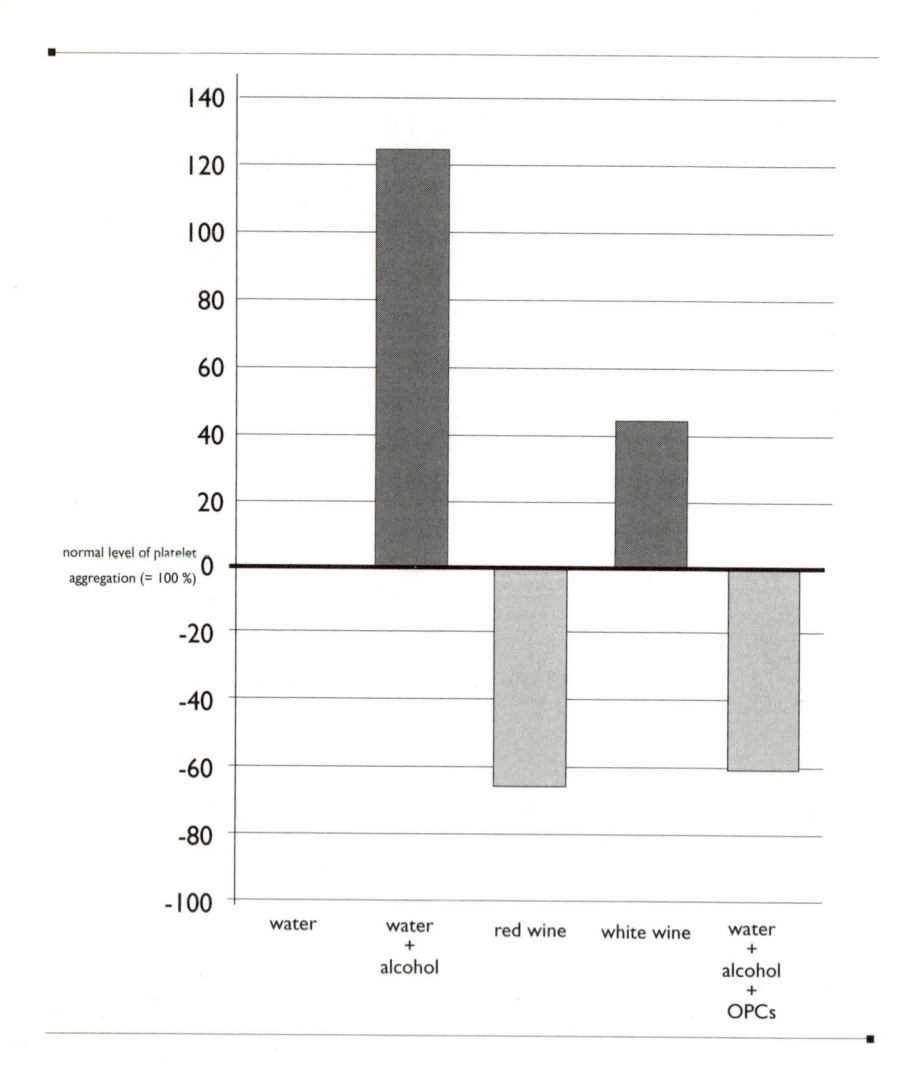

Through this unique experiment, Renaud isolated OPCs as the "red wine solid" that is able to produce by itself all the cardiovascular benefits attributed to red wine. No wonder red wine drinkers have a 30 to 40 percent lower risk of suffering from coronary heart diseases than do people who consume other alcoholic beverages.

Renaud's experiment also sheds light on a seemingly unrelated issue. From time to time, articles appear in newspapers and magazines about the health risks of long flights. After one passenger died of an embolism (occlusion of a vein or artery caused by a blood clot) at Heathrow airport following a long flight, the problem aggregated more serious attention than the swollen ankles of many economy-class passengers. In the boardrooms of the international airlines, the "Heathrow embolism" put the risks of incurring legal claims higher on the agenda. Immobility is a risk factor specifically related to blood clotting in the veins (venous thrombosis). That's why the more severe problems associated with long flights have become known as "DVT," which stands for deep vein thrombosis. People with DVT need immediate medical treatment. The less serious problems of long haul flying, such as swollen feet and ankles, have become known as the economy class syndrome.

Obviously, immobilizing people for 8 or 12 hours creates stress on their bodies. Economy-class seats are notoriously uncomfortable, and airlines show movies and serve meals to keep passengers seated while they are being transported to faraway destinations. On request, the cabin crew serves a variety of alcoholic beverages that help many passengers pass the time in a state of perceived comfort. Sitting on an airplane for many hours hampers and immobilizes the blood flow in the lower limbs. In immobilized blood, the particles involved in blood clotting become more active than they are in free-flowing blood. The sheer volume of the slow-flowing blood in the lower limbs tends to compromise the permeability and the integrity of the hair vessels in the legs' vascular system. This effect is enhanced by the fact that the heart exerts pressure on the blood to make it flow back in the upward direction. The upward flow of blood is impeded, however, because the legs are bent and not moving. This causes swellings of the legs and feet, which is the reason shoes don't fit as well at the end of a long flight. To combat this effect, passengers should stretch the whole body as much as possible during a long flight.

The alcohol that is consumed in flight seems to help because it reduces the tendency of the blood to clot. Renaud has shown this quite well in his tests. However, during the hours after the planes land, the rebound effect strikes passengers' blood of which the condition already worsened during the period of immobilization. It could be that cases of deep vein thrombosis and embolism associated with long flights were caused by more than the discomfort of the flight. It might well be that the rebound effect that followed the end of the alcohol consumption during a long flight lowered the blood's own capacity to undo the negative effects of immobilization. In other words, the rebound effect might amplify the platelet aggregation (clotting) processes set in motion during the flight. The rebound effect is a heretofore completely overlooked factor in the discussion about economy-class syndrome and thrombosis associated with long flights. Obviously, for all the reasons previously explained, my recommendation is to drink red wine and lots of water on board or take a sufficiently high dosage of OPCs to combat a long flight's discomfort and the risk of thrombosis.

It took some years before the medical world began to understand the implications of the rebound effect and the role it plays in the French paradox (see *chapter 31: Red Wine Drinkers Live Happier and Longer*). Overwhelmed by the enormous amount of positive press, the scientific evidence supporting it, and consumers' ready acceptance of the French paradox, most of those in the medical profession embraced the healthy effects of red wine. (Not in the least because many of them now had a good excuse to take a couple of glasses with each meal.) Unfortunately, some medical experts have decided to desecrate the phenomenon, and this is how the French paradox has not escaped from a rebound effect.

You may be surprised to learn that this particular rebound effect took place in the heart of the paradox's own country, France. "Grandeur and Decadence of the French Paradox" declared the *Le Monde* newspaper on October 17, 1999. One month later, on November 22, *Le Monde* followed with "The French Paradox Questioned." On the same day, in what seems to have been a concerted effort, the *Revue du Praticien*, a French medical magazine, quoted French Professor Amouyel as saying, "There exists no such thing as a French paradox; this term, which was coined at a time when cardiovascular diseases were attributed exclusively to cholesterol, is untenable now since coronary disorders are of multifactorial origin. Moreover, the death rate due to infarction drops with increasing efficiency of angioplasty [an operation for enlarging a narrowed coronary arterial lumen by peripheral introduction of a balloon-tip catheter and dilating the lumen on withdrawal of the inflated catheter tip] and intravenous injection of a fibrinolytic agent [medication that dissolves fibrinous clotting]."

With such criticism, promoters of surgery and medication inadvertently hit a mark, but not in the way they intended. Masquelier's primary response to the way the French paradox has been highlighted in the media is that the focus has been limited to the lowering of the mortality rate due to cardiac infarction. This remains a Pyrrhic victory as long as the general mortality rate remains high. Undeniably, the statistics presented by St. Leger demonstrate the positive relationship between red wine and cardiovascular health. But as Masquelier points out, 70 years ago, Dougnac demonstrated the much broader positive relationship between wine regions and life span. Masquelier came to the conclusion that the effects of the French paradox must not be limited to the discussion about cardiovascular mortality but expanded to the issue of general wellbeing and life span. Masquelier has always welcomed each and every opportunity to examine and explore all the health benefits of red wine and not confine the French paradox to the field of cardiovascular problems.

In his book *Le régime santé* Renaud writes, "Since oxidation of lipids presents a phenomenon that is related to coronary diseases as well as to cancer and aging processes, it is more easily understood why wine and health may be named in one breath." This remark fully supports Masquelier's opinion that the French paradox must not be confined to cardiovascular diseases. If it were, red wine would be struck by the fate that struck OPCs in their early decades of research and development. For a long time, OPCs were applied in an equally limited way; that is, as a vascular protector only. In truth, the antioxidant effect of isolated OPCs and red wine is not confined to cardiovascular health. The risk of radical oxidation exists in all body cells. The wine counteracts this process and thus prevents premature aging everywhere in the body. This is why the antioxidant properties of nutrients and other vegetal substances must be researched in the widest possible range of health applications.

In 1994, during a conference at the Free University in Brussels, Masquelier gave a lecture titled "French Paradox, Second Act." He ended with the following carefully chosen words: "The protection of the vascular system presents only one aspect of the broad range of applications which antioxidants present to modern medicine and health care." Again, Masquelier may find himself ahead of his time when he observes how the medical profession still has to fully understand the opportunity to apply the French paradox in fields of human health untouched by it so far.

Because the subject is dear to his heart, Masquelier always quotes the words of G. Portmann who said: "The enemies of wine are the people who do not know wine." Its friends should know it all the better. A major step in this direction was taken by the magazine *Vins et Santé (Wines and Health)*. In 1997, it published a guide presenting a selection of French wines, each of which was accompanied by a "test report" stating the quantity of polyphenols contained in the wine and categorizing the wines according to catechins and OPCs. Such initiatives show that the time may be ripe for applying a standard test that confirms the antiradical efficacy of individual wines. Red wines could be classified by their antioxidant capacity according to an index that would mark the wine for its antioxidant, free-radical-scavenging effect. Such an index should relate to the bioavailable antioxidants in red wine. Otherwise, readers might buy a wine that scores high in the laboratory but not in the body. Therefore, the best approach would be to calibrate the wine for its catechins and OPCs content. With the contents clearly marked on the label, consumers would be able to instantly determine a wine's antioxidant effect. It would add a modern feature to a product people have been consuming since time immemorial.

33. ALCOHOL, WHAT ELSE TO SAY?

Scientists, teetotalers, health authorities, doctors, officials, politicians, Mothers Against Drunk Driving, mothers and fathers of minors, police officers, and even some barkeepers warn us every day about the dangers of alcohol for two main reasons: traffic safety and public health. Leaving traffic safety to the police, let's see what there is to say about alcohol and health in the framework of this book. OPCs and alcohol are obviously in opposition with one another when it comes to their biological effects. On the whole, alcohol is a serious risk factor in the development of cardiovascular and cerebrovascular incidents. The initial blood-thinning effect of alcohol is completely lost in the rebound (see *chapter 32: OPCs and the Rebound Effect*). The vascular wall suffers and the blood clots faster. The liver is affected by the regular intake of substantial amounts of alcohol in yet another way. It responds to alcohol by producing the hydroxyl and superoxide oxygen radicals to eliminate the excess that cannot be handled by the liver's normal cleansing systems. When these oxygen radicals are involved in the elimination process, liver cells become hopelessly exposed to lipoperoxidation, which is another way of saying they "go rancid." Eventually, cells are destroyed and cirrhosis irreversibly reduces the function of the liver.

Oxidative stress due to alcohol intoxication does not confine itself to the liver because in fighting the free radical stress, the body depletes its enzymatic and nutritional antioxidant defenses elsewhere. French scientist Roger Nordmann and his colleagues observed that an alcohol attack on the liver is also felt in the brain. In a study published in 1985, Nordmann and his coworkers reported that within two hours after test animals' alcohol intoxication, the researchers were able to observe a significant increase in oxidation of brain cells. This "peroxidation" does not subside until six hours after intake. Nordmann found that the level of the antioxidant enzyme superoxide dismutase in the brain decreases in response to alcohol. Nordmann relates this to the fact that alcohol intake is followed "by a highly significant increase in liver mitochondrial superoxide production." Interestingly, but not surprisingly, he also found that the level of vitamin C in the brain decreases in response to alcohol intake. Levels drop because vitamin C is wasted in fighting free radicals. In his conclusion, Nordmann writes that his findings "suggest that the central nervous system is, like the liver, submitted to a free radical attack during alcohol intoxication."

The psychological and social problems caused by alcoholism and alcohol abuse fall outside the scope of this book, which focuses on the phytonutrient OPCs and their discoverer, Jack Masquelier. As a promoter of red wine, Masquelier has been confronted numerous times with questions about alcohol. He considers alcohol "the limiting factor" in wine consumption. Individuals have to determine for themselves how far they can go without risking any toxic effects. According to Masquelier, this is a completely personal issue because the elimination of alcoholic toxins is dependent on the scavenging enzymes. The body's production of these enzymes depends on an individual's genetic makeup, age, general health, and dietary habits. Standardized data about the average quantities of alcohol that can be tolerated by men or women are therefore meaningless. There is no such thing as normal alcohol consumption. As for traffic safety, the authorities have set strict limits in terms of parts per thousand for alcohol that may be found in the blood while a driver is operating a vehicle. In biochemistry, alcohol is a glucose fragment, and although the normal level of glucose in the blood is at 70 to 90 mg per 100 deciliters, there is no such normal level for alcohol. In fact, the normal level of alcohol in the blood is zero.

Did Mother Nature intend alcohol to be a normal constituent of food? No. Did Mother Nature create wine? No. In its original state, the vine is a liana. It reproduces with the help of birds that spread its seeds after having eaten the grapes. Wine was not anticipated in the program of nature. It is a purely human invention that nevertheless makes use of the natural process of fermentation and of the natural process that turns sugars into alcohol. In food, naturally produced alcohol is present in only small quantities in overripe fruits, in which the fermentation process changed sugars into alcohol. According to Masquelier, one might suppose that in the course of evolution, the liver developed a cleansing mechanism sufficient to deal with these incidental traces of alcohol. When humans started making and consuming wine, the body entered into a state of biological confusion because it can counter the excess of alcohol only by depleting itself of antioxidant enzymes and nutrients. This is a stopgap solution with bad consequences. Unless we drink alcohol in the form of red wine, it is a poison for the removal of which we need to make even more poison.

The ancient Greeks had already figured it out. For them, wine presented a biological intersection at which food, poison, and drugs met. This old Greek concept seems much more satisfactory to Masquelier than today's dualism in which wine is either a magical remedy or a poison that must be banned from our tables. The Greeks encouraged moderation, an attitude that made the Hellenic culture immortal. By restraining our desire to consume alcohol, we create the freedom to benefit from wine's medicinal properties. We should avail ourselves of this opportunity. The conflict between the beneficial and the damaging aspects of wine drinking can easily be overcome once the issue of quantity is taken into consideration. Consumed in small quantities, alcohol can easily be degraded by the liver and does not present any significant burden. A couple of glasses of wine consumed with a good meal can hardly cause any damage. Quite to the contrary they are beneficial for the organism. However, simular and larger quantities of alcohol (spirits) cause a problem and result in increased activity of free radicals. Substituting large daily quantities of alcohol with large quantities of red wine to try to shift away from the poisonous side of alcohol won't do. Red wine is healthy, but not in immoderate amounts. To paraphrase the chemistry of proanthocyanidins, as long as the number of glasses you drink is in the "oligo" range, you're fine. When you stumble into the "poly" range, you're losing what you gained.

34
WHY THE JAPANESE OUTLIVE THE FRENCH

In its May 30, 1986, issue, the *American Journal of Cardiology* published the results of a survey that ranked 14 industrialized countries in terms of mortality rate due to cardiac disorders. The study was based on figures from 1980 that were provided by the World Health Organization (WHO). Unlike the surveys that had given rise to the French paradox, this survey included Japan. Here are the resultst:

Country	Mortality Rate per 100,000
Finland	599
England	500
New Zealand	468
Australia	421
United States	398
Canada	390
Germany	314
Belgium	264
Argentina	250
Spain	225
Switzerland	216
Italy	212
France	137
Japan	65

Note: Based on a study of males aged 40 to 69 years.
Source: World Health Organization, 1980

Mortality Rate Due to Cardiac Disorders by Country, 1980

For those for whom the French paradox is the nutritional equivalent of the Gospel, the results of the WHO survey gave rise to the somewhat unsettling question: How could Japan rank ahead of France when so little wine is consumed in the Land of the Rising Sun? Was it the sushi or the sashimi? Was there some Japanese paradox that might overturn the French one? The French, who had only red wine to bring to the table, left the issue unmentioned. Maybe they were unaware of the survey. Maybe, in the slipstream of their public relations offensives for red wine, the fact that the Japanese invariably ranked more favorably in the same type of statistics was better left ignored and untouched. This attitude somewhat clouded a new and unique point made in the *American Journal of Cardiology* article: Japan had scored first in cardiovascular health!

When Masquelier read the publication, it would have been easy for him to have relaxed in complacency and to have continued harvesting the credits for his contributions to solving the French paradox without investigating the phytochemical roots of what looked like a Japanese paradox. What the epidemiologists or promoters of red wine would not or could not explain needed to be explained by the application of some sound phytochemistry, which seemed to Masquelier the best way to confront this issue. In fact, when he looked at the Japanese cardiovascular score, the simplicity and obviousness of the answer sprang to his mind right away. "Which food common in Japan," he asked himself, "also presents a protective effect on the heart?" The answer consisted of one simple word: tea. To be more specific, green tea, which is consumed in Japan in quantities equal to which the French consume wine. Masquelier's hunch was based on — you guessed it — what is usually referred to as the tannin content of green tea.

The use of the word tannin to describe the slightly astringent solids in a cup of tea is very common and broadly accepted. That you find tannins in tea is a "fact" that is as readily accepted as the fact that you find salt in the sea. But for someone like Masquelier, who has been "tanned" by erroneous use of terms and names during half a century of working in phytochemistry, a few corrective words must be spoken. The vine and the tea plant both produce catechins, which are indeed the building blocks of tannins. Tannins, as explained in *chapter 8: Colorless isn't Yellow or Red*, are the thicker clusters of proanthocyanidins, consisting of six or more catechin units. However, of the two plants, only the vine is able to combine the catechins into clusters of catechins, into oligomers and polymers of proanthocyanidins.

The tea plant lacks the enzyme that can cluster catechins. For that reason, tea does not contain proanthocyanidins. In other words, tea does not contain OPCs nor does it contain tannins. Tea contains only catechins. In red wine, we find catechins, OPCs, and tannins. The only ingredient red wine and green tea have in common is catechin. Although not as strong as OPCs, catechins do exert a protective antioxidant function. Green tea owes its antioxidant effect to its catechin content. It didn't take Masquelier very long to figure out that the catechins in Japan's national drink are responsible for the favorable cardiac condition of its population.

The Western reader may wonder, "When I take Masquelier's observations seriously, what explains the fact that cardiac mortality among the British, for whom "High Tea" is a sign of civilization, is 10 times higher than that of the Japanese? Might we be faced with a British counter-paradox?" Let me enlighten you.

The British do not benefit from the favorable effect that tea has on cardiovascular health because they and all other Western populations do not normally drink the unadulterated green tea. They prefer the black tea that is made through the fermentation and heating of fresh tea leaves. This treatment destroys the major part of fresh tea leaves' catechin content while developing flavors that are responsible for the black teas' aromas. In a way, the poor ranking of the British and other black-tea-drinking Western nations confirms the fact that catechins are the active principle in tea because in their tea, there are no catechins. Moreover, the Anglo-Saxon habit of drinking tea with a few drops of milk causes any potentially remaining catechin to bond with the milk's casein, thus losing its specific efficacy.

Already during 1942, the British biochemists Snow and Zilva discovered that vitamin C is rapidly destroyed by oxidation when added to black tea. Black tea works as an oxidant that depletes the body of antioxidants such as vitamin C and OPCs. Great Britain thus makes a big mistake if it wants to cheer up its residents with the false promise that a "nice cup of tea" has any cardiovascular benefits. The English cup of tea is not even a shadow if its Japanese equivalent. Nevertheless, Great Britain deserves credit because it was one of its citizens, the Welshman St. Leger, who bravely extolled the health assets of wine, a product his fellow citizens did not drink in sufficient quantities. For Masquelier's French colleagues and winemakers and promoters, their nestor's observations about the cause of the eminent cardiovascular condition of the Japanese population will have a reassuring effect. The presence of catechins is the antioxidant principle that red wine and green tea have in common.

There is a drawback to drinking green tea, though. Catechins display a certain level of toxicity. Although this is not a worry for those who don't drink excessive amounts of green tea, catechins' toxicity should not be completely neglected. It is the reason the catechins used by Lorenz and Reimann in their anti-ulcer experiment never made it to the shelves of pharmacies (see *chapter 26: Histamine, Stomach Ulcers, and Allergies*). The advantage of catechins' inhibition of ulcer formation is compromised by the fact that it burdens the liver. Because catechins impose themselves on the liver, they are known not only as antioxidant but also as hepatotoxic. In their isolated form, catechins in concentrated high dosages have been found to be unfit for use in medicine and nutrition. In this context, the term "theism" means tea poisoning. It refers to the fact that drinking green tea in large quantities can cause liver intoxication due to catechins.

What about the relatively smaller quantities of catechins we find in MASQUELIER's Original OPCs (ANTHOGENOL) and MASQUELIER's French Pine Bark Complex? Are they toxic? In all the toxicity tests performed with MASQUELIER's Original OPCs and MASQUELIER's French Pine Bark Complex, there was never any sign or indication that the catechins in these products caused any toxicity. For some reason, when present in the natural ratio in which they coexist with OPCs in the living plant, catechins do not show any toxicity, and they attain their optimum biological efficacy. Therefore, catechins need not be eliminated from the MASQUELIER's products.

Neither is there any reason to fear that any toxicity could be caused by the catechins in red wine, where they also coexist with OPCs. We owe this insight not only to scientists, such as Frankel and Teissedre, but also to their predecessors. One of them was Jean Lavollay, a biochemist and colleague of Masquelier during his younger days. Masquelier and Lavollay knew each other well and often went to congresses together. Lavollay was interested primarily in plants. He was very familiar with catechins, and during the 1940s, he had compared their structure with that of citrin's bioflavonoid components. It was in the days that Szent-Györgyi developed the concept of vitamin P. His ideas had created an atmosphere of enthusiasm in which scientists all over the world tried discover vitamin P, the cofactor of vitamin C. For that reason, Lavollay examined catechins and epicatechins. He was anxious to find out whether catechins had the same effect on capillary vessels as the effect that Szent-Györgyi had claimed for citrin. While the latter worked with extracts from citrus fruits and peppers, Lavollay worked with red wine. During 1943 and 1944, Lavollay conducted a series of tests in which he gave guinea pigs red wine, which he knew to contain catechins and epicatechins.

Michel Flanzy, a contemporary of Lavollay and Masquelier who worked in Narbonne, France, had already pointed out that red wine administered to guinea pigs had a strengthening effect on their capillary vessels. Lavollay's studies confirmed this insight. He showed that following the intake of several milliliters of red wine, the capillary resistance of guinea pigs doubled within one to two hours. This increase was many times more significant than the best results that were ever reached with citrin. Obviously, the wine that was applied by Lavollay and Flanzy contained not only catechins but also OPCs. But because at the time of their experiments they were able to identify only catechins, everybody attributed the wine's vitamin P effect to catechins. In fact, red wine's beneficial effects depend largely on its OPCs content. Yet, catechins contribute to the effect, as was confirmed later by scientists such as Teissedre and Frankel.

You may wonder: "When catechins are weaker than OPCs, how is it that the Japanese score so immensely high in cardiovascular health?" To answer this question, let's see if the Japanese miracle is also a paradox or just the result of an overall healthy diet. The French paradox is a paradox because when you look at the average dinner table fare in France, you would not expect the French to score so well. Sausages, butter, foie gras, ham, bacon, paté, mayonnaise, meat, cheese, sweetbread, eggs, and fried potatoes are common savory elements in the French diet. Frankly speaking, although the French paradox may be reassuring for wine drinkers and winemakers, the paradox rests on the correct observation that the French dietary habits without the red wine would be killing. Surely, in the southern parts of France, people eat what is called the Mediterranean diet, which is known for its fresh salads and vegetable oils. Many French people do take good care of their health, but statistically speaking, the French are saved by their elegant paradox that permits them to overcome the consequences of eating what they like so much. In this way, the French paradox stops being paradox where the Mediterranean diet fills the tables. Likewise, there is no paradox in Japan in that the consumption of catechins would have to compensate an unhealthy diet. In the traditional Japanese diet, there isn't much to compensate for. The Japanese tables are filled with fish and seafood, both containing lots of omega-3 fatty acids, rice, and raw vegetables. Under such favorable dietary conditions, the catechins, although weaker than OPCs, are capable of tipping an already balanced scale.

35 TANNINS, TOO BIG TO HANDLE

Compared with catechins and OPCs, tannins are huge molecules that turn from brownish-red to brown as they increase in size. In contrast to the red color of anthocyanins, it is not a bright red that gradually turns to brown. Tannins are "brownies," not "reddies." The discovery of colorless OPCs was difficult not only because the OPCs are hidden in the equally colorless protein part of plants (peanuts, cacao beans), but also because they are hidden in plant parts that are overwhelmingly browned by tannins (grape seed skins, peanut skin, pine bark). The problem of finding OPCs was confounded by the fact that OPCs and tannins are both procyanidins. Like OPCs, tannins turn red in the Bate-Smith reaction. In addition, tannins are much bigger and largely outnumber the OPCs in their natural plant environment, which makes Masquelier's discovery of OPCs that much more impressive.

How was it possible that by the use of simple table salt Masquelier separated the valuable phytonutrient OPCs from the antinutritional tannins? A significant amount of salt changes the tannins' solubility so that they precipitate. In fact, getting rid of the tannins by way of "salting them out" is a physical maneuver rather than a chemical one. Because OPCs are not physically affected in a salty environment, they remain in solution. This salting out of tannins has always been the essential preliminary step in the production of OPCs. Much later, in 1990, Masquelier described and patented another way of separating OPCs from tannins by influencing the solubility of tannins. In the laboratory, he had found that lowering the temperature of a solution tends to lower the solubility of tannins.

Those who spend time in the kitchen know that it is easier to dissolve substances in hot water than in cold water. Dissolve a spoonful of honey in a glass of hot water and then dissolve another spoonful in a glass of ice water. You'll see the difference. Before isolating OPCs from the crude teas made from whatever plant Masquelier and his colleagues were investigating, they used to get rid of the major part of the tannins by putting the liquid in the refrigerator for a night. The lower the temperature, the lower the solubility of the tannins, and after one night, the majority of the tannins had precipitated and could be filtered. It saved the researchers a lot of salt.

Studying the peanut, Masquelier originally wanted to determine whether the skin surrounding the nut might actually contain something toxic. In 1945, scientists were preoccupied with the problem of the toxicity of tannins — more specifically, with the problems of toxicity of tannic acids, which seemed to be chemically related to tannins. In those days, the precise chemical nature of these seemingly related substances was still a closed book. The fact that OPCs (chromogen at the time) resembled tannins wasn't a good sign. During the war the use of phosphor bombs had caused burns of an unprecedented severity among soldiers and civilians. The heavy fighting that took place at Tobruk during World War II in 1941 and 1942 was literally marked by phosphor bombs that killed and scarred many soldiers. For many years, such skin burns had been treated with tannic acid, a tremendously efficient therapy. The tannic acid "seals off" the wound and makes it impenetrable for bacteria. However, it became obvious that the victims of burns developed severe liver and kidney damage that resulted sometimes in death due to toxemia (blood poisoning) within less than six days. The damaging effect was attributed to tannic acid, an assumption that was confirmed in experiments with guinea pigs. The tests involved the topical treatment of experimental burns as well as the subcutaneous injection of tannic acid.

What exactly was this tannic acid that doctors used on the battlefield? It was an extract obtained from the oak gall apple (Allepo gall), which is the primary source of gallo-tannins. The chemical structure of this group of substances is based on the combination of gallic acid and glucose. Tannic acids are big heavy molecules. Unlike the tannins related to OPCs, tannic acid does not contain catechin units. Under the influence of heat and acid, tannic acid splits into its individual components: gallic acid and glucose. Technically speaking, gallo-tannins are characterized by their heteroside structure; that is, by the fact that gallo-tannins contain an "-ose" or sugar molecule. Relevant as this explanation may be for the biochemist, it didn't mean much to those physicians who dealt with the toxicity of this substance for treating burns. For the doctors, it was sufficient to always remember that tannic acid should be used with caution because the massive application of this substance on the skin causes severe damage to the liver.

Were OPCs to be used with the same level of caution? That was the question Masquelier had to answer when he was preparing for his doctoral degree. He noticed no reactions of a gallo-tannic nature when he administered the first OPCs to guinea pigs, neither following the topical application nor after subcutaneous injection. But what about the sugarless tannins, the thick proanthocyanidins? Are they as toxic as tannic acid? At the time, nobody really knew. Now we know the structure of catechins, OPCs, and tannins, and we also know that tannins are unrelated to tannic acid. Through his growing insight in this matter, Masquelier came closer and closer to explaining how it is that since the beginning of human history, people have been consuming catechins, OPCs and tannins and why these flavanol compounds have been human companions throughout the ages.

Tannins are responsible for the astringent taste in foods. They have a slightly antiviral effect, but this effect is of no further interest because tannins are not bioavailable. In Masquelier's opinion, tannins should be used for their only valuable property, a property that people have known about for a long time: their effectiveness against diarrhea. Because of their size, tannins cannot pass the intestinal barrier and are therefore not bioavailable. And this is good because the big size of the molecules makes tannins genuinely antinutritional. Like OPCs, they show an affinity for proteins, but because tannins are much bigger than OPCs, their affinity for proteins takes on such a magnitude that it cannot be sustained by the living protein structures in our body. Tannins are so powerful that they "crush" where OPCs gently stay in check with the delicacy of the tissues they protect. OPCs and the body's cells and structures are of comparable magnitude. Tannins are out of sync. Yet, when tannins overwhelm and neutralize diarrhetic putrefactive proteins by forming tanno-protein complexes in the intestines, tannins are of service for keeping these bad proteins out of our system.

Inside our system, tannins have a destructive rather than a healing effect. Apart from serving us as an antidiarrhetic compound, they are more useful for tanning leather. Hide, which consists of collagen, requires a strong tanning agent to protect it against decomposition. Fishing nets and sails, when they were still made of organic materials, were tanned with tannins, which is why, when well tanned, they displayed a brownish-red color. Leather tanning is now done with chemicals, and nets and sails no longer need tanning. When we speak the word "tan" today, we usually mean suntan because after exposure to sunshine, our skin takes on the color of tanned leather. However, the difference is that the tan created by the sun is not of a protective nature. On the contrary, sunshine is a massive source of free radicals, and it destroys our skin the way it destroys the page of a newspaper we leave on a garden table. (See *chapter 28: OPCs, The Mightiest Scavengers of Free Radicals*.) OPCs can be considered mild and much more delicate tanning agents for the human body in the sense that they protect cells (the skin!) the way tannins protect sails and nets.

Because of their molecular size, tannins cannot pass from the intestinal tract into the blood; rather, they block the passage. The body does not get along well with tannins. This is, by the way, the reason the saliva of typical plant eaters contains considerable quantities of the amino acids lysine and proline. These amino acids adhere themselves to tannins so that the complex of amino acid plus tannin will be eliminated through the intestinal tract. Humans and animals have another even simpler way of avoiding tannins. When a vegetal product or foodstuff contains an excessively high concentration of tannins, it produces a strong astringency. The food becomes distasteful, both for humans and for plant eaters, and it is left uneaten.

Yet, there's a drink that many of us are fond of for its tannin content. Wine connoisseurs know what it is. Many red wines are praised for their "ripe tannins," which give them a touch of astringency that, combined with all the other wonderful substances that can excite our taste buds, gives red wines their unique place on our dinner tables. In the wine industry, pure tannins are known to influence the character of wines. Tannin is added to the cheaper cognacs and to the cheaper red wines to give the impression of maturity and age. In a similar way, certain producers of grape seed extracts inflate their extracts by leaving tannins in their product not to influence the taste, but simply to dilute and yet give consumers the false impression that they are consuming OPCs. Speaking of tricks, most readers probably don't know that the reason red wines that have never seen a wooden barrel taste so wonderfully "oaky" is that producers hang pieces of oak in the vast stainless steel hectoliters of wine awaiting bottling. Though the French allow the use of tannins, the "oaking" of wines is considered a criminal act! As far as Masquelier is concerned, selling tannins as OPCs is an equally unfair practice.

36 GRAPE SEED EXTRACT, THE DREADED SCENARIO

Many herbal extracts or plant extracts are brought into distribution under the names of the plants from or with which they were made. Drugstores and health food stores offer products labeled, for instance, Kava Kava, Echinacea, and St. John's Wort. To the unsuspecting consumer, this may sound normal and perfectly acceptable. After all, the botanical names of many of these plants ring a bell in the minds of most consumers, and most people trust that herbal products sold through these trusted stores are safe, natural, and effective. The lack of essential information regarding an extract's components or active ingredients is often overlooked because people believe that the unidentified ingredients will somehow have a "synergistic effect."

In most cases, such botanical extracts are sold without any reference to their method of production and without any reference to a quality standard. If a quality standard is mentioned in terms of one component, it is often unclear whether the given quantity of this component was later added to an otherwise worthless extract or marks a known and researched extract. In most cases, even the trained observer is left guessing whether the manufacturer used the whole plant for extraction or used a certain part of the plant and, if so, which part. We aren't informed about the origin of the extract and about the name of the actual manufacturer. We're not told in which country the extract was made and according to what local standards it was produced.

Sellers of such unidentified and untraceable extracts put their own brand on a bottle to tell consumers that this is X's

Echinacea and Y's Kava Kava. And if X's St. John's Wort is half the price of Y's, then why buy X's? Companies X, Y, Z and their beloved competitors use the name of a plant that has become well known as the source of a standardized, proven, well-researched, and often trademarked product to sell something different that was nevertheless made with or from the same plant. The differences, if known at all to the seller, are conveniently left unmentioned, and consumers have little or no means to make the distinction. This is how outstanding, well-researched, high-quality extracts and phytonutrients are being discredited — coattail riders are selling unidentified and untraceable products.

A recent example is Kava Kava. When made as the people of the Pacific Islands make it, Kava Kava has a soothing effect on the human mind. In its original and working form, Kava Kava was brought to the United States by the American author and researcher Chris Kilham. In 2002, authorities in some European countries decided to ban Kava Kava because incidental reports had emerged about its potential toxicity. Although the Pacific Islanders have been happily drinking Kava for centuries without incident, all of a sudden, there was a discussion about Kava's safety. One of the things that was found during the investigations that followed was that a Hawaiian manufacturer had begun extracting the entire plant instead of only the roots and that potentially toxic components in the stem had thus ended up in the extract. Why? Because of the growing demand for the extract, this manufacturer simply figured that he could make more extract of the entire plant than from the roots only. The pharmaceutical lobby and its political friends smiled when the authorities blindly shot down a perfectly safe product that competes with regular tranquilizers and sleeping pills from which the same authorities happily accept the hazards and numerous side effects. The herbal products industry screamed, but in fact, authorities did what the industry does: lump unrelated products under the name of a plant.

The wondrous world of "grape seed extracts" presents another example of such unsavory practices. Consumers of dietary supplements and even many bona fide natural foods retailers have somehow come to believe that the term grape seed extract means something. Respected members of the health food industry have embraced the term as a supposedly meaningful one to describe unidentified and untraceable materials that have little more in common than that their production process somehow started with seeds of grapes. Pulled by the tractor called profit, the grape seed bandwagon began to live a life of its own, and manufacturers popped up as corn in a hot pan. As a result of the frenzy, we now find grape seed extract in cosmetic products of reputable manufacturers, probably because their marketing staff came to notice the growing demand for something that was named grape seed extract.

For Masquelier, this is a dreaded scenario because it is absolutely contrary to everything he stands for. For the discoverer of OPCs, it is a frightening thought that his scientific methods and accomplishments could have given rise to products that fail to comply with even the minimum of the requirements set for MASQUELIER's Original OPCs. After decades of scientific labor, Masquelier had finally freed OPCs from the curse of being erroneously classified as bioflavonoids. And then, when the American Natural Foods industry got wind of OPCs and of Masquelier's work, it engulfed OPCs under a tidal wave called grape seed extracts. There is no relevant pharmaceutical, nutritional, biochemical, or analytical definition of grape seed extract nor is there one standardized manufacturing method of producing it. There are no commonly accepted, clear analytical "fingerprints" for qualifying grape seed extract. In fact, the term is so broad and so vague that it could mean anything.

Nevertheless, this scenario has become a reality that will implode when those who inflate it find something else to knock off. Masquelier lives in another world. He feels that we cannot do without chemistry, without analytical due diligence, without safety tests, and without clinical trials when it comes to making claims for products that people buy to improve or sustain their health. Ever since he boiled his first peanut skins, Masquelier, his colleagues, and their coworkers have gone to great lengths to isolate, analyze, identify, qualify, and quantify OPCs. Most of the companies to which Masquelier and his colleagues entrusted the fruits of their scientific work have adhered to the same scientific criteria, at least for as long as these fruits were protected by patents that specified the criteria.

Now, imitators sell their products by implying and claiming in clever ways that their imitations have the same health benefits as Masquelier's OPCs. Some of these companies even have the effrontery to use Masquelier's name to unfairly promote an unrelated product by wrongly establishing credibility for a product that has never been touched by the inventor's scientific hand. In most such cases, sellers do not provide proof of their implicit or explicit claims. This is another practice for which the Natural Foods industry uses the euphemism "borrowing science." Normally, when you borrow a cup of sugar from your neighbor, you replace it the next day. In the Natural Foods industry, the science that is borrowed is never returned. And what's worse, it is being used to make claims for products that cannot even stand in the shadow of the tested product.

Consider a comparison of OPCs with vitamin C. Both materials are well-defined ingredients, but there is a difference. No pure vitamin C is extracted from lemons or oranges, which are known good sources of vitamin C. To the contrary, OPCs cannot be synthesized; they must be isolated from vegetal materials. Did you ever see an orange extract or a lemon extract being sold as vitamin C? I didn't. Why then would companies sell grape seed extract as OPCs? Vitamin C is made of starch. It is not being isolated from lemons or oranges because natural vitamin C would be much more expensive than the vitamin C that is synthesized from starch. Likewise, lemon extract or orange extract is much more expensive than the vitamin C that is being made from starch in massive quantities. So, there is no room here for making a quick buck and for cutting corners. In the case of MASQUELIER's Original OPCs, producing grape seed extract is infinitely less costly than isolating OPCs. In fact, the low quality of some grape seed extracts shows that these extracts are no more than the raw material from which OPCs are isolated.

During the first half of 2001, some of America's mainstream media reopened their recurring attacks on the natural foods industry. As recently as spring 2003, some of Europe's mainstream media did their best to discredit dietary supplements. During the same period, the media in Australia and New Zealand scandalized dietary supplements. Activist members of the health food industry see the dark hand of the "Pharma Kartel" behind these attacks. The more regular members of the industry respond to such attacks by showing that most of it is mere propaganda, intended to hurt rather than to inform. It may very well be that the methods and background of these propagandists are dishonest and serve the Pharmaceutical Masters or other vested interests that would love to see the demise of dietary supplements and free choice. What is disturbing is that the natural foods industry should have guarded itself against these attacks by selling certified, proven, researched, and clinically tested ingredients of traceable origin. Especially in the field of herbal extracts, integrity and honesty are vital ingredients when it comes to offering products to a public that has no way of controlling or inspecting food supplements. Selling low-priced, low-quality imitations that do not give consumers satisfaction creates the complaints that end up on the desks of authorities and journalists.

It also gives rise to warnings issued by respectable scientists. In the September 2000 issue of the English journal *Free Radical Biology & Medicine,* UC Berkeley Professor Martyn T. Smith and graduate student Christine F. Skibola warn that flavonoids sold in high doses as dietary supplements in health food stores "are likely to make you sick." More in particular, the Berkeley scientists warn against "popular products as ginkgo pills, quercetin tablets, grape seed extract, and flaxseed, which contain high concentrations of flavonoids." "When consumed in the diet, plant flavonoids actually have the capacity to become carcinogenic at higher levels," says Smith. In this respect, Smith even mentions a rare form of leukemia in young children, and he states, "I think some Americans could be poisoning themselves with these supplements."

The mutagenic effect of high doses of bioflavonoids such as quercetin and coumarin has been known for many decades. I have made reference to this earlier in the book. Gingko extracts contain high levels of bioflavonoids. Per the definition of grape seed extract that was officially adopted and promoted by the platform of the American health food industry, the American National Natural Foods Association (NNFA), the inclusion of grape seed extracts in what the Berkeley scientists call "risk" products is factually correct. Under the auspices of the NNFA, a white paper was compiled regarding grape seed extracts. In it, the NNFA defines grape seed extracts as products that "may consist of hundreds of known, and perhaps thousands of unknown, naturally occurring, biologically active substances that aren't OPCs, such as quercetin, ferulic acid, caffeic acid, coumaric acid, and myricitin." The paper's editor, Jim Roza, also writes, "The amount and types of compounds present in a particular grape seed extract can vary and is greatly influenced by the extraction process, as well as the source, variety, and storage of seeds used." The Berkeley inclusion of grape seed extracts in the category of risk products therefore fits the definition that is officially used by the NNFA.

Did Berkeley professor Smith bring something new to the table? With all due respect, I am afraid not. In July 1979, quoting peer reviewed scientific publications, Masquelier wrote, "Certain bioflavonoids are mutagenic in high doses." Masquelier's reason for publishing then what his Berkeley colleague published in 2000 arose from the need to distinguish the beneficial and safe OPCs from the not-so-harmless bioflavonoids with which OPCs were always confused. Masquelier's 1979 publication puts the Berkeley publication in an unexpected historic perspective. The matter also puts in perspective the issue that has dominated all of Masquelier's work: OPCs differ significantly from bioflavonoids not just on the point of mutagenicity, but also on the point of bioavailability and therefore on the point of efficacy. In fact, the risks of taking high doses of bioflavonoids are mitigated by the fact that most bioflavonoids are not bioavailable. In direct comparison with OPCs, Masquelier and his team demonstrated that the bioflavonoid rutin is not bioavailable. Our body protects itself against the mutagenic effect of bioflavonoids by breaking them down in the gastrointestinal tract. The perfect bioavailability of MASQUELIER's Original OPCs and the malabsorption of bioflavonoids mark one of the important differences between OPCs and bioflavonoids.

A few years ago, the unsurpassed record of safety of MASQUELIER's Original OPCs (ANTHOGENOL) was confirmed in a modern Reverse Mutation (AMES) mutagenicity test performed by BSL BIOSERVICE, an independent German test facility in Münich. In compliance with ever-stricter standards for nonmutagenicity, BSL BIOSERVICE performed a modern AMES Assay on MASQUELIER's Original OPCs. No sign of mutagenicity was found. The total lack of mutagenicity of MASQUELIER's Original OPCs stems from the fact that OPCs essentially differ from bioflavonoids. Even though grape seeds are used as the vegetal material for making OPCs, OPCs are not to be classified as a grape seed extract. MASQUELIER's Original OPCs (ANTHOGENOL) do not fall in the category of the risk products listed by Smith. The Berkeley scientists do not seem to have made an in-depth study of Masquelier's work. They persevere in classifying proanthocyanidins as flavonoids, yet the overall message of their publication unintentionally acknowledges

303

Masquelier's pioneering and innovative work, in which he relentlessly demonstrated and explained the differences between flavonoids and OPCs. Paradoxically, Smith and Skibola wrote an interesting chapter in the history of Masquelier's struggle for recognition of OPCs as a separate and safe set of compounds.

You may perhaps think that these words are written because a retired French professor harbors some old grudges against some charlatans who borrowed his science and made his life less pleasant. Independently performed tests that objectively confirmed the enormous differences between OPCs and grape seed extracts show that my evaluation of grape seed extract is not a matter of Masquelier's grudge or opinion. During 1997, an independent laboratory in Chelmsford, Massachusetts, performed a comparative analysis of MASQUELIER's Original OPCs (ANTHOGENOL), MASQUELIER's French Pine Bark Complex, and 10 grape seed extracts. The analytical methods used by the Chelmsford laboratory (PhytoChem Laboratories, named ESA Laboratories at the time of the testing) had previously been intensely explored and thoroughly applied by Dr. Marie-Claude Dumon of the University of Bordeaux.

In her 1990 doctoral thesis, Dumon explains in great detail how she exactly analyzed OPCs isolated from various plants according to Masquelier's method. PhytoChem embedded Dumon's work in a set of five state-of-the-art analytical tests. Combining the results of these five tests leads to the conclusion that a representative section of grape seed extracts broadly sold in the United States and elsewhere don't have much in common with MASQUELIER's Original OPCs and MASQUELIER's French Pine Bark Complex. The Special Reports in which PhytoChem's comparative work was published can be found on INC's website www.masquelier.com.

37
THE U.S. PATENT REVISITED

Dr. Masquelier's relationship with the largest dietary supplement market in the world has always been somewhat ambiguous. On April 9, 1985, he applied for his free radical scavenging patent at the U.S. Patent Office, well aware that there was an essential point he had long held in common with the National Academy of Sciences/National Research Council. In 1968, on the basis of the opinion of a review panel of the National Research Council, the Food and Drug Administration (FDA) had issued a statement saying that flavonoids are not effective in humans "for any condition." The FDA then initiated action to withdraw flavonoid drugs from the market. Under the title "Requiem for Flavonoid Drugs," the February 9, 1968, issue of a publication on drugs and therapies called *The Medical Letter* the following appeared:

> *"In fact, the evidence that flavonoids are effective is so meager that the package insert for one product (Hesperidin Methyl Chalcone with vitamin C © Lilly) states: "The pharmacologic activity of the flavonoids in man is not well established," and "Convincing evidence" of the efficacy of flavonoids in these [clinical] conditions is lacking."*

THE MEDICAL LETTER
a non-profit publication
on Drugs and Therapeutics

Published by Drug and Therapeutic Information, Inc., 305 East 45th Street, New York, New York 10017

Vol. 10, No. 3 (Issue 237)   February 9, 1968

REQUIEM FOR FLAVONOID DRUGS

The Food and Drug Administration has decided, on the basis of both its own investigations and the findings of a review panel of the National Academy of Sciences/National Research Council that flavonoids are not effective in man "for any

Masquelier could not have agreed more, but he feared that no difference would be made between flavonoids and "his" OPCs so that OPCs would also be swept under the FDA's carpet. Thus, there was also the risk that the examiner of Masquelier's patent application would refuse to grant the patent for OPCs' antioxidant effect. And this is exactly what initially happened.

The examiner of the U.S. Patent Office objected to Masquelier's patent application. He based his rejection on the opinion that OPCs were bioflavonoids and on the fact that the antioxidant effect of bioflavonoids had already been described in a 1981 article of the Frenchman I. Maridonneau. Maridonneau describes how he performed an antioxidant test with a product called Difrarel. Difrarel is a bilberry extract with a standardized content of anthocyanosides (same as anthocyanins), the red pigment of which OPCs are the precursors (see *chapter 8: Colorless Isn't Yellow or Red*). Anthocyanosides are found in red wine and in many berries, the best known of them being the bilberry or Vaccinium myrtillus. Anthocyanosides, or anthocyanins, are anthocyanidins to which nature has connected a sugar molecule. On request of Difrarel's manufacturer, Merck, Sharp & Dohme-Chibret, Maridonneau had checked "the effect of flavonoids," as Difrarel's anthocyanosides were called, on the oxidation of red blood cells. The test showed that outside the human body, in vitro, "flavonoids have antiperoxidative properties."

As far as Masquelier was concerned, the examiner's choice for the Maridonneau article was spot-on because Masquelier was completely familiar with the situation. Masquelier wrote the examiner that during 1980, Difrarel's manufacturer had approached him with a request "to remedy the serious shortcomings they had discovered in Difrarel." Although Masquelier declined the invitation, he did point out to Merck, Sharp & Dohme-Chibret that anthocyanosidic vegetable extracts are unstable. This effect is easily observed when red wine is kept without precautions. Soon one finds a reddish precipitate and the wine loses its intense coloring. "In a century-old bottle of a vintage wine, initially a red wine," wrote Masquelier to the examiner, "I have myself ascertained that the anthocyanosides had completely disappeared, being converted into an insoluble dark red deposit accumulated at the bottom of the bottle. This wine was practically colorless." The same effect can be observed in black currant liquor, which loses its clear, bright red coloring. All this because "anthocyanosidic molecules are fragile," not only in red wine and currant juices, but also in Difrarel. Masquelier informed the examiner that he had observed the complete perishing of Difrarel's anthocyanosides within five months after its date of production.

Furthermore, Masquelier explained to the examiner in a declaration made in December 1986, "There are at least 10 different anthocyanosides," and none of them were specified by Maridonneau. Masquelier also explained that anthocyanosides differ from OPCs in structure and function and that unlike anthocyanosides, OPCs cannot be classified as bioflavonoids. When Masquelier checked the results given by Maridonneau in an antioxidative test, he found, "Difrarel is inactive at the concentration at which PPBE produced a 50% inhibition." In other words, anthocyanosides are inactive at the concentration at which MASQUELIER's French Pine Bark Complex (PPBE) produces a 50% inhibition. With regard to the century-old bottle of red wine, Masquelier reported to the examiner that he found in it only proanthocyanidins that are colorless. What better evidence than a century-old red wine could possibly exist to show the differences between anthocyanosides and OPCs!

On October 6, 1987, the American government finally granted Masquelier U.S. Patent No. 4,698,360, which he had applied for two and a half years earlier. It formalized Masquelier's discovery that OPCs are capable of scavenging free radicals. The '360 patent, as it was soon called, protects the use of OPCs as a "therapeutic agent having radical scavenging effect and use thereof." To quote from the patent's abstract, "The invention provides a method for preventing and fighting the harmful biological effects of free radicals in the organism of warm-blooded animals and more especially in human beings, namely cerebral involution, hypoxia following atherosclerosis, cardiac or cerebral infarction, tumor promotion, inflammation, ischemia, alterations of the synovial liquid, collagen degradation, among others."

By granting Masquelier the '360 patent, the U.S. Patent Office implicitly confirmed Masquelier's findings that there is a difference between bioflavonoids and OPCs. For Masquelier, this provided perhaps an even greater satisfaction than the granting of the patent itself because for several decades, he had been preoccupied with the bioflavonoid issue. The actual invention and the fact that the U.S. Patent Office had granted Masquelier a patent for it was not received with utter delight by everybody. To Masquelier's surprise, the '360 patent was challenged in 1996, when an anonymous person or company filed a request for reexamination. Hundreds of pages were sent to the U.S. Patent Office, all relating to research that had been done with bioflavonoids. In the field of patents, there is something called "prior art." It has nothing to do with art, but it simply means that if the technique, product, or use an inventor claims to be an invention existed before the date of the inventor's claim, the inventor's invention is not patentable even when he was unaware of the prior art. So "Anonymous" and friends tried to overwhelm the Patent Office with what they claimed to be prior art. They sought to convince the examiner of the obsolete theory that OPCs are bioflavonoids — an issue the examiner had already examined in 1987.

This anonymous request for reexamination was handled by the same examiner who had examined Masquelier's patent application during 1985-1987. Dr. John W. Rollins was obviously the right man to take a decision in this reexamination because he had examined the same issues almost 10 years earlier. With the help of International Nutrition Company (INC), the worldwide supplier of the MASQUELIER's products, and its American patent lawyer, Norman Zivin, Masquelier diligently answered Rollins's questions the same way he had done 10 years before. In his final August 22, 1997, decision Rollins confirmed the validity of Masquelier's '360 patent, stating that none of the documents presented to the Patent Office by those who wanted to crack the '360 patent "teach or suggest" Masquelier's invention. "In addition," examiner Rollins stated, "prior to 1985, the skilled artisan did not know that proanthocyanidins possessed any free radical scavenger activity." Again, OPCs were separated from bioflavonoids.

Today, confusion undoubtedly exists in the field of nutritional supplements and dietary foods with respect to their actual antioxidant properties. Innumerable antioxidative ingredients and formulations are offered to the public. A single product may contain 10 or more substances that are all supposed to fulfill an antioxidative function. Our increased need for safe and bioavailable antioxidants has been addressed in previous chapters. Processed foods and profound social changes have altered our eating habits. The dinner table is no longer a place where the whole family meets and eats. Most people have completely lost track of the nutritional value or lack of value of the foods they consume. Health-conscious consumers looking for a natural, safe, bioavailable, well-researched, documented, and patented phytonutrient that can efficiently protect the most sensitive structures of the human body against free radicals make no mistake when they pick MASQUELIER's Original OPCs (ANTHOGENOL). After all, per U.S. Patent 4,698,360, ANTHOGENOL's free radical scavenging effect "may prevent, attenuate or inhibit the harmful effects of aging caused by an excess of free radicals."

38
CELEBRATE YOUR OWN 120TH BIRTHDAY

For those who had hoped that the discoverer of OPCs also discovered the Fountain of Eternal Youth, the text of the '360 patent contains a slight disappointment. According to Masquelier, the radical scavenging effect of OPCs "does not overcome aging, which is a biological process programmed in the genes." So, you may wonder, will OPCs prolong my life? The answer is that they may because in any individual case, OPCs could "prevent, attenuate, or inhibit the harmful effects of aging caused by an excess of free radicals." In other words, OPCs may prevent premature aging and premature death.

If your body is genetically scheduled for a life of 90 years but succumbs prematurely of a heart attack at 65, you miss out on 25 years of a lifetime that may still have brought you happiness, friendship, and satisfaction. OPCs can help you bridge the gap that separates the moment of your premature death from the moment at which your genetically programmed life span was scheduled to come to an end. Without a doubt, living a long and happy life was always a major preoccupation of our ancestors. The many generations before us feared sickness and premature death as much as we do. Looking at the history of the last 2 millennia, we can see that we've made good progress. In ancient Rome, for instance, half a generation had died by the age of 20. In 1900, the age level at which half a generation had died had shifted to approximately 65 years. The increase can be attributed to various factors, of which hygiene is certainly the most significant. This factor concerns not only personal hygiene, but also environmental hygiene: clean water and the disposal of sewage. Cleanliness in handling food, an understanding of good nutrition, and better health care through medicine and hospitals all contribute to a life expectancy that is longer than that of our ancestors.

For a long time, it was assumed that the theoretical limit of the human body's life was about 100 years. A French woman, Jeanne Calment, proved otherwise when she died at the age of 124 not too long ago. By celebrating her 124th birthday, Mrs. Calment confirmed what scientists had been figuring out more recently. Examining human DNA in terms of maximum life span, they now assume that 120 years is the limit for the human body. Celebrating your 120th birthday seems a good idea, but what if you've been sick since you reached 75? A long life doesn't mean much without quality of life. The ideal situation, of course, would be that you live in good health, without experiencing the agony of degeneration and sickness until a genetically disposed point in time and then die a natural death simply because your genes instruct your body to cease living.

Long before Masquelier devoted himself to the free radical scavenging effects of OPCs and to OPCs' effects on aging, the biologist Denham Harman had conducted a landslide experiment in the United States. In the early 1960s, Harman had found that the life span of mice could be prolonged when their food was supplemented with an antioxidant called BHT (Butylhydroxytoluene). BHT is an admitted antioxidant used in the food industry to protect foodstuffs from the damaging effects of oxygen, thus making them less perishable. BHT protects vegetable oils against rancidity, but it works equally well in synthetic rubbers and plastics. The mice with which Harman did the experiment were bred from the same family. Over a period of 10 years, they reproduced only among themselves, so that they finally displayed tremendous genetic similarities, almost as if they had been cloned. Because of their genetic similarity, all the mice in the Harman experiment had exactly the same life span of 18 months, which was considered typical for their species.

By feeding them BHT, Harman succeeded in prolonging the life span of his mice by as much as 45 percent, and the mice attained their genetically programmed life span. The mice, which were on record as having a normal life expectancy of 18 months, now lived an unexpected 24 months. BHT lifted the animals way over what now appeared to be a premature death at 18 months. This finding furnished solid evidence that fighting free radicals in the animal organism resulted in a significant prolongation of the life span. Harman assumed that when people's food was enriched with antioxidants, his results could be transferred to humans. However, to scientifically confirm Harman's opinion is difficult for several reasons:

- Even scientific researchers usually shy away from experiments concerning human life span because the scientists involved are not likely to live long enough to learn about the results of the required multigeneration studies. In reality, those who want to attain an eminent reputation in the sciences tomorrow work hard at producing studies whose results can be published today.
- Not all known antioxidants are innocuous and could therefore be taken daily during an entire lifetime.
- In view of our relatively long life span, a comparable experiment in humans would have to be conducted over a period of at least 50 years to attain reasonably

conclusive results. And then, if we'd want to redo the Harman test per the book, it could be done only with a group of people with an identical genetic makeup. Ethical implications, however, forbid that we inbreed until we have clonelike men and women who share an identical set of genes. Even if we would find first-generation volunteers, their second- or third-generation children may opt out of an experiment that will take several generations.

In *chapter 30: Tumor Prevention and Cancer,* we looked at the role of free radicals in cell formation and disease. After we've reached the summit of our life span, the aging process of the human body sets in. Newly formed cells are of a lower quality than the old cells being replaced. Eventually, the cells become shadows of their former selves. The major reason for this diminishing of new cells' quality is not that the genes are programmed to "span" your body's life from conception through birth, youth, adulthood, and maturity to old age, in a process that would ideally take 120 years. Very few of us make it to a 120 because our genetic material is constantly under bombardment by free radicals. In computer terms, when you expose your hard disk to a voltage that is too high, it loses its capacity to copy its contents. In the same way, free radicals shoot holes in genetic material and prevent it from copying its contents without mistakes.

With aging, the body's capacity to produce enzymes that scavenge free radicals slackens, giving free radicals more freedom to attack sensitive structures such as the genes. When the aging process accelerates beyond its normal pace, it begins to produce cells that are no longer in conformity. Normally, the immune system traces such deformed cells and destroys them. In an aging body, the immune system gets weaker and weaker. Earlier in the book, we noted that people who have been on immune-suppressing drugs have a fivefold chance of developing cancer. People who suffer from a deficient immune system, as in AIDS, often die of cancer or pneumonia simply because the body lacks the capacity to trace and destroy abnormal cells. Old age can work in a similar way — as an immune deficiency.

For obvious reasons, Masquelier cannot guarantee us Harman-type results, but it is his firm opinion that OPCs are the superior anti-aging nutrient. Will the daily intake of OPCs alone permit you to celebrate your 120th birthday? I wouldn't bet on it and neither would Masquelier. The famous movie classic *Some Like It Hot* ends with the words, "Nobody is perfect." Was Jeanne Calment, who died at a 124, perhaps perfect? Did she have a perfect set of genes? No one knows. Did she take OPCs every day? We have no record of her dietary habits, but because she was French, she probably drank a red wine from time to time. Like Mrs. Calment, each of us must cope with the influences that shorten our life spans. We have to make the best of the genes we have and protect ourselves against the stresses of decay and degeneration.

In physics, stress is an applied force or system of forces that strain or deform a body. Mentally or emotionally, stress is a disruptive and disquieting influence. Stress is not a phenomenon of modern times. We have evidence that the ancient Romans knew stress. Caesar, for example, was a victim of "tedium vitae," weariness of life, fatigue, "ennui," or tediousness. In modern life, the label of stress can be tagged to many situations. In France and many other European countries, labor unions consider working more than 35 or 36 hours per week stressful. Exams for students are labeled stressful. Being late for an appointment equals stress. This book is not the place to discuss mental stress, but as we all know, mental stress produces effects in the body. Fear or nervousness can make you break out in a sweat. Some people become red in the face when they're angry. Cancer is one of the most dreadful responses by which the body pays its toll to mental stress. It is well known that the outbreak of cancer is frequently related to a death in the family, a major financial loss, or some similar catastrophe.

Considering the influence of the psyche on the body made Masquelier think back to the days when he was preparing for his exams. "When I was still a student at the university, the examinations were taken once a year in the month of June. Those who had not already studied from the beginning of the year now started to hit the books really hard. They were terribly restless, nervous — in other words, stressed. In those days, tuberculosis was still a dreaded disease. During the examination period, the mortality rate due to tuberculosis was always on the rise. Likewise, it was also found that the number of cavities diagnosed in students by means of radiography almost doubled during that period. The mental stress — the fear of failing in front of the examination commission — manifested itself in organic disorder."

Mental stress can also trigger an inflammatory response in many parts of the body. An acute attack of rheumatic fever, for instance, may be of bacterial origin, but there is an equal chance that such a fever can be attributed to a sudden impact of stress. Mental stress may also result in ulcers. Immobilizing test animals induces the release of histamine in the lining of the stomach, as was shown by researchers Lorenz and Reimann when they checked the influence of catechins in ulcer formation (see *chapter 26: Histamine, Stomach Ulcers, and Allergies*). Rattling a bunch of keys above the heads of rats in a cage increases their use if vitamin C. Stress may reflect itself in real as well as in imaginary pain. The pain mechanism contains an exceptional mental component. Painkillers, such as morphine, are efficient in only 75% of the cases. In 25%, they do not produce any effects. Those 25% have a different system for perceiving pain.

The aging body is less and less resistant to mental and physical stress. The term "anti-aging vitamin" truly applies to OPCs in that OPCs counteract age-related damage in the organism. To the degree to which free radical scavenging enzymes are losing their protective effect against free radicals, we must find other means to prevent oxidative processes of destruction. OPCs are an excellent weapon for this purpose. I cannot tell what OPCs can accomplish with respect to the mental level, but with regard to the physical manifestations of stress in the human body, OPCs are clearly an important safeguard. They provide protection wherever stress is reflected in symptoms of deterioration and degeneration, especially when these developments are related to excessive oxidation and free radical formation. People who reach 40 or 50 years of age should begin to include OPCs on their list of dietary supplements to prepare for the period when the signs of aging may begin to manifest themselves. With advancing age, the stresses of a lifetime accumulate, especially because the body's own defense mechanisms are gradually running out of power. Masquelier suggests that a relief of oxidative stress gives more physical health, which in turn will give more mental comfort, meaning less stress.

39 OPCs, VITAMIN C, AND THE FACTS OF e-LIFE

The crucial aspects of the scientific works of Dr. Jack Masquelier and Dr. Albert Szent-Györgyi dovetail in a wonderfully complementary way. Szent-Györgyi coined the concept of vitamin P but failed to isolate and chemically define the actual vitamin compound. Masquelier discovered and isolated OPCs, the substance that perfectly fits the vitamin P "glove." But the meeting of the minds went much deeper than their vitamin P encounter. In April 1985, Masquelier filed his application for U.S. Patent 4,698,360, describing how OPCs scavenge free radicals. Surely, the discovery of OPCs' free radical scavenging had the practical consequence of opening the door to discuss OPCs' benefits in various degenerative diseases and premature aging; it is very well explained by Masquelier in his patent. But there's much more to it. Masquelier's discovery also opened the door to discussions about and an understanding of OPCs in terms used by Szent-Györgyi in an article he happened to publish when Masquelier was filing his "antioxidant" patent. Coincidence? Masquelier always says, "There's no coincidence when you pay attention."

In the very month when Masquelier filed the patent application that put OPCs in the spotlight as a prime antioxidant, Nutrition Today magazine published an article from Szent-Györgyi: "Cancer, Metabolism and Ascorbic Acid." Like your car, so wrote Szent-Györgyi, your body is a combustion engine that is driven by that same mysterious force we call "energy." The Hungarian Nobel Prize winner explains in very basic chemical terms that the body survives by using the energy that is stored in plants. In everyday language, the sugars, starches, and oils contained in our food are the fuel the body combusts to keep itself at 98.6° (37°C). An "energy bar" could well be the convenient food form epitome of the kind of stored plant energy that Szent-Györgyi had in mind. Plants don't make the contents of energy bars out of thin air. This energy is produced elsewhere, far away, in the sun by way of continuous atomic explosions. It reaches us as sunshine, which we experience as light or warmth. At night, this energy doesn't reach us at all, except as reflected by the moon. Closer to the sun, the enormous cosmic forces that this star so violently throws into space leave no room for life as we know it. Planet Earth is just far enough removed from the sun to catch sunlight in quantities compatible with organic life.

Organic life exists, explained Szent-Györgyi, because it has solved the problem of how to catch, handle, use, store, distribute, and release the sun's energy. Nature endowed plants with that unique capacity to handle sunshine. Organic life in its totality would not exist if plants were not capable of storing the sun's energy. Why not? Because there is no sunshine at night, and without energy, life ceases and its machinery disintegrates. Our body is incapable of directly converting or using sunlight in the production of energy. In other words, the body does not have a mechanism whereby the warmth that you feel when you're exposed to sunlight can be absorbed and utilized as a contribution to the body's internal energy production. This is why the plants that are capable of capturing and storing sunshine form the indispensable link between the nearest star and human life on earth. In fact, human civilization would not exist if there were no green plants. The plants that are capable of transforming sunshine are known by the green color of the pigment that makes the actual catch. Green plants, including algae and phytoplankton, contain chlorophyll — chloro means green — which is capable of using the sun's energy to make organic compounds out of inorganic substances. Green plants are "self-feeders," or autotrophs, because they make their own food and grow and maintain themselves autonomously. A major part of humanity's diet consists of self-feeders or of what we make of or extract from self-feeders. In the simplest of terms, the sugar in your coffee contains the sunshine that some green plant converted.

In duration sports, carbo-loading means stuffing the body with as much energy as possible right before an event. It's like filling the gas tank of your car to the brim before you go on a long trip. Carbohydrates, or carbs, are all the various combinations of carbon, hydrogen, and oxygen better known as sugars and starches. They make up the major part of the body's fuel. Carbohydrates are made by green plants out of water and the atmosphere's carbon dioxide. Chlorophyll combines hydrogen and some of the oxygen with carbon into carbohydrates and releases the rest of the oxygen. What does this have to do with energy? The splitting and combining is not a spontaneous process that needs to be watched only. No, chlorophyll has to work on this. For that work, it needs an energy input from an outside source. Chlorophyll has that unique capacity that it can catch sunshine and use it as the energy required to produce carbohydrates and oxygen.

The magic of it all is that the sunshine — energy — that is caught and used by the chlorophyll does not get lost in the splitting of water to make carbs. That energy still exists after the splitting is over because the splitting of things that have a great affinity for each other serves as a method to "store" that affinity in the form of a potential. For chlorophyll, the purpose of the action is the transformation of the warmth of the sun into a potential that can be released as warmth at some other time and place. The potential exists because of the high affinity between hydrogen and oxygen. The energy required to separate the two by the splitting water is the equivalent of the amount of affinity of the potential. It's like two lovers who have become separated. The hydrogen, which the chlorophyll has given a place in the carbohydrates, craves to be reunited with the oxygen that the chlorophyll released into the air. By consuming carbs and inhaling air, the combustion engine we call the body forms the instrument that facilitates the reuniting of hydrogen and oxygen. In return for that favor, the body gets energy to live on.

If this explanation seems confusing, just think of chemistry, potential, affinity, energy, and warmth in terms of human relationships, where they seem to work in the same way. The beauty of it is that organic life makes use of the mysterious metamorphosis that the life force we call energy is capable of. One moment this energy is an electric potential, the next moment that potential expresses itself as warmth. In the right form at the right place and time, energy can thus be stored in the form of a *warmth potential*, which can be released as actual warmth when it is needed. We can now overcome the periodic absence of sunshine and survive. Life thus makes smart use of that magical transformation from heat to electricity and from electricity to heat. This is how organic life keeps itself going. The "charging" of plants, the release of this charge in the human body, and the role of ascorbic acid in this process was one of the topics in Szent-Györgyi's scientific work.

Earlier we said that free radicals must not be regarded only as devastating particles we must find and destroy. Free radicals also serve a highly useful purpose because they are indispensable in bringing back together oxygen and hydrogen in energy production. The way the body uses oxygen to keep warm differs from the way oxygen is used to burn things such as wood, oil, or natural gas. Such direct use of oxygen would create enormous damage if it took place in the body. To avoid such harm, combustion in the body takes place by way of a gradual, step-by-step process, which involves radical — reactive — forms of oxygen and oxygen-hydrogen combinations. Without these intermediary radicals, the coupling of hydrogen and oxygen would not be compatible with the body's structures and functions. So, rather than demonize free radicals, we need to acknowledge that they are necessary to sustain life. Even those who eat a super-healthy diet and live in a stressless and perfectly clean environment are not without free radicals. We need them to stay alive as much as green plants need sunshine. And because they're volatile, we must make sure that they don't cause harm where they don't belong.

To complete this rather nutshell exposé of the facts of life, let's look at the electron. According to Szent-Györgyi, the electron "has very special properties which we cannot understand. Because by understanding, we mostly mean that we have seen something similar before." Not a very encouraging statement. Fortunately, even though we can't see electrons, scientists have developed definite ideas about what electrons do and what their place is in the makeup of the elements by closely observing certain chemical and physical phenomena. The fact that we cannot see an electron should not prevent us from understanding what electrons do and how they feel. Anyone who was ever hit by an electric shock understands the electron as something that does not produce a positive sensation.

An electron is an infinitely small particle that has a negative electric charge. In addition to flowing through the wires of your house as electricity, it "electrifies" organic life. Chemical elements consist of electrons that orbit a positively charged nucleus of positively charged protons and neutral neutrons. Elements, molecules, and compounds interact through the sharing or exchange of electrons. It makes life "*e*-life." What interests us here is that *e*-life exists because the catching, storage, transfer, and release of energy by plants, animals, and humans is performed by a number of compounds that are capable of doing this by alternately absorbing and donating an electron. In other words, electron donating and accepting compounds can exist in various states of charge, caused by fluctuations in the number of electrons. Compare it to a person who is capable of changing the number of dollars on his bank account by alternately receiving and paying money.

The whirling dance of electrons that we just named *e*-life knows two basic steps called "oxidation" and "reduction." When electrons — negative charge — exit a molecule, that molecule experiences a relative increase in the positive charge. It becomes "more +" or "less −". This process is called oxidation. Electrons joining a molecule produce a relative increase in negative charge ("more −" or "less +"). Although the number of electrons increases, we call this step reduction because more electrons add up as "more minus charge." When a compound is a giver and taker of electrons, it has a reduction-oxidation, or "redox," capacity. A redox compound can function only when it finds a compound to give an electron to (to reduce) and another compound to take an electron from (to oxidize). An oxidant is thus a taker of electrons, and a reductor is a giver of electrons. Antioxidants are reductors. In terms of bookkeeping and banking, an oxidant is a creditor (a property owner, for example) to whom you make a payment. A reductor is a debtor (an employer, for example) who makes a payment. The electron is the dollar.

The word antioxidant does not describe exactly what takes place during antioxidation. An antioxidant does not stop or inhibit oxidation, but it sacrifices itself to satisfy the need for an electron in the oxidant. Doing this, the antioxidant protects the compound from which the electron would have been taken otherwise. What we generally refer to as antioxidants are specific reductors that operate only in situations of unwanted oxidation. Antioxidants do not inhibit or stop the vital process of producing energy by oxidation. That would be rather catastrophic. The substances that have risen to fame as antioxidants have a knack for picking out just the oxidants that cause harm. They don't interfere elsewhere. In terms of money, an antioxidant is your rich uncle who pays the ransom when you've been kidnapped.

Masquelier's way of explaining how antioxidants manage to be so selective is to compare biochemical compounds with the cogwheels in an engine. One cogwheel causes the next cogwheel to turn in synchronization, with the second cogwheel possibly having a completely different function from the first. The latter may be connected to a third one that in turn may have different functions, and so on. In the human body, each of the many different biochemical pathways has its cogwheels, interconnecting with other pathways. What takes place in one pathway may affect another pathway, but only if there's a cogwheel connection. The simile of the cogwheel also allows us to understand why it is that cogwheels such as OPCs work in so many seemingly unrelated situations.

In a way, the enormously complex interplay of all the processes in living organisms rests purely on the supplying, distributing, monitoring, controlling, and guiding of electrons. Free radicals are to be feared because they heavily and indiscriminately interfere with the normal flow of electrons. Free radicals are completely out of balance. They crave electrons so much that they steal them from the nearest compound. When a free radical steals an electron from a compound that lacks the ability to replace it, permanent "free radical damage" will be the result. In terms of money, free radicals are thieves. They only take and make you go broke. Antioxidants are *e*-life's solution. They satisfy free radicals' hunger for electrons.

Keeping free radicals quiet by donating electrons to them is a skill that has been mastered by free-radical-scavenging enzymes *(see chapter 28: OPCs, the Mightiest Scavengers of Free Radicals)*. Nature has endowed the same skill to antioxidative nutrients such as OPCs and the vitamins C and E. It is obvious that the performance of this skill depends completely on the availability of the electrons that must be donated. What makes OPCs so special in this respect is that they contain many electrons that can be donated. Other compounds have the capacity to fill up with electrons to replenish the donated ones. A perfect example of such a giver and taker of electrons is vitamin C, or ascorbic acid. It can switch from a reduced state (charged with an electron) to an oxidized state (released of that electron) back to a reduced state and so on and so on. By filling up with electrons every time electrons are given, vitamin C is able to fulfill all its tasks many times over, including the task of giving electrons to free radicals. Vitamin C is a true reduction-and-oxidation (redox) compound.

Speaking of the many tasks fulfilled by the "cogwheel" vitamin C, according to Szent-Györgyi, vitamin C also plays a vital role in the production of energy. He even describes scurvy as a result of a deficiency in vitamin C in the production of energy. "If there is no ascorbic acid present," wrote Szent-Györgyi, "the whole energy production must stop and a terrible disease is produced, which is called scurvy." The Hungarian Nobel Prize winner takes us one step further when he continues by saying that a lack or low level of oxygen combined with a lack or low level of vitamin C will produce cancer. In other words, when vitamin C is amiss in the process that facilitates the recoupling of oxygen with hydrogen, an energy shortage will result. According to Szent-Györgyi, a low energy level prepares the way for the onset of cancer. During experiments carried out under Szent-Györgyi's supervision, the restoring of energy production by way of improving the oxygen supply in combination with the administration of vitamin C caused the remission of 80 percent of peritoneal (ascite) tumors in mice.

Most people probably never think of vitamin C in terms of its chemical structure and how that structure makes it a very dynamic "electrical" compound. If they'd have to visualize vitamin C, they would probably see it as a rather inert white crystalline powder. The fact that vitamin C is such a versatile redox compound makes it a dynamic and crucially active piece of biochemistry. At one moment it has an oxidizing effect, and in the next moment it goes into reverse, acting as a reducing agent. Since free radicals and their antioxidant opponents became common knowledge, vitamin C has become well known for its antioxidant effect. In reality, this is only one side of vitamin C's biochemical character. Vitamin C also acts as a pro-oxidant, a free radical. This is when it replenishes an electron that it gave away when it took a new electron from an external supplier. Fortunately, in the human body, vitamin C selects different targets for its antioxidative than for its pro-oxidative action. It is an antioxidant in some situations and a pro-oxidant in others. Because of this selective behavior, we have come to respect vitamin C as a benign antioxidant and not as a free radical, even though vitamin C does have a radical side.

By acting as an antioxidant, vitamin C loses its antioxidant property as it oxidizes itself. Giving away electrons, for instance, to neutralize a free radical, vitamin C depletes itself of them. This is how with every antioxidative action, the antioxidant capacity of vitamin C wanes. It must therefore be recharged with energy — electrons — to again perform its antioxidant function. Because vitamin C is a "busy" compound with a large workload, it is quickly depleted unless it is recharged. Vitamin C recharges itself by taking an electron away from a substance it oxidizes in the action. That substance acts as an antioxidant. Vitamin C needs an antioxidant to perform as an antioxidant. This isn't a senseless exercise because both antioxidants are cogwheels in different pathways and systems. OPCs, being rich in electrons that may be donated, are vitamin C's perfect antioxidant. In the absence of donors like OPCs, vitamin C depletes itself, and that is how scurvy comes about. In other words, scurvy isn't a problem only of a vitamin C deficiency. It is also a problem of vitamin C's not being able to recharge itself. This phenomenon was demonstrated by Masquelier when he kept guinea pigs alive and well by recharging a suboptimal dosage of vitamin C through OPCs. OPCs have no problem sacrificing themselves because they're abundantly rich in giveaway electrons. OPCs' "richesse" places them at the natural origin of many processes that they sustain by recharging cogwheels like vitamin C. Remember that the Portuguese sailors escaped scurvy by recharging their vitamin C with a daily ration of red wine.

A human is one of the five creatures on this planet that are dependent on the intake of external vitamin C; these five creatures somehow lost the ability to produce their own vitamin C. For a mouse, vitamin C is not a vitamin because the mouse makes vitamin C. Like the guinea pig and the bat, humans need to take vitamin C with their food to survive. If a depleted vitamin C molecule cannot be recharged, it must be replaced by a new vitamin C molecule via nutrition. As long as we consume a diet sufficiently rich in vitamin C, there are no problems. But as soon as supplies dry up or become depleted by an overload of tasks and demands, the body will show symptoms of a deficiency. Such symptoms are not confined only to the symptoms of scurvy so vividly described in the history books. Per the orthomolecular viewpoint from which this book is written, cancer, heart disease, bleeding gums, varicose veins, and all the other ailments that respond to an increase in nutrients in the diet are by definition deficiency diseases. The term "orthomolecular" was coined by Dr. Abraham Hoffer, a nutritionally oriented psychiatrist who found that large doses of vitamin B3 were very helpful in the treatment of schizophrenia. The old Greek word "orthos" means right, correct, and on target. In orthomolecular nutrition, the right quantities of nutrients an individual should take are the quantities needed by that particular individual at that particular moment.

In the human body, only a certain part of the total supply of vitamin C is available for providing antioxidative protection. Much of the vitamin C is involved in the making of fresh collagen. Historically, vitamin C is best known as the vitamin that is indispensable for making fresh collagen. The synthesis of collagen takes place through the bonding of two amino acids, lysine and proline. Technically speaking, this bonding takes place by way of hydroxylation, which is a very common approach used by nature as well as by chemists to couple molecules. First, a branch consisting of one hydrogen and one oxygen particle is added to each of the to-be-coupled molecules. These so-called hydroxyl branches function as locks that click the two molecules together. Thus locked, lysine and proline are fresh collagen. In nature, the locking of lysine and proline is facilitated by specific enzymes that require electrons to function. No compound other than vitamin C can assist in the hydroxylation of lysine and proline because ascorbic acid is the exclusive supplier of the electrons that keep the hydroxylating enzymes active. But vitamin C is not an unlimited electron reservoir. Every time it gives up an electron for the synthesis of collagen, it must fill up again. OPCs are able to recharge vitamin C so that, in turn, vitamin C can donate electrons to facilitate collagen production. This is how OPCs help in the making of collagen.

A lack of vitamin C thus causes a lack of collagen, which in turn causes failure of wounds to heal, cessation of bone growth, and fragility of blood vessel walls, the first signs of scurvy. With this we've come full circle. We're back on the common ground of vascular health that OPCs and vitamin C initially shared. Szent-Györgyi assumed that scurvy was a disease caused by a twofold deficiency: vitamin C and bioflavonoids. Had he delved further into the subject of flavonoids and had he found and isolated the OPCs, he, instead of Masquelier, would have been able to solve the entire riddle of scurvy.

Many nutritionists and doctors advise patients and healthy consumers to take (much) more than the 60 to 80 milligrams of vitamin C health officials propose as sufficient. Millions of people take 1,000 mg, 2,000 mg, or even higher doses of vitamin C every day, mostly in the form of a dietary supplement. Few people, even when seriously ill, do what Linus Pauling did. The great promoter of vitamin C mixed 18 grams of vitamin C powder with a couple of drinks every day. Surprisingly, Pauling never discussed the use of OPCs in the recharging of vitamin C. He went for replenishing the body's vitamin C supply with mega dosages.

Yet, replenishing vitamin C combined with recharging the vitamin C by way of taking OPCs seems a much more "elegant" approach. Pauling was a great fan of "orthomolecular" nutrition, of taking and prescribing the right nutrients in the right amounts. In most cases, this approach to maintaining or restoring health implies relatively high daily dosages of vitamins and minerals in the form of dietary supplements. In the orthomolecular tradition, high dosages of vitamin C are standard. However, in the taking and prescribing of orthomolecular amounts of vitamin C, one must not overlook the sustaining, recharging role and possible benefits of OPCs. In the perspective of the orthomolecular approach, OPCs have a balancing influence that may reduce the need for mega-intake of vitamin C, providing food for thought for orthomolecular consumers, doctors, and nutritionists who were unfamiliar with this aspect of OPCs.

40 APPLICATION, DOSAGE, AND SAFETY

MASQUELIER's Original OPCs (ANTHOGENOL) as well as MASQUELIER's French Pine Bark Complex fulfill the most exacting quality requirements. The production process is performed by the strict application of various essential criteria, which guarantee as high a quality level as possible. Solvents, procedures of filtering and centrifugation, temperature, freshness, and origin of raw materials are all subject to Masquelier's uncompromised standards, which evolved during half a century of scientific research. Every kilogram is analyzed before it leaves the extraction facility and released on the market. This comprehensive process ensures that OPCs produced according to Masquelier's quality standards correspond with the quality standards set for the products discussed in this book. The worldwide source of MASQUELIER's products is International Nutrition Company (INC), whose website, www.inc-opc.com, is also accessible under Dr. Masquelier's name as www.masquelier.com. These sites list the many names and addresses of the companies that make the MASQUELIER's products available offline as well as online.

The following recommendations and statements about the application, dosage, and safety of OPCs strictly and exclusively pertain to the MASQUELIER's products. Quite obviously, in France, they also apply to the Endotélon product, which is sold as a medicine and not as a dietary supplement. The recommendations do not pertain to grape seed extracts and pine bark extracts, not even when their manufacturers place the OPCs term on the label of such extracts. Outside the MASQUELIER framework, the single "OPCs" has lost the value and meaning it has when used in direct connection with Masquelier's name. Just because a company puts the term OPCs on a product's label doesn't mean that any of the words written in this book apply to that product. The wilderness you glimpsed in *chapter 36: Grape Seed Extract, the Dreaded Scenario* mushroomed on the quicksand of improper analytical methods and stretched definitions sprinkled with what is conveniently called "borrowed science."

The MASQUELIER's products are commercially available in the form of capsules, tablets, drops, and cream. They can be applied internally as well as externally. In his antioxidant patent, Masquelier states that the optimum daily dosage of OPCs is an average of 1 mg per pound (1.5 to 3 mg per kilogram) of body weight. This suggestion should be the yardstick to assess individual variations. May this dosage be lowered? If you are healthy and meet the following criteria, you may take the MASQUELIER's products in a dosage of 50 mg per day:

- You are not under a great deal of physical or psychological stress.
- You drink a lot of water.
- You eat fresh food.
- You don't smoke.
- You do not indulge in alcoholic beverages.

However, if any of the following is true for you, you should at least take 1 mg per pound (or at least 2 mg per kg) of body weight:

- You lead an active life.
- You work or live in a city.
- You are under stress.
- You sometimes enjoy the fast-food or microwave track.

- You smoke.
- You enjoy alcoholic pleasures.
- You lead an active sports life.

At the beginning of OPCs intake, people are advised to saturate all body tissues. To achieve this tissue saturation, take 300 mg during the first three days and then step down to the dosage you deem fit for yourself. Some people have asked whether they should take OPCs for the rest of their life. It depends how healthy and vigorous they want that "rest of their life" to be. OPCs are as essential as vitamins, nutrients, water, and oxygen. Do you get sufficient OPCs in your food? It is something you must decide for yourself or discuss with a nutritionist or with a nutritionally oriented doctor. My frank advice is to take OPCs every day for the rest of your life for the best possible protection against premature aging.

Do OPCs replace or interfere with other essential nutrients you are taking? First of all, OPCs have an autonomous place in the diet in that they do not require the synergism or help of other essential nutrients. OPCs do what they do, as is described in *Dr. MASQUELIER's Mark on Health.* You may be taking other nutrients to accomplish what OPCs can accomplish. It is then up to you to determine whether OPCs could do a better job. But then, you must assess whether the dietary supplement(s) you take perform more than one task in the body. Most nutrients have more than one function. In other words, few pairs of nutrients share the exact same functions. Just because OPCs work in many seemingly unrelated conditions doesn't mean that OPCs can replace the nutrients that make a contribution to those conditions. The more nutritional "cogwheels" the better. If your budget is limited, you must judge for yourself which nutritional cogwheels you will leave behind on the shelf. If your interest is purely condition oriented — that is, if you think of OPCs as a medicine rather than a dietary supplement — take OPCs for the conditions described in this book. Doing so may stir up some interest in other nutrients and dietary supplements.

In cases of acute need, such as when an allergy hits, OPCs may be taken in dosages of 200 to 300 mg per day. If OPCs are taken within the framework of a targeted therapy or regimen, the recommended dosage is as high as in acute cases. For varicose veins, the recommendation is 150 to 300 mg per day. In the event of hemorrhagic or hemorrhoidal crisis — that is, if an increased amount of blood flows from damaged vessels — the dosage can be raised to 500 mg per day. A further increase is not recommended for the simple reason that it would be wasted. In medical practice, excellent results were achieved with high dosages of 400 to 500 mg daily for the treatment of retinopathy, PMS, sports injuries, and post-surgical edema.

During many years of scientific research, no side effects for MASQUELIER's products have been determined. They show an unsurpassed long record of safety and non-mutagenicity. This record was once again confirmed in 2000 by BSL BIOSERVICE, an independent German test facility in München. To keep its MASQUELIER's Original OPCs (ANTHOGENOL) in full compliance with the ever-stricter standards for non-mutagenicity, INC commissioned this laboratory to perform a modern reverse mutation assay, commonly referred to as the Ames test, on ANTHOGENOL. The reverse mutation assay is but the modern and broader version of the test that was developed in the 1970s by Dr. Bruce Ames. The Ames test reveals whether a product or substance damages the DNA. DNA damage occurs under the influence of carcinogens and is generally seen as one of the main causes of cancer and other degenerative diseases. Performing the reverse mutation test serves as a screening of hazardous and toxic substances. This may seem unnecessary in the field of herbal and dietary supplements, which are normally perceived as natural and therefore safe, but not everything that is natural is automatically safe. The ANTHOGENOL product passed the test without the slightest sign of mutagenicity.

For a brief moment, the testing brings us back to the differences between OPCs and bioflavonoids. As long ago as July 1979, Masquelier publicly proposed to distinguish OPCs from the plant substances known under the common denominator bioflavonoids. In his article he wrote, "Until recently, flavonoids were considered as generally non-toxic. Certainly, some rutin preparations had caused accidents, the low solubility of most of these substances making their use in therapy difficult. But in 1977 Bjeldanes and Chang demonstrated mutagenic effects with various flavonoids, and several authors confirmed this fact. Quercetin, so broadly found, showed the highest mutagenicity, even without microsomal activation. Its heterosides are less dangerous but become mutagenic in contact with intestinal flora. Finally, according to Umezawa, quercetin induces malignant transformations in embryonic hamster cells."

Because OPCs used to be (wrongly) classified as bioflavonoids and because their products had to pass pharmaceutical standards in France, Masquelier and his colleagues were very keen on demonstrating the non-mutagenicity of OPCs. In

1979, in the same article, they reported how OPCs had passed their first Ames test, which was performed by the Pasteur Institute in France. The Pasteur Institute "noted the total absence of mutagenicity" when OPCs were Ames tested before and after metabolic activation. The tests were performed on various species of animals. During later years, the reverse mutation assay was broadened from time to time to diminish the chance of error. The mutagenicity test that was performed on MASQUELIER's Original OPCs (ANTHOGENOL) in 2000 was done according to the most up-to-date standards. More than two decades after the Ames test was first performed, the safety of MASQUELIER's Original OPCs still stands unchallenged.

In rare cases, people complain of flu-like symptoms when they start taking OPCs. Most people who experience such a body response will find that the discomfort changes into a significant feeling of well being and an increase in vitality. These very rare symptoms are not a side effect of OPCs in the way that drugs have side effects. The discomfort can be explained by the increased blood flow in the organism. It can stimulate the excretion of toxic substances deposited in the cells and tissues, a process that may result in a certain indisposition. In fact, the experience is related to detoxification, which may produce not only headaches, but also irritated, reddened skin because the body uses the skin as an organ to excrete toxins and waste materials. If you experience such a response, there is no reason for concern. On the contrary! Your body is getting rid of waste products it may have harbored in cells and tissues for a very long time. Drink 2 liters of water every day and abstain from coffee and other stimulating drinks until all the signs of detoxification have disappeared. If feelings of discomfort do not go away, you may want to reduce the dosage.

If reducing the dosage does not make the discomfort disappear, stop taking OPCs for a while and then try again, beginning with a low(er) dosage. Although OPCs are safe and efficacious, it is not advisable to try to cure serious diseases without the assistance of a nutritionally oriented doctor. Never hide from your physician or specialist the fact that you are taking OPCs or another dietary supplement. You must always openly communicate about these things. Some doctors may disagree with the taking of food supplements because they still think that dietary supplements do not contribute to your health. But when you put yourself in the care of a physician, you must either fully heed that physician's advice or look for a new doctor. The fact that in France, many doctors recommend OPCs in the form of a medicine should reassure those critical doctors who know MASQUELIER's products only as a dietary supplement.

The speed at which the ingested OPCs spread throughout the body may be subject to individual fluctuation, but OPCs' bioavailability is so high that individuality of the consumer isn't really a factor. A laboratory test showed that just 15 minutes after oral intake, OPCs could be found in the saliva. Keep in mind that these OPCs were in a sealed capsule whose contents were released only in the stomach. It took the OPCs found in the saliva only 15 minutes to get there via the digestive tract, the blood, and the salivary glands. Because OPCs have a high affinity for proteins and although the issue was never clarified in scientific detail, it is best to follow these simple rules:
- Do not take OPCs together only with protein-rich food such as yogurt or milk.
- Do take OPCs with a glass of water or fruit juice, preferably between meals.

Sometimes people's preferences cannot be well explained by scientific analysis. Even Masquelier remains silent when asked why some people do better on MASQUELIER's French Pine Bark Complex while others do better on ANTHOGENOL (MASQUELIER's Original OPCs). When pressed for an answer, he explains that the products share OPCs and catechins as their major active principles, but because they are made from different vegetal materials, the fingerprints of the "niches" of the products are not 100 percent identical. In fact, a sharp analyst with a profound botanical or biochemical background can determine the vegetal source when looking at the fingerprints' niches. It may be that some people are so sensitive, they can feel the difference and respond better to one or to the other product. Although both products have impeccable autonomous records in benefits and safety, a blend is sometimes proposed to leave no ingredient out and to completely dovetail the research that was done on both products.

LITERATURE

Abord Thérapeutique des troubles fonctionnels des membres inférieurs par un microangioprotecteur l'Endotélon; L. Sarrat; Bordeaux Méd. 1981; 11: 685-8.

Action Comparée de Divers Facteurs Vitaminiques P sur l'Oxydation de l'Acide Ascorbique par les Ions Cuivriques; J. Masquelier, Bulletin de la Société de Chimie Biologique, Extrait du Tome XXXIII, No 3-4, 1951.

Action Comparée de Divers Facteurs Vitaminiques P sur l'Acide Ascorbique-Oxydase; J. Masquelier, Bulletin de la Société de Chimie Biologique, Extrait du Tome XXXIII, No 3-4, 1951.

Action des Oligomères Procyanidoliques sur le Cobaye Carencé en Vitamine C; J. Laparra, J. Michaud et J. Masquelier, Travaux originaux, Université de Bordeaux, 1976.

Action du leucocyanidol sur l'hyaluronidase; M.F. Tayeau et Mme G. Lefevre.; Bull. Soc. Pharm. Bordeaux, 1956, 95, 132-136.

Action protectrice du vin sur l'ulcère gastrique; J. Masquelier. p. 61: RESULTATS.

Alcool et radicaux libres; Roger Nordmann, Catherine Ribière, Hélène Rouach, Jamal Sinaceur et Dominique Sabourault, Bull. Acad. Natle. Méd., 1985, 169, No 8, 1201-1206, séance du 19 novembre 1985.

Antioxidants: Elixers of Life or Tonics for Tired Sheep, Barry Halliwell, The Biochemist, Feb/Mar, 1995.

Collagen treated with (+)-catechin becomes resistant to the action of mammalian collagenase; R. Kuttan, Patricia V. Donnelly and N. Di Ferrante; Experientia 37 (1981). Birkhauser Verlag. Basel. Schweiz.

Condensed Proanthocyanidins from Cranberries and Cola Nuts; K. Weinges and K. Freudenberg, Universität Heidelberg und Forschungsinstitut für die Chemie des Holzes und der Polysaccharide, Heidelberg, Germany, Chemical Communications, nr 11, 1965.

Condensed tannins scavenge active oxygen free radicals; Uchida, Edamatsu, Hiramatsu, Mori, Nonaka, Nishioka, Niwa and Ozaki; Med. Sci. Res. 1987; 15, 831-832.

Contribution à l'étude des oligomères procyanidoliques: Endotélon, dans la rétinopathie diabétique (à propos de 30 observations); J.L. Arne; Gaz. Med. de France - 89, no 30 du 8-X-1982.

Dietary Antioxidant Flavonoids and Risk of Conory Heart Disease. Michael G.L. Hertog, Edith J.M. Feskens, Peter C.H. Hollman, Martijn B. Katan, Daan Kromhout; The Lancet, Oct. 23 1993.

Dosage Colorimétrique des Leucoanthocyannes dans les Vins Rouges; J. Masquelier, G. Vitte and M. Ortega, Bull. Soc. Phar. Bordeaux, 1959.

Dosage des Leucoanthocyannes du Vin Blanc - Emploi de la Poudre de Polyamide, J. Masquelier, Bull. Soc. Pharm. Bordeaux, 1963.

Dosage des Procyanidols dans les Extraits Végétaux Destinés à la Préparation de Médicaments; Marie-Claude Dumon, Jean Michaud and Jack Masquelier, Bull. Soc. Pharm. Bordeaux, 129, 1990.

Endotélon dans le traitement des troubles veino-lymphatiques dy syndrome prémenstruel. Etude multicentrique sur 165 patientes; M. Amsellem, J.M. Masson, B. Negui, F. Sailly, J. Sentenac, A. Siou, J.C. Tissot; Tempo Médical/no 282 - Novembre 1987.

The Effect of Procyanidolic Oligomers on the Composition of Normal and Hypercholesterolemic Rabbit Aortas; J. Wegrowski, A.M. Robert and M. Moczar; Laboratoire de Biochimie du Tissu Conjonctif, Université de Paris, 6 june 1984.

Effet de l'Endotélon dans les oedèmes post-chirurgicaux. Résultats d'une étude en double aveugle contre placebo sur trente-deux patientes; J. Baruch; Ann Chir Plast Esthét. 1984 - vol XXIX - no 4.

Effet de l'Endotélon sur l'indice de fragilité capillaire dans une population spécifique: les sujets cirrhotiques; F.X. Lesbre et J.D. Tigaud; Gaz. Med. de France - 90, no 24 du 24-VI-1983.

Effets Physiologiques du Vin; Jack Masquelier, Exposé présenté au Symposium International sur "Le Vin et la Santé", Mendoza, Argentina, November 1987.

Essai thérapeutique d'un angioprotecteur périférique, l'Endotélon; C. Beylot et P. Bioulac; Gaz. Med. de France - 87, no 22 du 13-6-1980.

Etude de l'Endotélon dans les manifestations fonctionelles de l'insuffisance veineuse périférique. Résultats d'une étude en double aveugle portant sur 92 patients; J.F. Thébaut, P. Thébaut et F. Vin; Gazette Médicale 1985, 92, no 12.

Etude des effets des oligomères du procyanidol sur la résistance capillaire dans l'hypertension artérielle et certaines néphropathies; G. Lagrue, F. Olivier-Martin, A. Grillot; Sem Hop Paris, 18-25 septembre, 1981.

Etude en double aveugle de l'endotélon dans l'insuffisance veineuse chronique; P. Delacroix; La Revue de Médicine no 27-28 - 31 août - 7 sept. 1981.

Etude pharmacocinétique des oligomères flavanoliques; J. Laparra, J. Michaud et J. Masquelier; Plants médicinales et phytothérapie, 1977, Tome XI, no spécial, p. 1331-142.

Etude Pharmacocinétique des Oligomères Procyanidoliques Totaux du Raisin; J. Laparra, J. Michaud, M.F. Lesca, P. Blanquet and J. Masquelier; Acta Therapeutica 4 (1978).

Evidence by in vivo and in vitro studies that binding of pycnogenols to elastin affects its rate of degradation by elastases; J.M. Tixier, G. Godeau, A.M. Robert and W. Hornebeck; Laboratoire de Biochimie du Tissue Conjonctif, Université de Paris, 25 june 1984.

Evolution de la résistance capillaire, spontanément ou artificiellement diminuée par l'action d'une substance capillaro-toxique chez des personnes âgées; G. Dubos, G. Durst et R. Hugonot; La Revue de la Gériatrie, Tome 5, no 6, septembre 1980.

Factors associated with cardiac mortality in developed countries with particular reference to the consumption of wine; A.S. St. Leger, A.L. Cochrane, F. Moore; The Lancet, MAY 12, 1979.

The Fate of Total Flavanolic Oligomers (OFT) Extracted from Vitis Vinifera L. in the Rat; European Journal of Drug Metabolism and Pharmacokinetics, 1978, no 1, p. 15-30.

Fixation sites of procyanidolic oligomers in the blood capillary walls of the lungs of guinea pigs; A. Pfister, M.T. Simon and J.M. Gazave; Acta Therapeutica no 8 (1982).

The Flavonoids: Advances in Research, Chapman and Hall, Edwin Haslam, Proanthocyanidins, London - New York.

The Flavonoids. A Class of Semi-Essential Food Components: Their role in Human Nutrition; Joachim Kühnau; Wld. Rev. Nutr. Diet., vol. 24, pp. 117-191; Karger, Basel 1976.

Flavonoids et pycnogenols; J. Masquelier, J. Michaud, J. Laparra et M.C. Dumon, Internat.J.Vit.Nutr.Res. 49, 1979.

Fractionnement des Leucoanthocyannes du Vin; J. Masquelier, J. Michaud and J. Triaud, Bulletin de la Société de Pharmacie de Bordeaux, Tome 104, 1965.

Histamine and Acute Haemorrhagic Lesions in Rat Gastric Mucosa: Prevention of Stress Ulcer Formation by (+)-catechin, an Inhibitor of Specific Histidine Decarboxylase in vitro; H.J.

Reimann, W. Lorenz, M. Fischer. R. Frölich, H.J. Meyer; Birkhauser Verlag, Vol 7/1 (1977), University of Marburg/Lahn, Germany.

Identification of Leuco-anthocyanins as "tannins" in food; E.C. Bate-Smith and T. Swain, Chemistry and Industry, April 18, 1953.

Inhibition of oxidation of human low-density lipoprotein by phenolic substances in red wine; E.N. Frenkel, J. Kanner, J.B. German, E. Parks, J.E. Kinsella; The Lancet, VOL 341; FEB 20, 1993.

Inhibitory Effects of Tannins on Hyaluronidase Activation and on the Degranulation from Rat Mesentry Mast Cells; Kakegawa, Matsumoto, Endo, Satoh, Nonaka and Nishioka; Chem. Pharm. Bull. 33(11)5079-3082(1985).

État des Leucoanthocyannes dans le Rhytidome de Pinus Maritima LAMK; J. Masquelier and J. Michaud, Bull, Soc. Pharm. Bordeaux, 1965.

Le Leucoanthocyane des Cépages Blancs de Vitis Vinifera; J. Masquelier and G. Point, Bull. Soc. Pharm. Bordeaux, 1956.

Mise au point: Procyanidines ou proanthocyanidols; Michel Bourzeix et Vladimir Kovac, IIe Rencontre Internationale de Coursan, I.N.R.A. Institut des produits de la vigne, Narbonne, France, Faculté de technologie, Novi Sad, Yougoslavie.

Natural Proanthocyanidins, The Flavonoids, E. Haslam, Chapman and Hall, Londen.

Observations on Anthocyanins, Otto Rosenheim, The Biochemical Journal, Volume XIV, 1920, Cambridge University Press.

Oedema-inhibiting Effect of Procyanidin: G. Blaszo and M. Gabor; Acta Physiologica Academiae Hungaricae, Tomus 65 (2) pp. 235-240 (1980).

Les oedèmes post-traumatiques chez le sportif: essai contrôlé de l'Endotélon; J.J. Parienti et J. Parienti-Amsellem; Gaz. Med. de France - 90, No 3 du 21-1-1983.

Les oligomères procyanidoliques dans le traitement de la fragilité capillaire et de la retinopathie chez les diabétiques. A propos de 26 cas; M. Fromantin; Méd. Int. - Vol. 16 - no 11 - Novembre 1981 - pp. 432 à 434.

Oligomères procyanidoliques (ENDOTÉLON) dans le traitement des lymphoedèmes post-thérapeutiques des membres supérieurs; A. Pecking, J.P. Desprez-Curely, G. Megret; Symposium Satellite, Congrès International d'ANGIOLOGIE, Toulouse (France), 4-7 octobre 1989.

Étude Pharmacocinétique des Oligomères Procyanidoliques Totaux du Raisin; J. Laparra, J. Michaud, M.F. Lesca, P. Blanquet and J. Masquelier, Acta Therapeutica, 4, 1978.

Les pigments de la graine d'Arachide; Bulletin de la Société de Chimie Biologique, Francis Tayeau and Jack Masquelier, 1949, 31, No 1.

Potential Health Impacts of Excessive Flavonoid Intake, Christine F. Skibola and Martyn T. Smith, Free Radical Biology & Medicine, Vol. 29, Nos 3/4, pp. 375-383, 2000.

Plant Extract with a Proanthocyanidins Content as Therapeutic Agent having Radical Scavenger Effect and Use Thereof; United States Patent, No. 4,698,360; Jack Masquelier; Oct. 6, 1987.

Plant Proanthocyanidins. Part I. Introduction; the Isolation, Structure, and Distribution in Nature of Plant Procyanidins; R.S. Thompson, D. Jacques, E. Haslam; Dpt of Chemistry, University of Sheffield, U.K., J.C.S. Perkin I, 1972.

Platelet Rebound Effect of Alcohol Withdrawal and Wine Drinking in Rats; Relation to Tannins and Lipid Peroxidation; Jean-Claude Ruf, Jean-Luc Berger, Serge Renaud; Arteriosclerosis, Thrombosis, and Vascular Biology, Vol 15, No 1 January 1995.

Procyanidine aus Früchten; Klaus Weinges, et al. Zur Kenntnis der Proanthocyanidine, Liebigs A.. Chem. 711, 184-204 (1968).

Les Procyanidols du Vin, Jack Masquelier, IIe Rencontre Internationale de Coursan, Paris, 1989.

Propriétés bénéfiques des vins rouges du bordelais; Thèse pour le doctorat en médecine; Martine Baspeyras; 10 Avril 1985; Université de Bordeaux.

Pycnogenols: Recent Advances in the Therapeutical Activity of Procyanidins; Prof. Jack Masquelier; Hyppocrates Verlag, 1981, Stuttgart; Natural Products as Medicinal Agents.

Radical scavenger capacity of different procyanidins from grape seeds; J.M. Ricardo Da Silva, N. Darmon, Y. Fernandez, M.T. Canal and S. Mitjavila. Resumé du poster présenté au Symposium Free Radicals in Biotechnology and Medicine, Royal Society of Chemistry, Londres, janvier 1990, 79-80.

Radical Scavenging Action and its Mode in Procyanidins B-1 and B-3 from Azuki Beans to Peroxyl Radicals; T. Ariga and M. Hamano; Agric. Biol. Chem., 54 (10), 2499-2504, 1990.

Recherches Biochimiques et Pharmacologiques sur le Leucocyanidol de la Pruche, Pierre Claveau, Thèse pour le Doctorat de l'Université, 1964.

Recherches sur les Anthocyanogènes Oligomères de la Vigne et du Vin; Philippe Lacaze, Thèse pour le Doctorat de l'Université, 16 Janvier 1970.

Recherche et dosage des Oligomères Flavanoliques dans les Aliments d'Origine Végétale; J. Masquelier, J. Michaud et K. Bronnum-Hansen; Faculté de Pharmacie, Bordeaux.

Recherches Analytiques sur les Pycnogenols; THESE; Marie-Claire Dumon, 28 Juin 1990, Université de Bordeaux.

Recherches Comparatives sur l'Activité de Diverses Substances Vitaminiques P, Jack Masquelier and Francis Tayeau, Bulletin des Travaux de la Société de Pharmacie de Bordeaux, 1950.

Résistance capillaire en gériatrie. Etude d'un microangioprotecteur = Endotélon; J.Y. Dartenuc, P. Marache et H. Choussat; Bordeaux Médical, 1980; 13: 903-7.

Rétinopathies et O.P.C.; MM. Ph. Vérin, A. Vildy et J.F. Maurin; Bordeaux Médicale, 1978, 11, no 16, p.1467.

Sens lumineux et circulation choriorétinienne. Etude de l'effet des O.P.C. (Endotélon); Ch. Corbé, J.P. Boissin, A. Siou; J. Fr. Ophtalmol. 1988, 11. 5. 453-460.

Stabilisation du collagène par les oligomères procyanidoliques; J. Masquelier, J. Dumon et J. Dumas.; Acta Therapeutica 7 (1981) pp. 101/105.

Les substances Vitaminiques P des Vins Blancs - Extraction et Dosage, J. Masquelier and G. Point, Bulletin de la Société de Pharmacie de Bordeaux, 1956.

Vascular effects of oxygen-derived free radicals; Gabor M. Rubanyi; Free Radical Biology & Medicine, Vol. 4, pp. 107-120, 1988.

Un nouveau Facteur Vitaminique P isolé du Pin des Landes, J. Masquelier and G. Sansous, Bulletin de la Société de Pharmacie de Bordeaux, Tome 91, 1953.

Wein-kompendium; Prof.e.Dr.K.G. Bergner; Wissenschaftliche Verlagsgesellschaft mbH, Stuttgart, 1993.

Intake of Wine, Beer, and Spirits and the Risk of Clinical Common Cold. Bahi Takkouche, Carlos Regueira-Méndez, Reina García-Closas, Adolfo Figueiras, Juan J. Gestal-Otero and Miguel A. Hernán. American Journal of Epidemiology. Vol. 155, No 9, 2002.

Wine, alcohol, platelets, and the French paradox for coronary heart disease; S. Renaud, M. de Lorgeril; The Lancet, VOL 339; JUNE 20, 1992.

42. PUBLICATIONS AND PATENTS OF DR. JACK MASQUELIER

1948

Recherches sur les pigments de la graine de l'Arachide. Thèse de Doctorat ès-Sciences naturelles (Etat.), Drouillard imp., Bordeaux, 1948.

Recherches sur les pigments de la graine de l'Arachide. I. Mise en évidence d'un chromogène. En collaboration avec F. Tayeau. C.R. Acad. Sciences, 1948, 227, 602.

Recherches sur les pigments de la graine de l'Arachide. II. Mise en évidence d'une flavanonne. En collaboration avec P. Blanquet. C.R. Acad. Sciences, 1948, 227, 641.

Recherches sur les pigments de la graine de l'Arachide. I. Le chromogène. En collaboration avec F. Tayeau. Bulletin Société chimique de France, 1948, 15, 1167.

Recherches sur les pigments de la graine de l'Arachide. II. La flavanonne. En collaboration avec P. Blanquet. Bulletin Société chimique de France, 1948, 15, 1172.

Étude chimique sur les pigments de la graine de l'Arachide. III, Le tannoïde et la phlobaphène. Bulletin Société chimique de France, 1948, 15, 1175.

1950

Recherches comparatives sur l'activité de diverses substances vitaminique P. En collaboration avec F. Tayeau. Bulletin Société de Pharmacie de Bordeaux, 1950, 88, 168.

1951

Procédé d'extraction du leucocyanidol caractérisé par ce qu'on traite l'écorce de pin (pinus maritima), cette application nouvelle permettant d'isoler aisément le leucocyanidol à l'état pur. Brevet d'invention. No 1.036.922. Demandé le 9 mai 1951. Délivré le 29 Avril 1953.

Dosage du Leucoanthocyanidol de l'Arachide. En collaboration avec F. Tayeau et Mme G. Lefevre. Bulletin Société de Pharmacie de Bordeaux, 1951, 89, 5.

Action Comparée de Divers Facteurs Vitaminiques P sur l'Oxydation de l'Acide Ascorbique par les Ions Cuivriques. Bulletin de la Société de Chimie Biologique, 1951, 33, 302.

Action Comparée de Divers Facteurs Vitaminiques P sur l'Acide Ascorbique-Oxydase. Bulletin de la Société de Chimie Biologique, 1951, 33, 304.

1952

La localisation des composés catéchiques phlorogluciques dans les organes végétatifs du Pin maritime. En collaboration avec R. David. C.R. Académie des Sciences, 1952, 235, 1325.

1953

Un nouveau facteur vitaminique P isolé du Pin des Landes. En collaboration avec G. Sansous. Bulletin Société de Pharmacie de Bordeaux, 1953, 91, 16.

Recherches sur l'action vitaminique P du vin. En collaboration avec Mme H. Jensen. Bulletin Société de Pharmacie de Bordeaux, 1953, 91, 20.

Recherches sur l'action bactéricide des vins rouges (première partie). En collaboration avec Mme H. Jensen. Bulletin Société de Pharmacie de Bordeaux, 1953, 91, 24.

Recherches sur l'action bactéricide des vins rouges (deuxième partie). En collaboration avec Mme H. Jensen. Bulletin Société de Pharmacie de Bordeaux, 1953, 91, 105.

1954

A propos du flavonoside des raisins blancs. En collaboration avec G. Point. Bulletin Société de Pharmacie de Bordeaux, 1954, 92, 33.

1955

Les substances vitaminiques P des vins blancs. Extraction et dosage. En collaboration avec G. Point. Bulletin Société de Pharmacie de Bordeaux, 1955, 94, numéro spécial, page 80.

1956

Identification et dosage des facteurs vitaminiques P dans diverses boissons fermentées. Bulletin Société de Chimie Biologique, 1956, 38, 65.

Le leucoanthocyane des cépages blancs de Vitis Vinifera. En collaboration avec G. Point. Bulletin Société de Pharmacie de Bordeaux, 1956, 95, No 1, 6-11.

Note sur les constituants polyphénoliques du Cynara Scolymus L. Étude du Scolymoside. En collaboration avec J. Michaud. Bulletin Société de Pharmacie de Bordeaux, 1956, 95, 65-67.

1957

Note sur les constituants polyphénoliques du Cynara Scolymus L. Étude du Scolymoside. En collaboration avec J. Michaud. Bulletin Société de Pharmacie de Bordeaux, 1957, 96, 103-105.

1958

Leucoanthocyannes ou Leucotannoïdes ? In "Volume commémoratif Braemer." A. Coueslant Edit., Cahors, 1958.

Sur un pigment flavonique extraits des graines de Phoelipaea ramosa. En collaboration avec C. Izard. C.R. Académie des Sciences, 1958, 246, 1454-1456.

Essais d'indentification dy Cynaroside. En collaboration avec J. Michaud. Bulletin Société de Pharmacie de Bordeaux, 1958, 97, 77-81.

Sur quelques propriétés biologiques des anthocyannes de la vigne. Qual. Plant. Mat. Veg., 1958, III-IV, 481-490.

1959

The bactericidal action of certain phenolics of grapes and wine. The Pharmacology of Plant Phenolics, Oxford, Academic Press, 1959.

Recherches sur les pigments de la graine de Tournesol. I. L'Acide chlorogénique. En collaboration avec J. Sechet et F. Tayeau. Bulletin Société de Chimie Biologique, 1959, 41, 1059-1065.

Recherches sur les pigments de la graine de Tournesol. II. L'Acide caféique. En collaboration avec J. Sechet et F. Tayeau. Bulletin Société de Chimie Biologique, 1959, 41, 1067-1070.

Dosage colorométrique des leucoanthocyannes dans les vins rouges. En collaboration avec G. Vitte et M. Ortega. Bulletin Société de Pharmacie de Bordeaux, 1959, 98, 145-148.

1960

Sur la stabilité des leucoanthocyannes dans les médicaments galéniques. En collaboration avec J. Roux. Bulletin Société de Pharmacie de Bordeaux, 1960, 99, 65-72.

A propos de l'action vaso-constrictive et particulièrement coronaro-constrictive d'un tannoïde du vin. En collaboration avec J. Patay. Bulletin de l'Académie Nationale de Médecine, 1960, 144, 716-721.

1961

Acquisitions récentes sur les facteurs vitaminiques P. Origine de la notion de vitamine C2. Journ. Méd. Bordeaux, 1961, 213-218.

Les constituants du vin présentent une action hypocholestérolémiante. Extrait C.R. Congrès Méd. International Étude Scientifique Vin et Raisin, Bordeaux, 1961.

A propos de l'action d'un tannoïde du vin. En collaboration avec R. Patay. Bulletin de l'Académie Nationale de Médecine, 1961, 145, No 14-15, 322-325.

Caractérisation de la sinapine dans la graine de Colza, Brassica campestris L., var. oleifera. En collaboration avec M. Oliai. Bulletin Société de Pharmacie de Bordeaux, 1961, 100, 238-240.

Présence du complexe leucocyanidol-catéchine de Forsyth dans le chocolat. En collaboration avec Mlle Golse. Bulletin Société de Pharmacie de Bordeaux, 1961, 100, 241-247.

Sur la toxicité d'un tannoïde extrait des parties ligneuses de la grappe de raisin. En collaboration avec R. Patay. 86e Congrès des Sociétés Savantes, Montpellier, 1961.

1962

Remarques sur l'emploi de l'éther saturé d'eau comme procédé d'extraction du rutoside. En collaboration avec B. Mochayedi. Bulletin Société de Pharmacie de Bordeaux, 1962, 101, 225-228.

1963

Étude chromatographique des constituants cinnamiques du vin. En collaboration avec R. Ricci. Bulletin Société de Pharmacie de Bordeaux, 1963, 102, 3-6.

Dosage des leucoanthocyannes du vin blanc. Emploi de la poudre de polyamide. Bulletin Société de Pharmacie de Bordeaux, 1963, 102, 51-52.

1964

Procédé pour l'obtention des hydroxyflavanne 3-4 diols à partir de matières végétales telles que l'arachide ou l'écorce de pin. Brevet d'invention. No 1.427.100. Demandé le 14 décembre 1964. Délivré le 27 décembre 1965.

Action cholérétique des constituants cinnamiques du vin. En collaboration avec J. Laparra. Bulletin Société de Pharmacie de Bordeaux, 1964, 103, 121-122.

Chromatographie des dérivés cinnamiques du vin. En collaboration avec R. Ricci. Qualitas plantarum et materiae vegetabiles, 1964, 11, No 2-4, 244-248.

1965

Le traitement des affections veineuses, vasculaires et capillaires par un nouveau bioflavonoïde ou facteur vitamine P contenant essentiellement à titre de produit actif le tétrahydroxy 5,7,3',4' flavanne 3,4 diol. Brevet spécial de médicament. No 4.482. Demandé le 12 mars 1965. Délivré le 3 octobre 1966.

État des leucoanthocyannes dans la rhytidome de Pinus Maritima Lamk. En collaboration avec J. Michaud. Bulletin Société de Pharmacie de Bordeaux, 1965, 104, 33-36.

Fractionnement des leucoanthocyannes du vin. En collaboration avec J. Michaud. Bulletin Société de Pharmacie de Bordeaux, 1965, 104, 81-85.

Action bactéricide des cides-phénols du vin. En collaboration avec Mlle D. Delaunay. Bulletin Société de Pharmacie de Bordeaux, 1965, 104, 152-156.

Révélation différentielle des acides-alcools des depsides hydroxycinnamiques sur les chromatogrammes d'extraits végétaux. Bulletin Société de Pharmacie de Bordeaux, 1965, 104, 233-238.

Hydroxyflavan 3,4 Diols and Medicaments based thereon. Jack Masquelier. Patent Specification 1,092,269 – The Patent Office London, Dec. 3, 1965.

1966

Métabolisme du leucocyanidol chez le Rat. En collaboration avec P. Claveau et Mlle J. Golse. Bulletin Société de Pharmacie de Bordeaux, 1966, 104, 193-199.

Vitaminothérapie P moderne et rétinite diabétique. En collaboration avec P. Verin et J. Le Rebeller. Symposium international sur l'Oeuil Diabétique, Bordeaux, Octobre, 1966.

Recherche systématique de leucoanthocyannes dans l'écorce de douze espèces de conifères. En collaboration avec P. Claveau. Naturaliste Can., 1966, 93, 345-348.

1967

Effet du leucocyanidol sur le catabolisme auxinique. En collaboration avec D. Grenier. Bulletin Société de Chimie Biologique, 1967, 49, No 12, 1807-1812.

1968

Synthèse du leucocyanidol monomère. En collaboration avec J. Michaud. Bulletin Société de Chimie Biologique, 1968, 50, No 7-8, 1346-1348.

1969

Hydroxyflavin 3,4-Diols, a Method of Producing Them and Medicament Based thereon. United States Patent, 3,436,407. Patented Apr. 1, 1969.

Étude du pigment rouge isolé des fruits d'Actaea rubra Wild. En collaboration avec G. Favreau et Y. Raymond. Naturaliste Can., 1969, 69, 191-202.

Phytosynthèse de rutoside marqué au 14C. En collaboration avec J. Michaud, Mlle M.F. Lesca, Mlle M.F. Harmand et P. Blanquet. Bulletin Société de Pharmacie de Bordeaux, 1969, 108, 133-142.

1970

Procédé d'extraction des oligomères flavanoliques totaux des végétaux, et produits obtenus. Brevet d'invention. No 2092743. Demandé le 15 juin 1970. Délivré le 28 janvier 1972.

Method of Manufacturing Chemically Pure Flavanediols. En collaboration avec Jean Michaud. United States Patent 3,549,661. Patented Dec. 22, 1970.

Effets physiologiques des constituants non alcooliques du vin. Cahiers de Nutrition et de Diététique, 1970, 5, 57-64.

1971

Activité levuricide du leucocyanidol en présence de cuivre. En collaboration avec J. Dumas. Annales de l'Institut Pasteur, 1971, 121, 69-73.

Fractionnement des oligomères flavanoliques du raisin. En collaboration avec J. Michaud, P. Lacaze. Bulletin Société de Pharmacie de Bordeaux, 1971, 110, 111-116.

1972

Les produits de dégradation de la catéchine et leur activité antivitaminique. En collaboration avec J. Michaud et Mlle M.F. Lesca. Annales Pharmaceutiques françaises, 1972, sous presse.

1977

Étude Pharmacocinétique des Oligomères Flavanoliques. En collaboration avec J. Laparra et J. Michaud. Plantes Médicinales et phytothérapie, 1977, Tome XI, Numéro spécial, 133-142.

1978

Étude Pharmacocinétique des Oligomères Procyanidoliques Totaux du Raisin. En collaboration avec J. Laparra, J. Michaud, M.F. Lesca et P. Blanquet. Acta Therapeutica, 4, 1978.

1979

Action des Oligomères Procyanidoliques sur le Cobaye Carencé en Vitamine C. En collaboration avec J. Laparra et J. Michaud. Travaux Originaux, Laboratoire de Matière Médicale, Faculté de Pharmacie de Bordeaux, 1979.

Flavonoides et pycnogenols. En collaboration avec J. Michaud, J. Laparra et M.C. Dumon. Internat.J.Vit.Nutr.Res., 1979.

1981

Stabilisation du Collagène par les Oligomères Procyanidoliques. En collaboration avec J. Dumon et J. Dumas. Acta Therapeutica, 7, 1981.

Pycnogenols: Recent Advances in the Therapeutic Activity of Procyanidins. Natural Products as Medicinal Agents. Hyppocrates Verlag, 1981.

1987

Plant Extract with a Proanthocyanidins Content as Therapeutic Agent having Radical Scavenging Effect and Use thereof. U.S. Patent 4,698,360. Oct. 6, 1987.

Effets Physiologiques du Vin, Exposé présenté au Symposium International sur "Le Vin et la Santé." Mendoza, Argentina, November 1987.

1989

Les Procyanidols du Vin, IIe Rencontre Internationale de Coursan. Paris, 1989.

Procédé de préparation d'extraits polyphénoliques du type flavan-3-ol purifiés et extraits obtanus. Jack Masquelier. Demande de Brevet d'Invention. No. 89 01947. 15 février 1989.

1990

Dosage des Procyanidols dans les Extraits Végétaux Destinés à la Préparation de Médicaments. En collaboration avec Marie-Claude Dumon et Jean Michaud. Bulletin Société de Pharmacie de Bordeaux, 1990, 129, 51-65.

ABOUT THE AUTHOR

Bert Schwitters was born in Holland in 1945. He started his journalistic career producing and directing documentary programs for Dutch Television. The author of several non-fiction books, he has dealt with subjects such as Interpol, psychiatry, and human health. In 1993, in cooperation with Dr. Jack Masquelier, Schwitters wrote *OPC in Practice*. In 1994, his first collection of poetry, *Where I Live*, was published in Holland. He published a second collection called *Without Naming* in 2003.

Since 1980, Schwitters has been focusing his attention particularly on health and nutrition and has been playing an active role in the promotion and free availability of dietary supplements. As an investigative journalist and businessman, he has met and come to know many innovators in the fields of medicine, health, and nutrition. Since the late 1970s, he has been an independent supporter of alternative medicine and of the orthomolecular approach to health.

DISCLAIMER

The information in this book is offered for general interest and educational purposes and is based on data from published and unpublished sources. The information in this book is not intended as a medical advice or as a substitute for consulting a physician. Any attempt to diagnose and treat an illness should come under the direction of a competent health professional. Always let your doctor or nutritionist know about any dietary supplements or herbs you are taking. In case of doubt, always consult a competent health professional.

COLOFON

Printed matter: 1st edition, January 2004, by Hentenaar-Boek, Nieuwegein, The Netherlands

Pre-press production: Monique Willems, Dr. Tanouja Rama, Linda Devine, Anne Simons.

Design and lay-out: Monique Willems

Copyright: Bert Schwitters

All rights reserved.
No part of this book may be reproduced or utilized in any form or by any means, electronic or mechanical, including photocopying, recording or by any information storage and retrieval system, without written permission from the publishers.

ISBN 88-86035-20-9

Publishers:
Alfa Omega Editrice
23 Via San Damaso
00165 Rome
Italy

Distributors:
ABC Media
410-412 Van Diemenstraat
1013 CR Amsterdam
The Netherlands